Insectopedia

The secret world of southern African insects

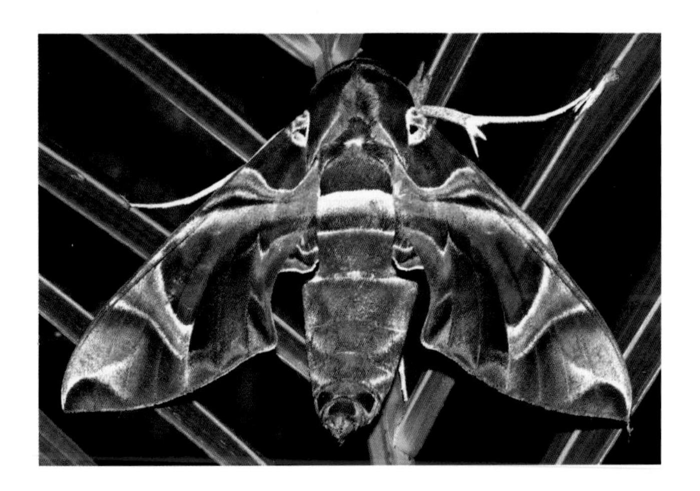

Insectopedia

The secret world of southern African insects

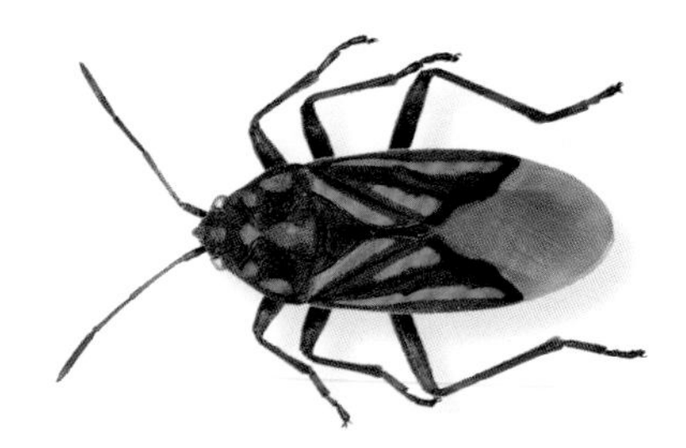

ERIK HOLM

Published by Struik Nature
(an imprint of Penguin Random House South Africa (Pty) Ltd)
Reg. No. 1953/000441/07

The Estuaries No. 4, Oxbow Crescent, Century Avenue,
Century City, 7441
PO Box 1144, Cape Town, 8000 South Africa

Visit **www.penguinrandomhouse.co.za** and join the Struik Nature Club for updates, news, events and special offers.

First published as *Insectlopedia of southern Africa* by LAPA Publishers (Pty) Ltd, 2008

Fully updated, revised and redesigned edition published as *Insectopedia – The secret world of southern African insects* by Struik Nature, 2017

10 9 8 7 6 5 4 3 2 1

Copyright © in text, 2017: Erik Holm
Copyright © in photographs, 2017: As credited below
Copyright © in illustrations, 2017: Erik Holm
Copyright © in published edition, 2017: Penguin Random House South Africa (Pty) Ltd

Illustrations in Chapter 12 are reproduced from *Insects of southern Africa* by Clarke H. Scholtz and Erik Holm with the kind permission of Protea Book House, Pretoria.

Print: 978 1 77584 198 2
ePUB: 978 1 77584 200 2
ePDF: 978 1 77584 199 9

Publisher: Pippa Parker
Managing editor: Helen de Villiers
Project manager: Roelien Theron
Editors: Liz Sparg, Roelien Theron
Designer: Janice Evans
Typesetter: Deirdré Geldenhuys
Proofreader: Emsie du Plessis
Indexer: Emsie du Plessis

Reproduction by Hirt & Carter Cape (Pty) Ltd
Printed and bound in China by C&C Offset Printing Co., Ltd.

All rights reserved. No part of this publication may be reproduced, stored in a retrieval system or transmitted in any form or by any means, electronic, mechanical, photocopying, recording or otherwise, without the prior written permission of the publishers and copyright holders.

Also available in Afrikaans as *Insektopedie – Die geheime wêreld van Suider-Afrikaanse insekte*
ISBN 978 1 77584 224 8

Front cover: Elegant grasshopper
Half-title page: Hawk moth
Title pages (p. 2, left to right, clockwise): Flea beetle, pear slug caterpillar, moth egg basket, ladybeetle, stink bug nymphs, acraeas, hover fly; **(p. 3):** Cotton stainer
This page: Ground beetle
Contents page (top to bottom): Flea beetle, bolboceratid beetle, clerid beetle, blue, aphids, hover fly, fruit chafer
Back cover: Emperor moth caterpillar, dragonfly

Picture credits: (t=top, b=bottom, m=middle, r=right, l=left)

All photographs by **Erik Holm**, except: **Lambert Smith**: front cover; **Kate Braun**: pp. 156 tm; 179 br; 193 tr; 194 bl; 197 r; **Duncan Butchart**: p. 195 tr; 196 tm; **Nigel Dennis/Images of Africa**: pp. 122 l; 125 bm; **Hein Gebhardt**: p. 137 bl; 171 bm; 183 mb; 185 m both; 187 bm; 193 bl; **Charles Griffiths & Mike Picker**: p. 80 meloid-mimicking jewel beetle; **Leonard Hoffmann/ Images of Africa**: pp. 8 t; 13 br; 15 r; 19 t; 27 r; 56 t; 72 br; 76 tl; 125 br; 126; **Jeremy Hollman**: p. 119; **Honey Bee Research Extension Laboratory**: p. 182 bm; **Elize Lundall-Magnuson**: pp. 53 locusts all; 72 tr, mr; 121 tl; 130 tr; **Public Domain/pixabay.com**: p. 118 br; **At Schoeman**: pp. 2 bl, r all; 4; 5 all; 6; 9; 10 b; 12 t; 16; 18 l; 20 tl, bm; 21 tl, bm; 22 tr; 23 mr; 24 br; 25 ml, bl, mr, br; 26 tl, br; 29 r; 31 m, b; 32 bl, tr; 33 tr, br; 34 b; 35 m, br, l; 36 tl, tm; 37; 38 tm, tr, ml; 39 ml; 42 tl, br; 43 t, m, r; 44 t, bm; 45 tl, tr, br; 47 m both; 48 tr; 50 m both, bl; 52 ml, bl; 56 bl, br; 57 all; 58 bl, br; 61 t; 65 mr, br; 66 br; 68 ml, bl; 69 ml; 71 t both, ml, b; 72 ml; 73 bl, br; 74 t, bl; 75 t, br; 76 tr; 77 tr, bl, bm both; 78 tr; 79 tm, bl, br; 80 tl, b all, tml, tr; 81 b; 82 br; 83 tl, bl, br; 88 t; 90 bm, br; 91 b; 93 t; 98 t, mr; 99 bl; 102 all; 104 tl; 109 tr; 111 ml, bl; 113; 114 both; 115 all; 116 all; 118 bl; 121 tr; 129 mr, br; 130 tl; 131 bl, bml; 132 t; 134 tl, br; 135 all; 136 tl, ml, bl, bm; 137 br; 138 both; 139 tr, bl; 140 tm; 141 r; 142 bl, br; 143 tl, tm, bl; 144 l, br; 145 l; 146 both; 147 all except l; 148 tm; 149 tl, mm, bl; 150 all; 151 ml, tm, mm; 152 tm, ml; 153 l, m, br; 155 br; 156 rm; 157 tl, mm, bl, br; 158 tl, bl; 159 mt, bm; 161 tr; 162 bm, br; 164 l, mt, mb; 66 mb; 167 bl; 168 m all; 169 l both, mt; 170 tm; 171 mm, br; 172 m both, r both; 173 m both; 174 all; 175 tl, m, tr; 176 tl; 177 l all; 178 bl, bm; 180 r both; 181 mm, bm; 182 tl, tm, br; 183 mt, br; 184 m, r; 185 l; 187 br; 188 bm, br and above; 189 rm; 190 bl, bm; 191 tl, bm; 192 all except tl; 193 tl, lm, mb, br; 194 m; 195 m, br; 196 tl, bm; 197 bl, mm; 198 bl, tr; 199 tm, br; **Shutterstock.com: A.G.A**: p. 120; **Nattawat Kaewjirasit**: p. 7 reptile; **Dr Morley Read**: p. 7 centipede; **woe**: p. 7 shell; **Rory Stott**: p. 7 flower; **Roelien Theron**: p. 7 mushroom; **Braam van Wyk**: pp. 1, 30 bl both; 34 m; 62 b; 81 tl, tr; 101 both; 127 flowers; 128; **Hein von Hörsten/ Images of Africa**: p. 125 bl; **Wikimedia Commons: Alvesgaspar, CC BY-SA 3.0** p. 63 b; **Charlesjsharp, CC BY-SA 4.0** p. 22 br; **Didier Descouens, CC BY-SA 3.0** p. 173 l; **Bernard Dupont, CC BY-SA 2.0** p. 22 tr; **Peter Webb**: pp. 165 r; 183 tr; **Steve Woodhall**: p. 193 mm

Contents

Acknowledgements

Several people worked harder than I did on this book.

Riaan Stals of the South African National Collection of Insects at the Agricultural Research Council worked extensively on the first edition. Not only did he improve the language, but he also brought the nomenclature up to date and corrected the many sloppy errors made by his ex-professor.

With endless perseverance and forbearance, my daughter Louise processed and re-processed every word and every photograph that appeared in the first edition and handled all correspondence for this new edition.

Senior editor Roelien Theron, designer Janice Evans and the team at Struik Nature made sure this edition is a totally new and updated version of the original book published in 2008.

To all of you, thanks!

In addition, I would like to thank all those people who supported me during the many hectic months it took to complete this project. These were spent either writing or hunting down insects to photograph on crazy expeditions all over the country. A special thanks goes to my wife Elsabé and my children Nike, Kora and Erik; Riaan Conradie, Henk Terreblanche and Anthony Loubser, who supported me on barely legal expeditions in the Cape provinces and Namibia; and all those hospitable farmers who helped along the way (especially the Strauss-gang on Kanaän). With your support, I'd do it all over again!

I also wish to thank all my colleagues who contributed their invaluable photographs and often amazing information, which I had no hope of assembling on my own. A special thanks goes to At Schoeman and Dawid Jacobs for their photographs and comments as well as Henk Geertsema for his constructive criticism. Thank you for your selfless help and loyalty.

Alta Joubert, my assistant on and off for 50 years, helped me compile the revised manuscript. She is a glutton for punishment with a short memory for pain, suffering and hard work!

ERIK HOLM

Spittle bug nymphs are covered in foam made of their own excrement, protecting them from predators and from drying out.

Introduction

Planet Earth is undoubtedly the domain of insects. An estimated three-quarters of all living species are insects (see pie charts right), and no terrestrial ecosystem could function without them.

Insects are of immense and unimaginable importance in the ecology of our world – more so than all the other animals on our planet combined. As pollinators they play a critical role in sustaining the web of life. Without species such as bees, wasps, ants, butterflies, moths and beetles, the world's ecosystems would in all likelihood collapse.

Despite their many benefits, insects can justifiably also be regarded as pests. Even with all the knowledge and technology at our disposal, we cannot prevent them from devouring at least 20 per cent of agricultural crops grown for human consumption. It may be better to relinquish this share voluntarily, as the cost of using chemicals or other means to control insect pests is often equal to, or higher than, the cost of crop losses.

Insects also carry diseases. It is estimated that more people have died from contracting illnesses such as malaria, yellow fever, typhus and plague, transmitted by insects, than from all other causes of death combined.

Why is our knowledge of these creatures so limited? Probably because they are so much smaller than we are; it's the bigger creatures, such as the huge land mammals, which make up only one tenth of all vertebrates, that we notice. Most insects are about two millimetres in length and are, therefore, relatively inconspicuous. However, for us to ignore them would be unwise, not least because they are among the most fascinating and extraordinary of nature's many wonders.

Insects have 'technology' that we could only dream of, such as the ability of fireflies to produce completely cold light, and mechanisms of flight that are beyond our understanding.

The intention of this book is not to identify the roughly 80,000 insect species in our region in the manner of an ordinary field guide – this would be an impossible task. Rather, it is to describe the incredible behaviours and activities of insects, which outstrip some of the best efforts of humans.

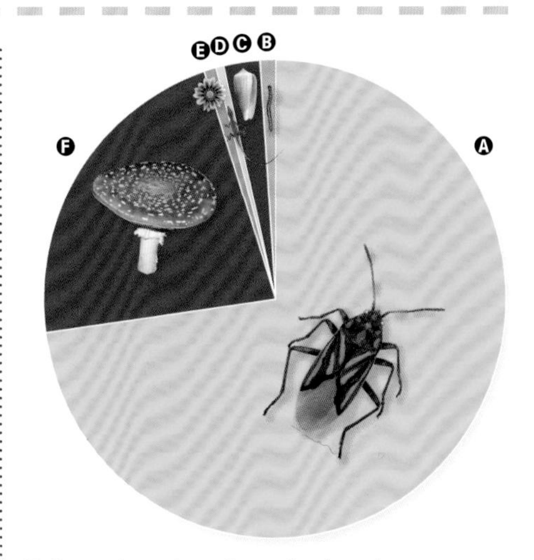

Estimated number of species in existence

- A **Insects:** 20,000,000 (73%)
- B **Other arthropods (spiders, crustaceans, etc.):** 250,000 (1%)
- C **Other invertebrates (molluscs, worms, etc.):** 600,000 (2.5%)
- D **Vertebrates (birds, mammals, etc.):** 50,000 (0.5%)
- E **Plants:** 300,000 (1%)
- F **Microbes & fungi:** 6,000,000 (22%)

Species presently known and described

- A **Insects:** 751,000 (52%)
- B **Other arthropods (spiders, crustaceans, etc.):** 130,000 (8%)
- C **Other invertebrates (molluscs, worms, etc.):** 140,000 (9%)
- D **Vertebrates (birds, mammals, etc.):** 44,000 (3%)
- E **Plants:** 250,000 (17%)
- F **Microbes & fungi:** 160,000 (11%)

Introduction to the world of insects

Dragonfly

IN THE BEGINNING

About 350 million years ago, during the Carboniferous period, the first vertebrates and arthropods crawled from the oceans and began colonising the new continents. Fifty million years earlier, plants had started growing on land. The marine arthropods were partly scorpion-like, partly worm-like, and had numerous legs. From them the first terrestrial arthropods and the first known insects developed – the first primitive fish moths, mayflies, dragonflies and cockroaches.

Several insect orders that had originated during the Carboniferous period, as well as half of all species on earth, perished 100 million years later, at the end of the Permian period. This extinction was the result of catastrophic carbon dioxide poisoning of the atmosphere. Before this disaster happened, insects had diversified enormously: virtually all the insect orders we know today originate from that period, with some members of these orders having survived the catastrophe (see diagram on page 9).

Two other mass extinctions, both caused by meteorites, apparently had little effect on insect diversity. The first of these occurred towards the end of the Triassic period (about 210 million years ago) and caused the extinction of our primitive mammal-like reptiles (Karoo fossils) and most of the gymnosperm plants. The second occurred at the end of the Cretaceous period (about 65 million years ago) and led to the extinction of, among others, the dinosaurs on land and the ammonites in the oceans.

The classification of insects, like that of all living organisms, is based on similarities and differences in structure and behaviour and, more recently, is inferred from genetic analysis. From fossils we can more or less deduce when certain branches of the family tree split off, and missing data are reconstructed using logic.

INSECT FOSSILS

The insect fossil record is not as continuous as that of vertebrate animal skeletons. Insects left recognisable fossils in only a few geological layers. The best layers are in the coal of the Carboniferous period and the fossilised tree resin (amber) of later periods. In between, there are a few layers with good insect fossils in very fine slate (petrified mud).

Dragonfly fossil in coal layer

OUR LIVING FOSSILS

Oldest insect order

Our oldest existing insect order is probably the fish moth, which dates from a time before insects developed wings. Several relict species and groups occur only in southern Africa and, like the coelacanth, cling to survival in small areas in

GENEALOGY OF THE INSECT ORDERS

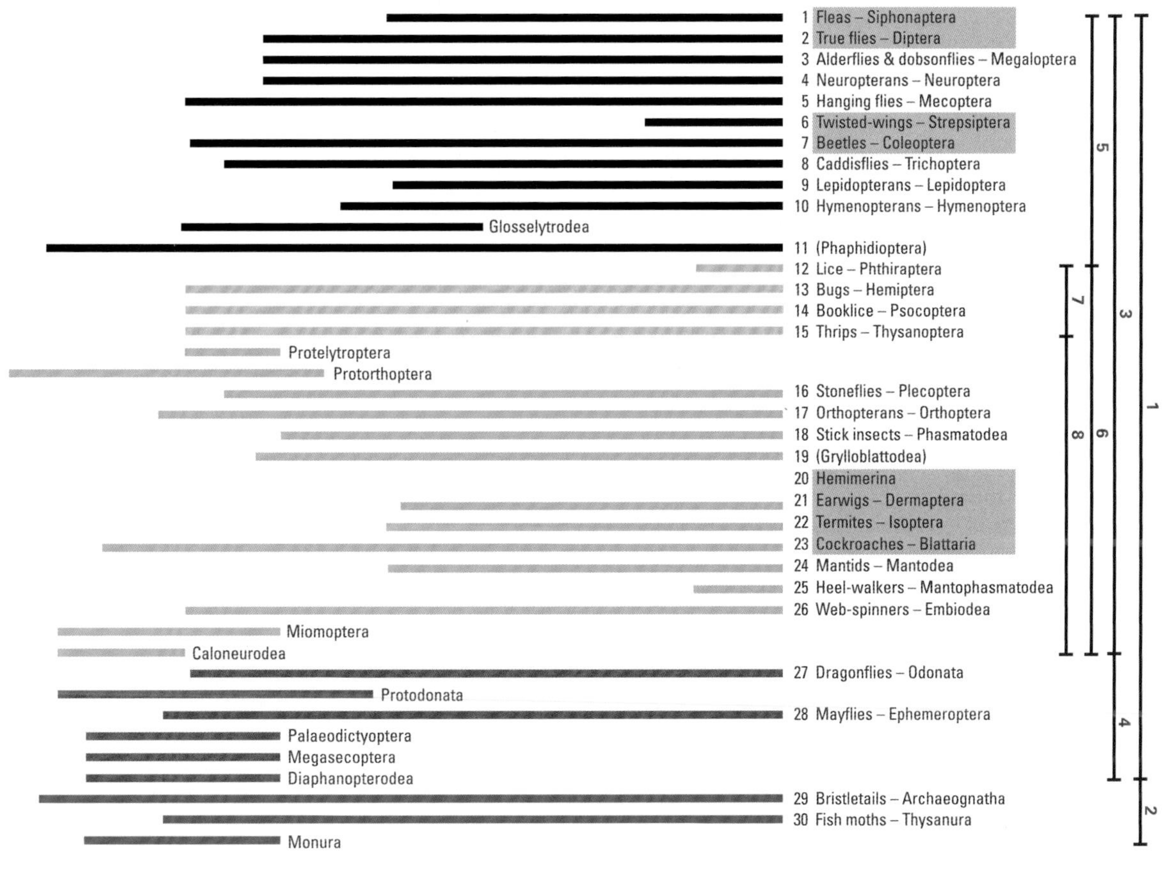

362 Carboniferous | 287 Permian | 251 Triassic | 208 Jurassic | 144 Cretaceous | 65 Caenozoic | 2 Pleistocene

MILLION YEARS AGO

The numbered red vertical bars (above right) indicate groups of orders (in colours) as follows:

1 Pterygota (winged insects)

2 Apterygota (primitive wingless insects)

3 Neoptera (advanced wing type)

4 Paleoptera (primitive wing type)

5 Endopterygota (with pupal stage in metamorphosis)

6 Exopterygota (without pupal stage in metamorphosis)

7 Hemipteroid orders (without posterior appendages and with complex sucking mouthparts)

8 Orthopteroid orders (with posterior appendages and simple biting mouthparts)

KEY TO GENEALOGY DIAGRAM (ABOVE)

- The lengths of the coloured bars illustrate when each order originated, based on the oldest known fossil.
- Two orders are in brackets (Phaphidioptera and Grylloblattodea); these do not occur in Africa.
- Eight orders are paired in grey: some experts consider each pair to be a single order.
- The diagram also contains extinct orders; more than half of them perished at the end of the Permian period.

specific regions. These 'living fossils' are part of our unique natural heritage, and although many of them are inconspicuous and known only to subject specialists, they are absolutely fascinating.

Unique to Africa

Of the roughly 30 insect orders currently found on earth, one order, the heel-walkers, was discovered and described only in 2002. Since then, several new species have come to light. The order seemed to be limited to Namibia and the Richtersveld and West Coast in South Africa, but another species was recently discovered in Tanzania. Heel-walkers are 10–20mm long and always lack wings. All of them appear to be predators. The direct ancestors of these insects were discovered in 40-million-year-old amber in Europe, and our present-day 'living fossils' have changed little since that time.

Rare and endangered

Seventeen species of one stag beetle genus are restricted to high mountain peaks in the Western Cape. They are wingless and can therefore not move far. Each species lives on one mountain peak only and all 17 species are exceptionally rare and endangered. They belong to the genus *Colophon*, and their closest relatives are found in South America, which separated from Africa and drifted away more than 100 million years ago. These living fossils had to move up the mountains as the climate changed in the geological past and now survive only on the bleakest of mountain peaks, in the most disagreeable of climates. Although strict laws protect the *Colophon* beetles, unscrupulous collectors plunder them because they fetch high prices on the black market.

Extraordinary and rare: Stag beetles (*Colophon* genus) are endemic to the Western Cape.

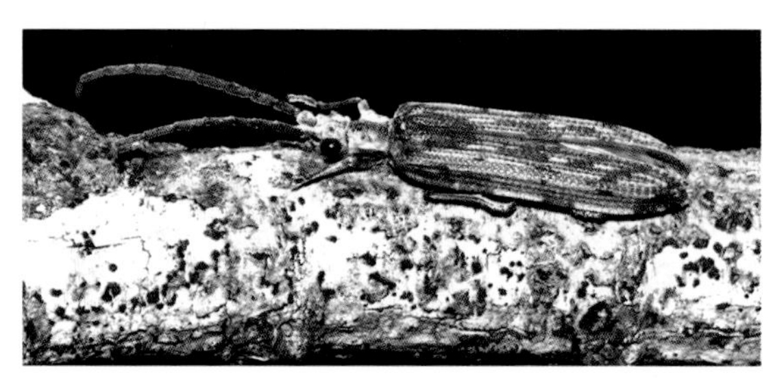

Oldest living beetle family: The only species of Cupedidae in Africa is found in the southern Cape.

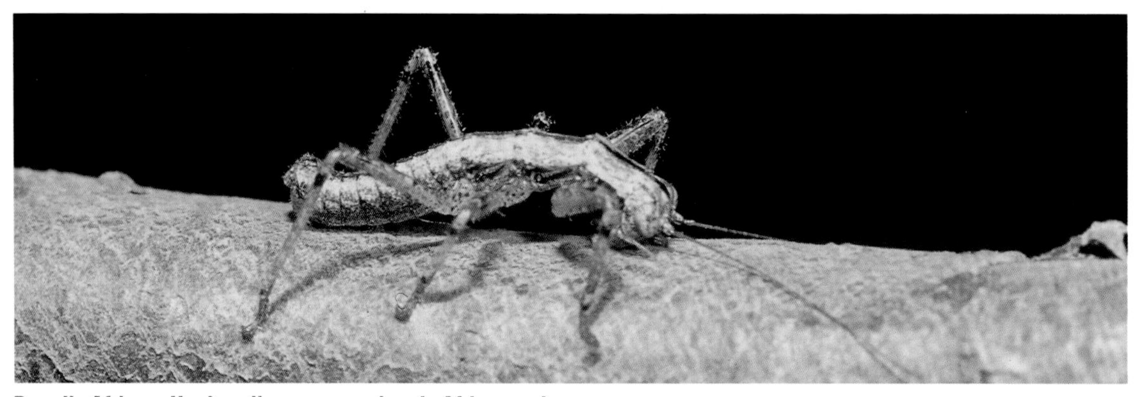

Proudly African: Heel-walkers are a uniquely African order.

The family Cupedidae, the oldest living beetle family, is known from fossils dating back at least 280 million years. There is one surviving species in Africa, which is restricted to forests in the southern Cape.

Most primitive moths

Ghost moths are among the most primitive moths. Although several species of this ancient family still survive throughout the world, we boast the most sensational of them all. The enormous keurboom ghost moth (*Leto venus*) is coloured fine silver and chestnut and it has a wingspan of 150mm. This species is found only in the coastal area of the southern Cape, where its larvae burrow into the wood of the keurboom tree. The closest relatives are found in Australia – and Australia and Africa drifted apart some 130 million years ago!

THE STRUCTURE OF AN INSECT

Insects' skeletons and muscles, and their circulatory, nervous, digestive, glandular and reproductive systems, are well adapted to their survival.

HOW WEIRD IS THAT?

Compared to humans, insects are put together the wrong way round:

- An insect's skeleton, which consists of tubes and sheaths, is situated on the outside, with the muscles attached to the inner surfaces.
- Insects' spinal nerves are located on the belly side, and a sort of heart pump is located where humans have their backbone (see page 12).

The digestive system is more or less in the 'right' position, with a mouth in front and an anus behind. The genitalia and eyes are also in the expected positions, but the rest of the sense organs are located in unexpected places:

- Most insects smell with their feelers (antennae), but some (like flies) smell with the soles of their feet.
- Hearing organs can be situated on the sides of the abdomen (moths), on the forelegs (crickets), on the feet (toktokkies) and on the feelers (male mosquitoes).

Most insects are covered with fine hairs, some of which are sensitive to touch, while others register airflow or vibrations.

Most primitive: The keurboom ghost moth

Life inside a shell

Having a shell on the outside naturally provides insects with excellent protection against the elements and even against enemies. The shell is covered in a layer of wax secreted by fine pores and protects the insect against both water penetration and water loss. It consists of chitin, a very strong, elastic substance similar to keratin, of which the hair, nails and horns of mammals consist. Chitin can be hardened or 'tanned' to varying degrees. In an insect's joints, the chitin remains untanned and can therefore form soft, flexible membranes. The toughness of insect shells differs dramatically, ranging from the extremely hard armour of weevils to the much softer shells of cockroaches and caterpillars.

Once the shell of an insect has hardened, it cannot expand, and the insect must discard its skin before it can continue growing. Much of its shell is then dissolved on the inner side, while soft, new skin forms beneath it. The insect swallows air, pumping itself up until it is as large as possible so that it literally bursts through the remainder of the old shell. The inflated new skin then hardens into a new shell through its exposure to air. The insect grows to fill the new shell, and eventually has to moult again. Insects have to moult like this several times before they reach adulthood.

Fascinating fact

Adult insects of the same species can vary considerably in size. This has nothing to do with their age, but with the amount of food they were able to absorb and the growth they could manage as larvae.

INSECT DESIGN

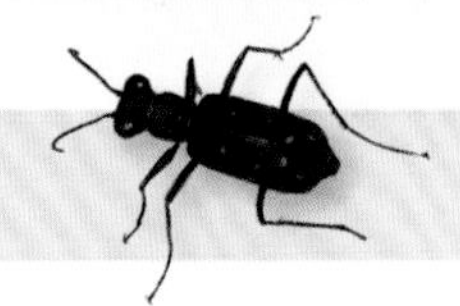

- The bodies of adult insects are divided into three distinct sections: head, thorax and abdomen.
- The thorax always has six legs, each consisting of a hip joint (coxa), upper leg (femur), lower leg (tibia) and foot (tarsus). The shape and structure of the legs are determined by function.
- The number of segments of the abdomen, the feet and the feelers can vary significantly.
- Variation is also found in the shapes of all body parts, as well as in colour, texture and hairiness. Appendages at the end of the abdomen and ovipositors are sometimes present and can differ remarkably.
- The shape of the wings is an important feature in classification. However, wings are frequently absent.
- The feelers (antennae) are also often distinctive, with some important differences in shape.

Structure of an insect

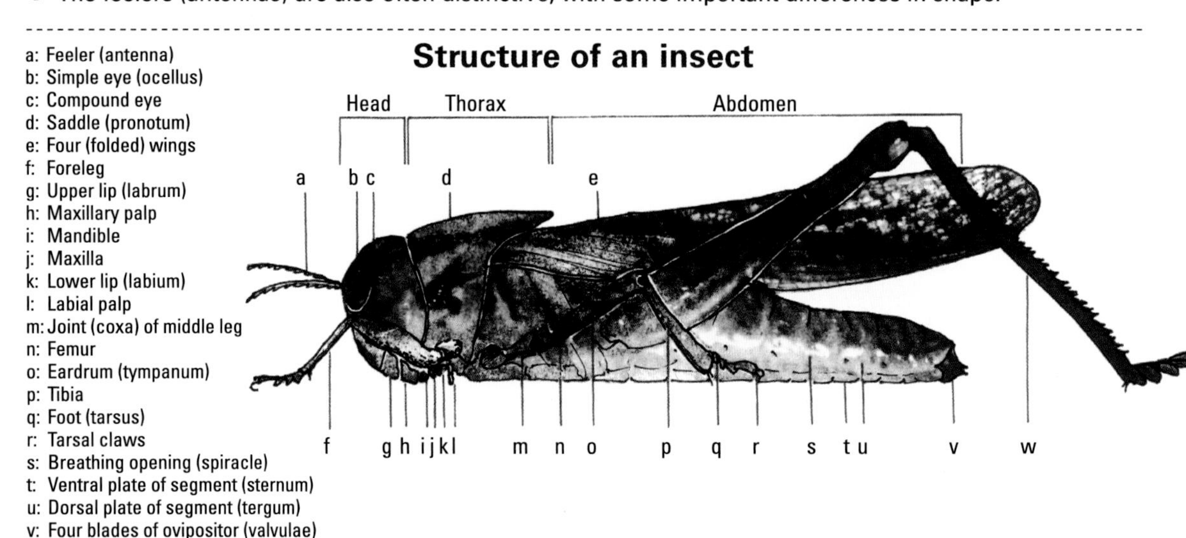

Internal organs of an insect

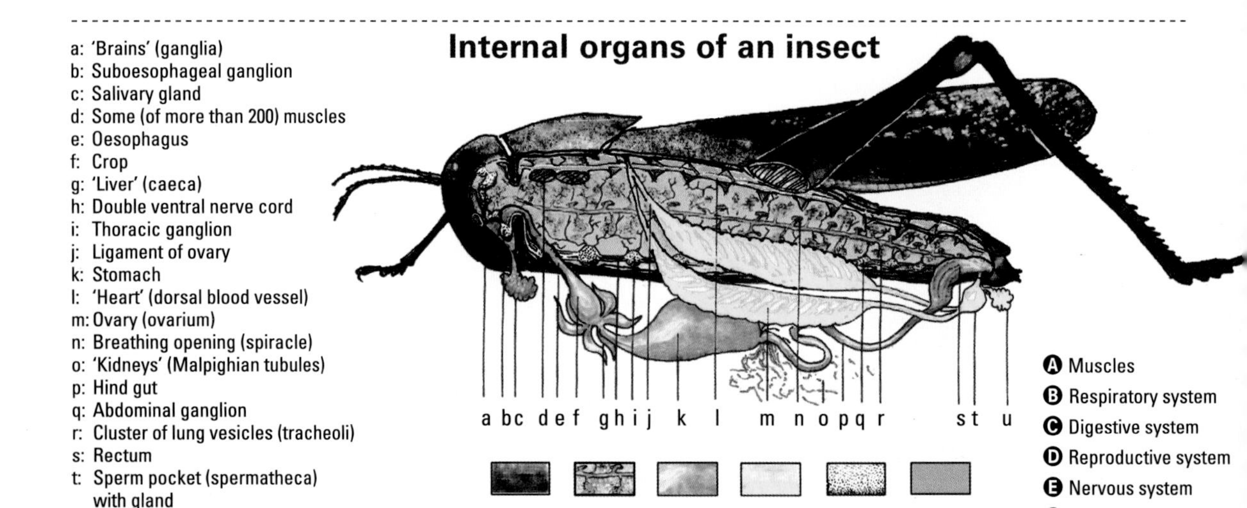

Leg modifications in insects

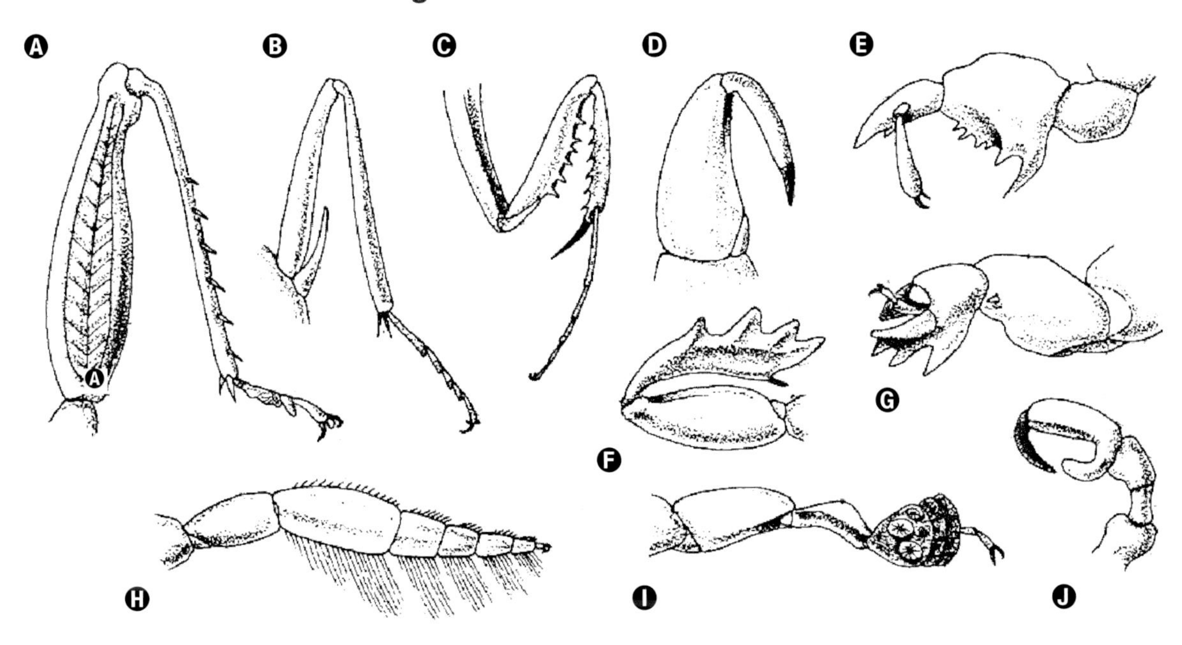

- A Jumping leg (cricket)
- B Walking leg (ground beetle)
- C Grasping leg (mantid)
- D Clinging leg (giant water bug)
- E Digging leg (cicada nymph)
- F Trowelling leg (dung beetle)
- G Burrowing leg (mole cricket)
- H Swimming leg (hind leg of predaceous water beetle)
- I Suction-leg (foreleg of male predaceous water beetle)
- J Clasping leg (louse)

The legs of insects are always paired and jointed, but significant variations in the structure of the legs occur. The front legs of mantids (left) are enlarged to grab and hold on to prey, whereas jumping insects, such as crickets (above), have large hind femurs to propel them over long distances.

Modifications of feelers (antennae) in insects

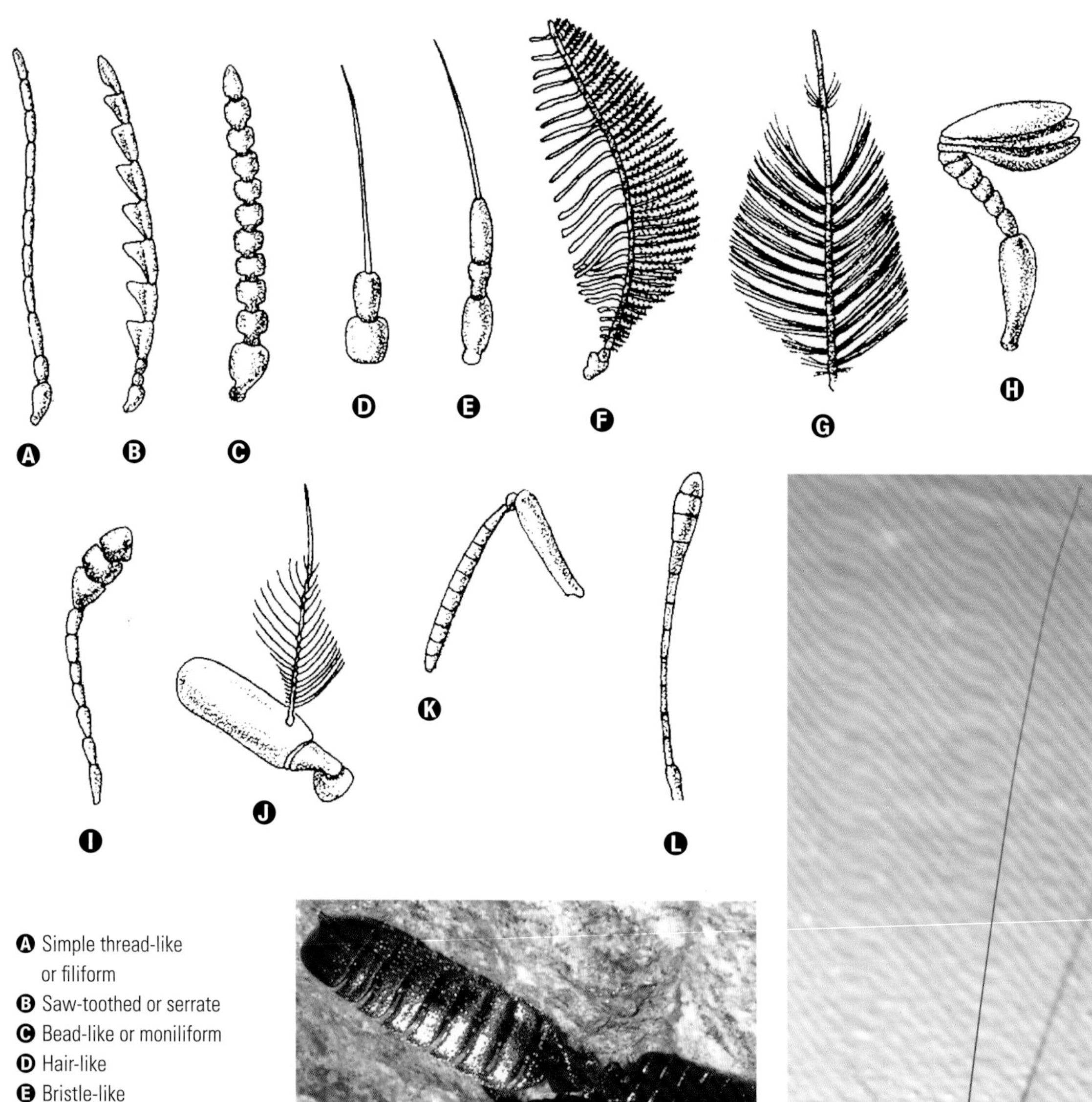

- A Simple thread-like or filiform
- B Saw-toothed or serrate
- C Bead-like or moniliform
- D Hair-like
- E Bristle-like
- F Compound or pectinate (left simple, right branched)
- G Plumed
- H Book-like or lamellate
- I Club-shaped or capitate
- J Haired or aristate
- K Elbowed or geniculate
- L Thickened or clavate

Insect antennae come in various forms. Ant beetles (above) have pectinate (comb-like) feelers and bush crickets (right) possess long thin filiform antennae, consisting of similar-sized segments.

Types of insect mouthparts

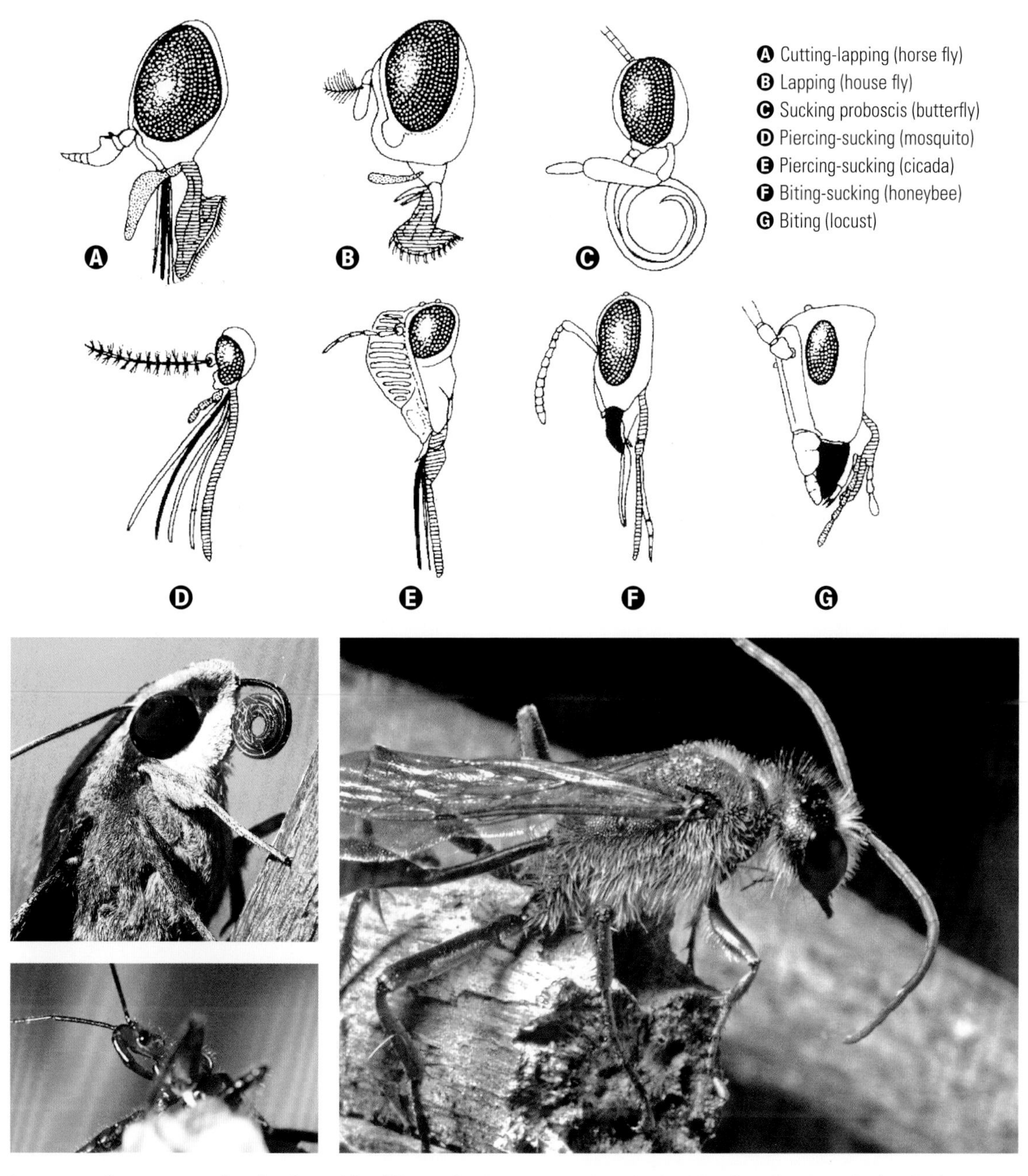

Insect mouthparts are variously adapted for different food sources and methods of feeding. Hawk moths (top left) have a long sucking tube (proboscis) to suck up liquids, while the assassin bug (above left) uses its curved proboscis to pierce its prey and suck the contents from the body. The mandibles of the wasp (above right) are adapted for biting and chewing.

Muscle power

An insect has almost as many muscles as humans have, although it is difficult to imagine this in a midge. The appendages of insects are actually tube systems in which the muscles have to operate with poor leverage, and around corners. The ability of these insects to perform 'power stunts' is baffling; one wonders how they manage such feats.

The answer is found in the fact that the strength of a muscle depends on its cross-sectional area, and not on its mass or volume. This means that – relative to its mass or volume – the bigger a muscle is, the weaker it is; and the smaller it is, the stronger it is. It is puzzling that the dinosaur *Brontosaurus* could stand or walk at all: relative to its mass, its muscles would barely have been able to support it! An elephant is incapable of carrying an object equivalent to its own mass, but a human can do that relatively easily, and an ant can carry about 1,000 times its own mass; however, the muscle strength of all three is the same per square millimetre sectional area.

An ant can handle about 1,000 times its own mass.

'Blood' and 'lungs'

Insects have a blood cavity (haemocoel), which means that their blood (haemolymph) simply flows about their organs and tissues and is not channelled in arteries or veins. To assist circulation, a muscular tube with a number of one-way valves along its sides is located in the insect's abdomen. This 'heart' contracts rhythmically and pumps blood from the abdomen to the thorax and head. From there it simply flows back to the area of lower pressure in the abdomen, and keeps circulating this way. Narrow appendages, such as feelers and legs, have additional little 'heart pumps' to effect blood circulation in these extremities.

When flying insects emerge as adults, and spread their wings to harden, they increase the blood pressure in their wing veins. Most flying insects do this only once to harden their wings. However, beetles, web-spinners and earwigs inflate the veins of their hind wings every time they spread them, and let the blood flow back when they close them again.

The 'lungs' of an insect are distributed almost throughout its body, boosting the delivery of oxygen to offset the insect's sluggish blood circulation. There are small openings (spiracles) with valves on the sides of the thoracic and abdominal segments. These holes open into a type of lung tube that runs lengthwise on each side of the insect's entrails. From the lung tubes, little clusters of lung vesicles (tracheoli) branch out everywhere among the tissues. The blood in the blood cavity continually washes over these tracheoli, absorbing oxygen and discharging carbon dioxide. Insects have a variety of blood cells similar to our own, but they lack red blood cells with haemoglobin to carry oxygen (with the exception of bloodworm maggots living in mud). In the majority of insects oxygen is transported internally, simply dissolved in the blood. Some insects have a green oxygen carrier, and hence green-coloured blood.

When insects want to accelerate their breathing, they use their muscles to pump the abdominal segments, like the pumping movement of an accordion. This can sometimes be observed when bees are drinking water, or when locusts are chirping.

Preparing for flight, a longhorn beetle unfolds its hind wings by pumping blood into its wing veins.

'Brain' and 'nerves'

Instead of having one brain located in the head, insects have a decentralised nervous system. In fact, primitive insects have a 'brain' or ganglion for each body segment, but gradually, through evolution, some of these small 'brains' have fused. All the ganglia are situated on the underside of the insect and are connected by two thick, longitudinal 'spinal' nerve cords.

The largest nerve bundle is located behind the eyes and appears to be involved exclusively with vision and the interpretation of impulses from the thousands of little eyes that form the compound eyes. Behind this area is a three-lobed nerve bundle that is generally called the 'brain'. Below this are several brain centres responsible for the secretion of hormones. Below these again, the oesophagus passes between the two 'spinal cords'. This then leads to the large suboesophageal ganglion, which is akin to the brain stem in humans.

These head ganglia are involved in most of the co-ordination of movements and muscle actions. However, this 'brain' is not essential for the independent movement or other functions of the various body parts. All the subsequent 'brains' – which, in turn, are connected to each other – can function quite independently of the central 'brain'. A fine example of this is the ability of a male mantid to mate effectively after having been decapitated (see Chapter 2).

Insects may be intellectually challenged, but their senses are brilliant – see Chapters 6, 7 and 8; also see 'Insect records' on pages 20–24.

Despite their extremely primitive central nervous system and 'brains', insects may display remarkably complex behaviours and they may appear very intelligent. However, their behaviour patterns are genetically fixed and derived from a lengthy evolution process, rather than from own experience. Still, there are insects that can learn certain things (very specific things, admittedly) and have a good memory (for example bees and ants, as discussed in Chapter 11).

Eating and digestion

At the front, an insect has a mouth. It consists of a lid-like upper lip (labrum) and two jaws (mandibles) that move in a horizontal plane. Below those are two more comb-like or brush-like jaws (maxillae) that also move horizontally and carry a small feeler (maxillary palp); and, lastly, a flat, lower lip or labium with two small feelers (labial palps) attached to it. These basic parts remain more or less unchanged in chewing insects, such as grasshoppers and beetles, but show remarkable variations in other insects. Sucking or lapping mouthparts, coiled tubes and all kinds of combinations have developed, due to modification of one or more of the six basic parts.

Behind the mouthparts is the entrance to the digestive tract, with a mouth cavity and oesophagus, often followed by some kind of crop in which food is temporarily stored. As in humans, a valve is found where the oesophagus or crop opens into the stomach. Behind this valve, a number of caeca, blind tubes secreting enzymes and clumped around the gut like a bunch of bananas, are found. More glands are found where the stomach opens into the gut, but these are long, thin threads, floating in the blood cavity, and they function as liver and kidneys. They extract waste products from the blood and dump it in the intestinal canal. Lastly, there is a closable anus, preceded by a rectum that reabsorbs water from the intestinal waste, similar to that of vertebrates.

Glands

All insects have salivary glands in their heads, but many can secrete other useful substances apart from saliva. These substances include anti-clotting agents and anaesthetics in blood-sucking insects; glue for papier-mâché and masonry in paper wasps and termites; silk for cocoons in

Scale insects produce wax from glands on their backs.

larvae of moths, butterflies, ants and fleas; and digestive enzymes, for example in assassin bugs and the larvae of neuropterans or net-winged insects.

Glands perform a very important function in insects – something that makes them rather similar to mammals but drastically different from other cold-blooded organisms, such as reptiles. Insects have different glands that secrete wax, resin and other substances onto the integument ('skin'), as well as a large variety of glands that produce scents for fending off or attracting others (see Chapter 8). Social insects have glands that produce scents with which they communicate (see Chapter 8). Beeswax, shellac and the wax of scale insects are all products of glands.

The drugs that ant nest beetles and some assassin bugs use on their prey (see Chapter 8) are also products of specialised glands; so are the shells of insect eggs and the egg parcels of mantids and cockroaches. Then there are some insects with glands that secrete a concentrated food: the 'nuptial gifts' of male crickets, the 'baby's milk' of paper wasps and honeybees and the 'pseudo placenta' of some cockroaches are examples of this (see Chapters 2 and 11).

A surprisingly large part of an insect's body is thus dedicated to glands.

The female mantid produces a foamy egg case from the secretions of specialised glands in her abdomen.

Reproductive system

The reproductive system of insects is essentially the same as that of other animals: gonads, ducts and a copulatory opening. The difference between males and females is that their gonads are, respectively, testes and ovaries. Additionally, the males have a copulatory organ (penis).

The sex organs of closely related male insects sometimes differ drastically from each other. Each of these fit only into the copulatory duct of females of the same species, much like a key that fits only one lock. These differences make life easier for the taxonomist who has to identify different species. Closely related insect species often can be identified with certainty only by examining the male genitalia, as in the case of the two fruit chafers illustrated with their respective genitalia (see below).

The female insect may have an ovipositor and/or sperm pocket (spermatheca) in which live sperm cells are kept and fed, and accessory glands with which to produce eggshells and egg packets. In some cases, sperm pockets can keep sperm alive for years on end, as in the queen honeybee (*Apis mellifera*).

The male genitalia of these closely related species of fruit chafer differ substantially.

INSECT SUCCESS

Why have insects been so successful during evolution that they make up three-quarters of all living species? A number of possible explanations have been proposed, but it is difficult to decide which of them is the most important. Insects have had certain advantages along their evolutionary course.

The first to arrive

It is a law of ecology that the first species to fill an ecological niche gains such an advantage that it is difficult for any later arrivals to compete with it (the 'founder principle'). Arthropods were some of the first land dwellers, and were therefore able to monopolise terrestrial niches.

Flight

For tens of millions of years, the only organisms capable of flight were insects, and that enabled them to be the first arrivals in many places, thereby thoroughly exploiting the founder principle. They were also faster to reach and exploit food sources and could better escape from disaster and danger – all competitive advantages, compared to organisms that could only walk or swim.

Neat eaters

Another reason why insects fared so much better on land than the other arthropods, such as scorpions, spiders and centipedes, is that they developed an added lower lip (labium) (see page 15). A lower lip never developed in these other arthropod groups, restricting them to a somewhat messy way of feeding, or to sucking. Insects, however, have the ability to feed on solid foods on land, without the food falling from their mouth.

Small and tough

The protection against drying out that arthropods gained by having an external skeleton was a great advantage from the beginning. Since such a construction can be quite small and light, insects can occupy numerous niches that are not available to larger animals. For example, a single tree that can sustain only a handful of vertebrates can support a multitude of insects that are root feeders, bark feeders, woodborers, leafcutters, leaf feeders, pollinators, flower feeders, seed feeders, fruit feeders or detritus feeders (see Chapter 11).

Changing identities

Those insect orders with a pupal stage, especially beetles, butterflies, moths, flies and hymenopterans (sawflies, wasps, bees and ants), came into existence at a later stage than the primitive insects, meaning that the founder principle worked against them. The great advantage of metamorphosis, however, is that the larvae and adults of the same species do not compete for resources, and therefore a species can double its numbers. This advantage is fully realised with the 'complete' metamorphosis that is made possible by a pupal stage.

THE BEETLE ENIGMA

Beetles came into existence later in evolutionary history, and their phenomenal success as an order remains something of a riddle. Their hardened forewings serve as excellent armour plating, yet there are examples of other bugs and wasps (such as Chrysididae and Mutillidae) that have equally hard protective 'shields', but which have been less successful. For now, a convincing explanation for the evolutionary success of beetles still eludes us.

Blister beetle

INSECT RECORDS

Longest

The longest insects are stick insects. In South Africa the body length of some stick insects exceeds 200mm.

Stick insect

Heaviest

The heaviest insects are the Goliath beetles (*Goliathus* spp.), found in Central Africa, which weigh about 75g. In South Africa, we have one Goliath beetle species which is, however, much smaller – more or less the same mass as the largest king crickets and dung beetles.

South African Goliath beetle

Widest wingspan

The widest wingspan (up to 280mm) belongs to certain tropical moths. In southern Africa, large emperor moths with wingspans of up to 180mm are found.

Emperor moth

Smallest

Parasitic wasps that develop inside the eggs of other insects are the smallest insects. The smallest adult parasitic wasp measured was 0.014mm long.

Parasitic wasp on other insect eggs

Longest-living

The insects that live the longest are the woodborers. A jewel beetle from the Cape is the record holder: *Bulis bivittata* (shown here) emerged from yellowwood boards that were older than 60 years. As these beetles only lay their eggs in living trees, the eggs must have been even older than that!

Jewel beetle (*Bulis bivittata*)

The queens of some ants and termites may live beyond the age of 30 years. One ant queen was recorded to have lived for 28 years.

Free-living adult insects seldom survive for longer than a year, but some of our wingless toktokkies and weevils have survived as adults in captivity for over 20 years. As their legs cannot regrow, they are gradually worn to stubs!

Toktokkie

Shortest-living

Aphids are small and can give birth to live offspring (nymphs). Under ideal food and temperature conditions, they can complete a whole life cycle in 4.7 days. Mosquitoes can manage the same in less than a week. The shortest adult life span is that of mayflies, which generally mate, lay eggs and die within a day of emerging from the nymph. One mayfly species in America has only five minutes to do everything, before dying!

Adult mayfly

Largest eggs

Carpenter bees lay the longest eggs (up to 16x3mm) but those of our large jewel beetle (*Sternocera* sp.) may be heavier, with dimensions of up to 10x7mm.

Eggs of the jewel beetle

Most copulations

This is a difficult record to establish, but a queen of the Oriental honeybee (*Apis dorsata*) that was studied mated with 53 different males, and a female leaf beetle mated 60 times, but with some males more than once.

Mating leaf beetles

Most progeny

The eggs of some parasitic wasps belonging to the family Encyrtidae divide numerous times inside the host and multiple identical offspring are produced (polyembryony). The largest number of parasitic wasps recorded to develop from one original egg in this way was 3,055.

Red driver ant colony

A female red driver ant (*Dorylus* sp.) has produced 150,000 eggs per day in one cycle of 25 days. Termite (Isoptera) queens lay some 50,000 eggs per day, continuously. In both cases, the total number of descendants produced over a lifetime of more than 20 years is astronomical.

Most moults

Since fish moths keep on moulting as long as they live, they moult many times more than the four or five times that are average for other insects. Sixty moults have been counted in the domestic fish moth (*Thermobia domestica*). Mayflies moult the most times in the nymphal stage – some of them more than 40 times.

Fish moths

Largest swarms and colonies

In terms of numbers and mass, the desert locust (*Schistocerca gregaria*) forms the largest swarms. In 1954 a swarm in Kenya covered 200km^2, with an estimated billion individuals – more or less 100,000 tonnes of locusts. In South Africa, in 1784, a swarm was estimated (probably not very accurately) to be 30 times as large. Such a swarm would eat 900,000 tonnes of plant material per day.

Desert locusts

By comparison, a large swarm of honeybees would have around 60,000 individuals, and a large red driver ant (*Dorylus* sp.) swarm would total about 20 million ants.

Honeybees

The largest number of head lice counted on a single (human) head was 1,434. On a human, there is more space for body lice: 3,800 of them have been counted on one person.

Fastest

On land, the tiger beetles would certainly be the fastest beetles, measured at a speed of 9km/hour over short distances.

A Namib toktokkie (*Onymacris* sp.) weighs 10 times as much as a tiger beetle, but can run at a speed of 5.5km/hour over long distances.

Tiger beetle

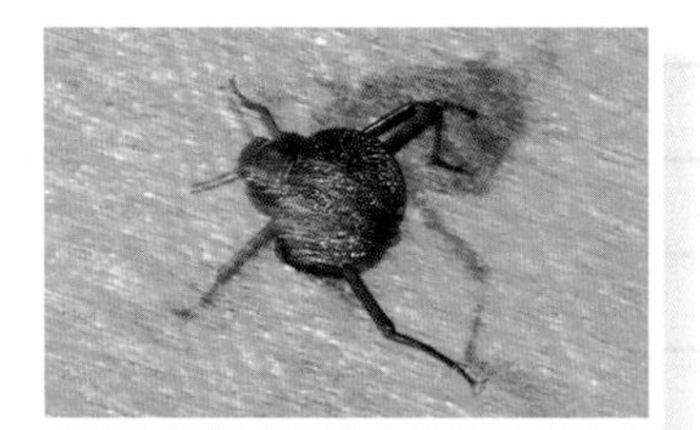

Namib toktokkie (*Onymacris* sp.)

There are several records for hawk moths flying faster than 70km/hour, but these measurements were made from the ground and the influence of wind speed was not taken into account. The air speed of migratory locusts has been clocked at 28km/hour, and that of certain moths in excess of 100km/hour. It is, however, almost impossible to measure the speed of the brief, rapid movements of dragonflies and certain flies.

A midge has the fastest wing beat, recorded at 1,046Hz (beats per second). The buzzing of a fly at 352Hz is, by comparison, rather slow.

Hawk moth

Highest

Among jumping insects, fleas must be the record holders – leaps of 400mm high, with a body length of only 1.5mm have been recorded. This is equal to a human jumping as high as 350m!

Flea

Longest migration

Once, in ancient times, a swarm of locusts lost their way and flew right across the Atlantic Ocean (4,500km). The American monarch butterfly migrates as far as 4,000km, a trip that can take up to 75 days, comparable to the true migrations of birds of passage. The monarch butterfly manages successfully to produce a new generation at each end of the migration, in the same year.

The brown-veined whites (*Belenois aurota*) in southern Africa migrate about 3,000km from the southern Karoo to the northern parts of Zimbabwe. They usually fly in a north–north-easterly direction across the interior of South Africa in

Brown-veined white

December and January. In some years, they reach impressive densities. Like locusts, these butterflies fly only by day and sleep in trees at night, sometimes covering the tree completely. Birds and other insectivores harvest the swarms of butterflies liberally, and by February they start disappearing from the region in significant numbers.

Most airpower

A robber fly can carry as much as three times its own mass through the air, and a mosquito can fly away with more than 2.5 times its own mass in its stomach!

Robber fly with prey

Most land power

Relative to its mass, the smaller an insect is, the stronger it will be. This is because muscle power is a factor of the cross-sectional surface area of the muscle, and not its volume. Therefore, we find that ants can drag up to 1,000 times their own mass, and a dung beetle can lift up to 850 times its own mass.

Ants

Keenest sense of smell

The males of the emperor moth have plumed feelers with which they can smell the pheromones of females at a distance of up to 15km. Their sense of smell is 1,500 times keener than that of humans.

Plumed feelers of a male emperor moth

Best vision

The eyes of dragonflies consist of up to 28,000 'facets', or tiny eyes, and these insects probably see three-dimensional hologram images. The eyesight of some flies is probably as sharp as that of dragonflies. Moths, such as the death's-head moth (*Acherontia atropos*), have night vision comparable to that of dragonflies and flies.

Eyes of a fly

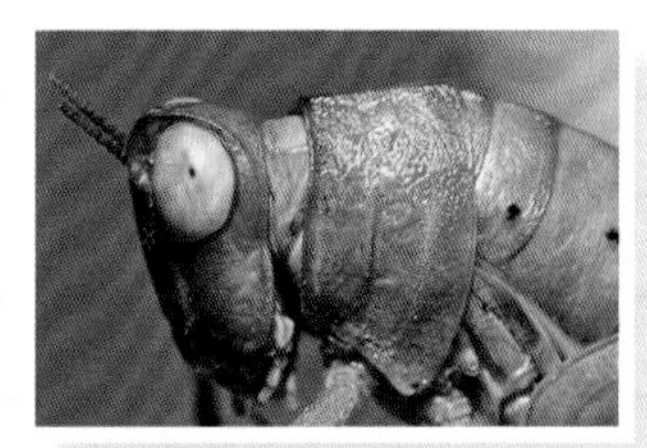

Eye of a grasshopper

Loudest noise

Cicadas create the loudest noise – the song of the African *Brevisana* sp. has been measured at 106.7 decibels.

Cicada

Most genetic forms

There are more than 30 different colour varieties in females of the mocker swallowtail butterfly (*Papilio dardanus*), each of which mimics a different poisonous butterfly. This variation overshadows the 12 different castes that certain species of ant can produce.

Colour varieties in female mocker swallowtail butterflies, with poisonous models on the left

Most hosts

The tsetse fly will bite any vertebrate animal and is probably the least specialised bloodsucker.

Similarly undiscriminating, one tiger moth is known to have at least 636 plant species as hosts.

Most heat resistant

The insects that are most resistant to heat are found in the Namib Desert. One of the Namib ants (*Ocymyrmex* sp.) can still be active when the surface temperature reaches 60°C. Some heat-seeking jewel beetles can tolerate this temperature too.

Most cold resistant

Various insects can remain active at temperatures below freezing, but one kind of bloodworm – the larval stage of Chironomidae – can survive temperatures as low as -270°C. To accomplish this, the bloodworm loses 97 per cent of its body moisture.

Toughest

Some insects have become resistant to virtually any commercial insecticide. The ultimate toughness in an insect this author has witnessed was when a student prepared a rice weevil for electron microscopy. The weevil was kept in 90 per cent alcohol for two days, after which it was coated with carbon and gold in a vacuum. The weevil then began walking around in the vacuum chamber of the microscope!

Jewel beetle

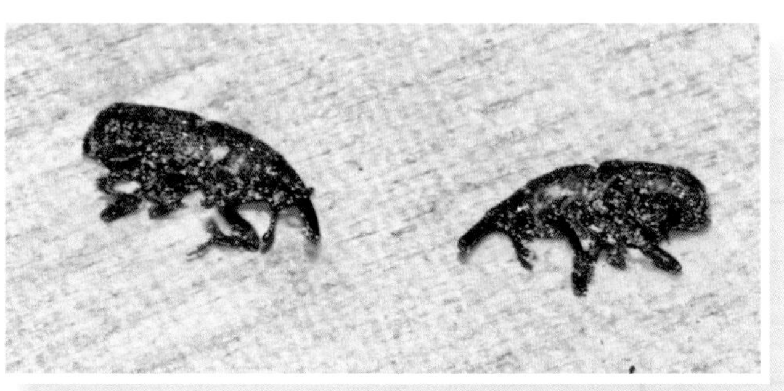

Rice weevils

FANTASTICAL FLOURISHES

Many insects look a little strange to the human brain, but two contenders for the title of 'most fantastical' are emperor moth larvae and twig wilters. The emperor moth larva (right) is usually green and decorated with colourful warts, hairs or spines – most of which seem squandered on such a short life phase. The lace-like adornments of the twig wilter (far right) make this bug almost unrecognisable as an insect. They also most certainly impede its movements.

2

Reproduction

Because insects are so small, mating is an extraordinary challenge. They need acute senses, and at least one of the sexes must have the ability to move over relatively vast distances.

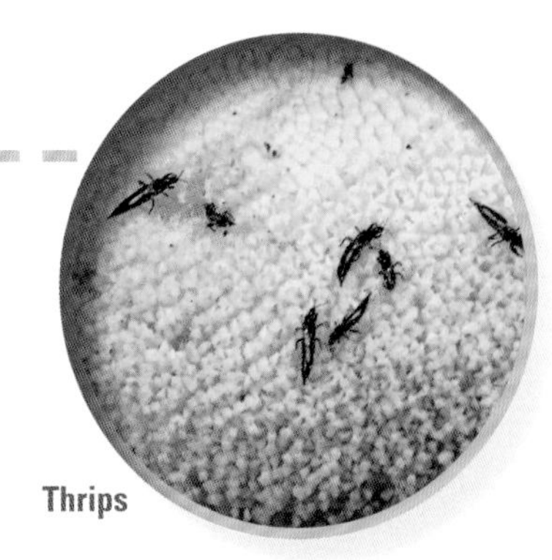
Thrips

ASEXUAL REPRODUCTION

Most insect species have both male and female sexes, but a few species have females only.

Walking sticks

Stick insects are large, clumsy and slow, and depend solely on camouflage for their defence – which also means that they move as little as possible. Such a lifestyle is not conducive to socialising. Females of most species can, therefore, lay viable eggs without fertilisation, and some species have lost their males altogether. Where males do occur they are much smaller than the females.

Other groups in which parthenogenesis is common are thrips, bagworm moths, fish moths, roaches, weevils, waxy scales and ground pearls.

Many species of waxy scale do not have males.

Adult ground pearl (left), with immature stages encapsulated in 'pearls' (right)

Part-time virgins

Aphids have combined the advantages of 'virgin birth' (parthenogenesis) and sexual reproduction. Whereas some tropical species, including the giant willow aphid (*Tuberolachnus salignus*), are truly parthenogenetic throughout the year, most aphids have developed different reproductive strategies that coincide with different seasons.

During spring and summer, when there is plenty of food and the weather is warm, females will reproduce without their eggs being fertilised. The eggs hatch inside them, and they give birth to nymphs on the plant they occupy, enabling them to multiply rapidly. In the autumn winged males and

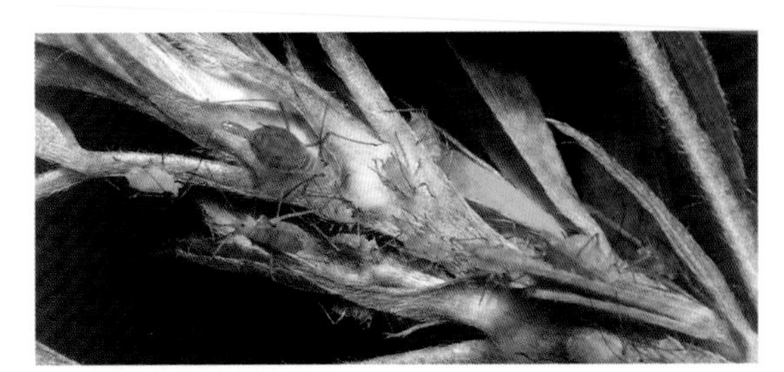
Many aphid species alternate between sexual reproduction and parthenogenesis.

Giant willow aphids never produce males.

Winged male and female aphids

females appear, which migrate to new host plants where they mate and the female lays her eggs. The fertilised eggs go into a winter resting phase (diapause), and in spring wingless females are born that once again reproduce parthenogenetically.

In this way, aphids are able to exploit favourable weather conditions by reproducing extremely fast, and still retain genetic variability, mobility and a dormant egg phase by alternating sexual and asexual generations.

Short-changed males

In the order of wasps, bees and ants (Hymenoptera), all males are produced parthenogenetically. Although they are of the opposite sex, they are clones or blueprints of their mother.

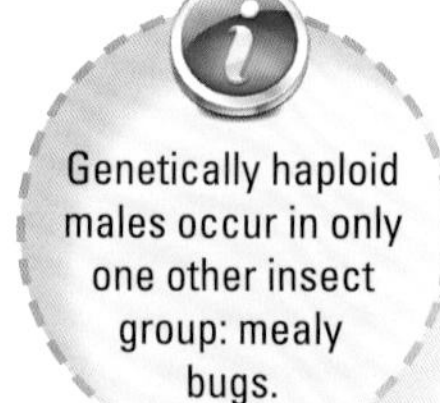

Genetically haploid males occur in only one other insect group: mealy bugs.

The eggs and sperm of all animals are haploid (contain a single set of chromosomes). In wasps, bees and ants, if an egg remains unfertilised, it develops into a haploid male. If it is fertilised, it develops into a diploid female, which has a full set of chromosomes – one from each parent.

Female hymenopterans normally have a special sperm purse (spermatheca) in which they can keep sperm alive for a considerable period after mating. The queen ant or bee can store millions of sperm in her sperm purse for years on end. To keep the sperm alive for long periods, she feeds them, using special glands in the sperm purse. The female can determine the sex of her offspring by releasing a sperm from her sperm purse or withholding it.

CHOOSING MR RIGHT

While the male is generally the more mobile of the sexes and goes in search of a mate, it is usually the female's privilege to select her suitor. First, she must ensure that her consort belongs to her own species. Second, if there is an oversupply of males, she may also have the opportunity to pick for quality. Often males will sort out their ranking among themselves. When a male mates with a female, he will do everything in his power to monopolise her and to keep other males away from his conquest.

Advertising for a mate

Much of the fantastic variety of colour and shape in insects exists just to send identification signals to the opposite sex. Insects often display their visual characteristics in special mating 'dances' or 'display posturing'.

A queen bee surrounded by sterile (female) workers

A fruit fly displays by wiggling its wings.

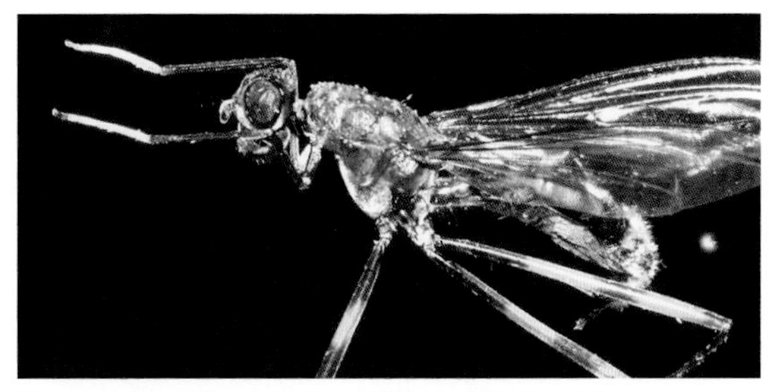

A semaphore fly signals with its white front legs.

A male mantid displays his species-specific colour signals on his front legs.

Many butterflies bob to a certain rhythm in a species-specific pattern of flight or wing beat that allows mating partners to recognise each other. Fruit flies wave and twist their wings in a specific pattern while sitting, and semaphore flies have white glove-like front feet with which they wave and signal to attract a mate.

Predatory insects have particularly elaborate displays, because not being recognised as a mating partner could be lethal, especially for the males, which are generally smaller. The male mantid gives an extensive display, involving species-specific colour signals on his front legs. This 'dance' is performed within sight of the female but out of her physical reach to ensure that she does not mistake him for a potential meal! Male fish moths and earwigs also perform mating dances.

Defending the territory

Many insect males must conquer a physical territory needed by the female and her offspring before the female will mate with them.

Male dragonflies occupy the lookout posts in their territories in the morning and then spend their day keeping watch. The male will immediately intercept anything entering his territory and then subject it to a strict order of priorities. First, he will try to mate with it; if unsuitable, he will try to eat it; if impossible, he will try to chase it away with all his might, especially if it takes the form of a competing male.

As the third option is most often the case, aerial dogfights between male dragonflies are a common sight close to any water. These males chase each other until a compromise 'border' between their territories has been established, much in the same way as dogs do on neighbouring properties.

A male dragonfly keeps watch over his territory.

Fascinating fact

Most insect genitalia have 'lock and key' structures that prevent a mismatch between different species (see Chapter 1). For example, the tail claspers of male dragonflies and earwigs have to fit the neck area of their respective females before mating can proceed.

Pecking order

In many species, males eliminate each other from the mating competition by fighting to establish their rank. Those who do not make the grade often lose all sexual interest and may even become sterile.

When house crickets are kept at high densities, males will fight for positions in the pecking order. In the Far East, there is an old tradition of rearing fighting crickets to compete in prizefights, with large amounts of money being bet on worthy contenders. Oddly, the biggest and strongest male cricket will not necessarily emerge as the winner.

A series of classical experiments can be used to explain the outcome of these contests. First, 10 male crickets are placed in a cage that is too small to allow for individual territories. In a series of duels, they will quickly sort out a pecking order from one to 10. Fights may be determined by simple threats and posturing, or may escalate into hitting, kicking and biting. In all cases, the winner eventually does a 'victory song' that thoroughly humiliates the loser and effectively dissuades him from further hostility.

After one or two nights of fighting, the pecking order is established. When the crickets become active in the evening, the seniors will briefly remind their juniors of their rank when they meet, and thus the order from one to the lowly number of 10 is re-established.

Most surprising is that the pecking order does not correlate with the crickets' physical size or strength. Number one may be a rather average cricket, whereas the strongest cricket may be much lower down in the rankings.

This phenomenon can be further examined in another experiment, where numbers five and six are removed from the cricket cage. While together in isolation, number five will humiliate number six every evening. An unexpected thing happens when these two crickets are returned to the main cage. Number five now has a 'superiority complex' and immediately beats up numbers four to one, becoming the new leader. Conversely, number six has developed an 'inferiority complex' and promptly drops out to number 10.

Male house crickets will fiercely compete to establish a ranking order. The action starts with a duel (top), followed by the winner (centre, with the victor on the right) performing a 'victory song' (above).

This experiment can be extended using any number of 'morale boosters', such as females, food or shelter, and their inverse (deprivation of these elements). It will always produce the same result: success in ranking fights is based on self-confidence, which, in turn, is based on recent experience. This absolute correlation between self-esteem and success in the pecking order could be applied to political leaders: all they need to get to the top of the pile is a misguided belief in their own superiority!

A very peculiar form of ranking competition is found in stalk-eyed flies, where males 'outstare' each other. They have consequently selectively developed ridiculously wide heads.

Bridal gifts

Male dung beetles that assemble large dung balls and trundle them off are not collecting booty for themselves; they are, in fact, assembling a wedding gift. Patrolling females have a connoisseur's eye for a quality dung ball, and will attach themselves to the best specimen they can spot, while it is rolled along by the male. Males roll the dung ball as fast and as far away as possible from the dung pad, since thieving males are always on the prowl, looking to steal a prize dung ball – often with the attached female who has no particular preference for a specific male. The winner becomes owner of both the dung ball and the female and has the honour of mating with her. The couple bury the dung ball in a breeding chamber, and the female then lays her egg, fertilised by the male, in the supply of dung.

Males of many roaches, katydids and armoured ground crickets have special abdominal glands that produce a protein-rich secretion, designed to entice females to mate, and females will refuse males who do not offer such a gift. The compulsory gift also weeds out inferior males who cannot accumulate the necessary energy surplus to produce this secretion, and enhances the reproductive success of both male and female by channelling more energy and nutrients to their offspring.

However, the male mantid pays the highest price for mating success. The female will often simply turn around and start devouring the male from the head down. This happens so frequently that male mantids have adapted to the situation and mate equally well with or without a head and thorax. The hind legs and abdomen of the male are autonomously programmed so that, if one should turn the hind body upside down on the female, the legs will feel around and bring the hind body into position again. The hind body will then re-engage and continue copulating.

A female dung beetle secures herself to a dung ball.

A male dung beetle tries to steal another beetle's dung ball.

Fascinating fact

A male hanging fly has to offer captured prey to his prospective 'bride' before she will mate with him. However, males are not always honest, and they often suck the juices out of the prey for themselves before handing it over. By the time that the fooled female realises her mistake, it is too late.

Male hanging fly

Male fruit chafers wait for females at a sap flow.

Singles pubs

Many insects have sites where 'nubile' females are likely to turn up. Males assemble at these sites, some even trying to monopolise them. Typical examples are the sap flows on *Combretum molle, Ziziphus mucronata* or *Tipuana* trees, where males of a variety of fruit chafers will assemble and try to fight each other off. These males are less interested in the sweet, fermenting juice oozing from the tree 'wounds' than they are in the females of their species that will predictably be attracted to the site. The sap flows are infected by bacteria and may ferment and fester for days, becoming fixed rendezvous sites for fruit chafers in the area.

Fascinating fact

The *Dalechampia* flower actively encourages a rendezvous between solitary bees: it not only rewards bees with resin, it also folds over at night to enclose and protect visiting males. The eventual arrival of a female bee means both male bee and flower have achieved their fertilisation aims.

The *Dalechampia* flower (left) offers protection to visiting bees when it closes at night (right).

Midge and chafer males and honeybee drones often congregate in large mating swarms, making it easier for females to find them. In summer, a large swarm of up to 10,000 honeybee drones from different hives gather each day in a fixed area. It is not clear how these sites are selected, but virgin queens know exactly where to go! The queen flies through the swarm and is promptly followed by hundreds of drones, forming what looks like the tail of a comet. Up to 30 drones mate with her, filling her sperm purse, and the fertilised queen returns to the hive with enough sperm to fertilise her eggs over the next few years. In this way, adequate genetic variation in her offspring is guaranteed, thereby enhancing the survival of the swarm.

Endurance racing

In the Namib, a whole train of male suitors of some toktokkies will follow a female around. This procession will run when the female runs and stop when she stops to feed, following her for days on end. The males do not get a chance to feed and have to be very tough to stay 'in the running'. Only when the female is ready to lay eggs will she allow the first in line to mate with her. Occasionally, some males will drop out from hunger or exhaustion. Curiously, the males do not attempt to get in front of each other in the line.

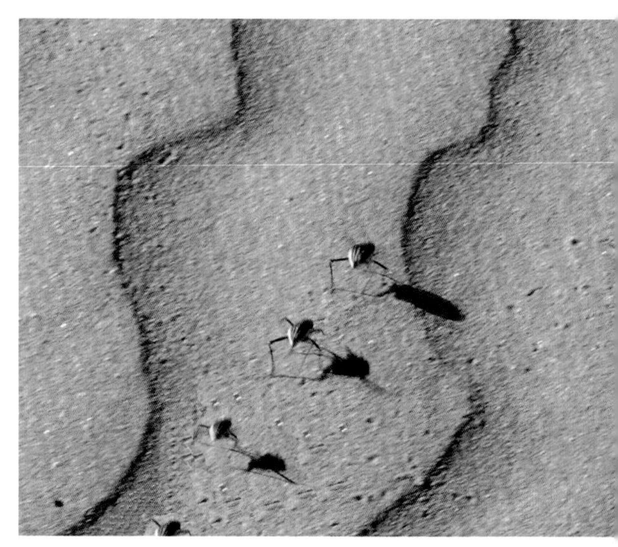

Male Namib toktokkies line up behind a female.

Dirty tricks

Adult fish moths regularly shed their skins, and with every shedding, the contents of the female's sperm purse are discarded – making it impossible for males to monopolise females.

Many males exploit the mating songs of their competition (see Chapter 7). However, male bedbugs exhibit the most violent mating parasitism. They inseminate the female by jabbing their dagger-like penis in between her body segments and squirting their semen into her blood cavity. The aggressive sperm then swim to the ovaries and dig through the ovary wall to the eggs to fertilise them.

Male bedbugs will sometimes rape other males in the same way. Their sperms then 'hijack' the testes of the raped male, who in his next mating session will spread the sperm of his rapist, and not his own!

The monopoly game

A male will go to great lengths to monopolise a female once he has secured her. Male grasshoppers will often spend days riding on the female they have fertilised, simply to prevent other males from mounting her. In this time, they cannot feed and are often exposed to the hot sun. Eventually they will drop off, giving another male the opportunity to mount the female, mate with her and monopolise her.

Male stainer-bugs take the monopoly game to a different level by simply refusing to disengage for days on end. Forced to run backwards during this period, they have evolved to run equally well in both directions.

Beetles also show this monopolising behaviour and female Namib toktokkies may benefit significantly from the shade provided by jealous males on their backs. To monopolise the female, some crickets have developed stoppers that they insert into the female's genital opening after mating. In the course of evolution, however, competing males have come up with 'corkscrews' to remove these stoppers. The whole rigmarole of 'stoppers' and 'corkscrews' has become a fixed but redundant strategy.

Extreme monopolisation occurs in some parasitic wasps, where the male not only fertilises the female, but inseminates all her female offspring as well, while they are still in the egg stage.

Male locust monopolising a female

Stainer-bugs engage in a mating game that can last for days on end.

Fascinating fact

Sometimes, in spite of a male insect remaining mounted on a female to prevent competition from other males, a second contender may try mounting the first – rarely with any success.

Two male mantids jostle for mating space.

INSECT KAMA SUTRA

Tail to tail

Research has shown that primordial insects mated tail to tail. This is still the mating position of most bugs, flies, butterflies, moths and earwigs.

Compact grasshopper species also mate tail to tail, but in slender types, the male mounts the female. The male then has to contort his abdomen through 180°. This same form of contortion is seen in mantids and heel-walkers.

Craneflies

Butterflies

Mantids

Compact grasshoppers

Twisted inside

To overcome their specific mating challenges, males of all species in the beetle order, including toktokkies and weevils, have inverted genitalia, tucked inside the abdominal cavity. This enables them to mate comfortably in the mounted position without having to invert the abdomen.

Some male beetles need special adaptations to stay mounted on their females. Toktokkies in the *Psammodes* genus have velvet pads on the abdomen to stay on top of the

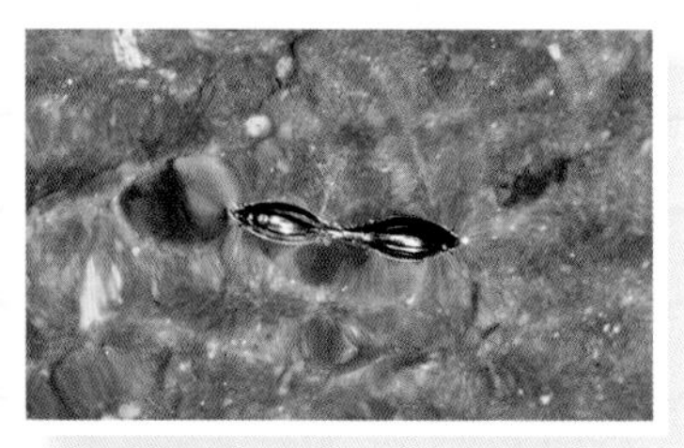

Whirligig beetles

Acacia weevils

White-legged toktokkies

smooth, round female. Water beetles have special suckers on their front legs to cling to the slippery female.

A whirligig male cannot mount a female on the surface of the water, and the pair have to mate back to back through a 'second inversion' of the male's genitalia.

The males of many flies and wasps also have inverted genitalia and mate in a mounted position.

Mating by proxy

The female dragonfly flies low over open water, dipping her abdomen into the water to lay her eggs beneath the surface. This ensures that the eggs remain submerged and do not dry out. During this risky procedure, the male flies in tandem by holding the female behind the head with his abdominal claspers. The male dragonfly is unable to mate with the female in this position, so before a mating flight he deposits his sperm into a special

Flying in tandem

Female dragonfly collecting sperm from the male's pocket

sperm pocket behind his thorax. The female dragonfly can supply herself with sperm from the male's sperm pocket, which she can even do while they are flying in tandem.

Fish moths also mate indirectly. The male does a mating dance and deposits a sperm packet (spermatophore) on the substrate, which the female picks up.

Female on top

In house crickets, the male backs up underneath the female during copulation, possibly because of the long ovipositor of the female.

Mating house crickets

KEY CHOICES TO ENSURE SURVIVAL

Where and how insects lay their eggs may be the single most important factor in their survival. Eggs and freshly hatched larvae are particularly small, vulnerable and immobile. Insect eggs provide small predators, ants and wasp parasites with easy, nutritious and defenceless pickings. Eggs are, furthermore, vulnerable to desiccation, fungal infection and excessive heat or cold.

Some moths produce a type of cocoon to protect their eggs.

Nursery food

The most common strategy of an insect mother is to deposit her offspring on or near the food they will require. Few insects will simply drop their eggs randomly – although stick insects are a notable exception.

Plant-feeding insects lay their eggs on exactly the right host plant. This is logical for beetles and bugs, where adults generally live on the same host plant as their larvae or nymphs. Bugs usually secure their eggs to the plant with a glue-like substance, to counter the removal of the eggs by ants.

Leaf beetles (left) glue their eggs (right) to the leaves of the host plant of their future larvae.

Although adult butterflies and moths feed on food that is totally different from that of their caterpillars, such as nectar (a), fruit juice (b) or even mammals' eye moisture (c), they unfailingly lay their eggs on the host plant their larvae need.

Some female cicadas, damselflies, crickets, sawflies and beetles have hard ovipositors that can drill into plant tissue. Eggs deposited in this manner are protected from predators and desiccation – although, once the eggs have hatched, the nymphs or larvae may feed on the outside of the plant.

The female cycad weevil (*Antliarrhinus zamiae*) has taken ovipositing inside plants to the extreme. She has a snout several times her own body length with which she drills a hole through the thick cycad cone, down to the seeds. She deposits an egg in the tunnel and shoves it right down with her long snout, so that the hatching larva can burrow straight into the seed.

Parasitic insects need to take extra care to lay their eggs within reach of the host and this is often a dangerous task. Nest parasites of bees, wasps and ants need special protective devices to enter the nests of their armed and lethal hosts. Cuckoo wasps and velvet ant wasps are therefore heavily armoured against the sting of their mason wasp hosts, and have impressive stings themselves.

A bee fly hovers above a wasp tunnel, 'bombing' it with an egg.

Female velvet ant wasps parasitise other wasps' nests with their own offspring.

Bee flies often parasitise the ground tunnels of digger wasps. Because bee flies are unarmed and defenceless, they have developed a special strategy to lay their eggs in such tunnels. The female bee fly waits until the owner is nearby and has opened up the tunnel, and then hovers perfectly still while 'bombing' her eggs from a safe height into the narrow nest opening. If the egg misses the 'target', the bee fly sees it with her large and sharp eyes and tries again!

One egg, many offspring

Some parasitic wasps that lay their eggs in caterpillars have developed a unique way to ensure that the maximum number of offspring can develop. The wasp lays just one egg in the caterpillar, but the egg will subdivide into a number that is exactly attuned to the species and age of the caterpillar and its projected growth potential, thus ensuring that the larvae have enough food. This is a rather complex predictive calculation, and yet the original egg will always subdivide into the correct number of eggs! The larvae will eventually devour their host from the inside, and emerge to pupate on the outside of the caterpillar.

Some caterpillars have evolved appendages on their skin that mimic 'parasite pupae' to ward off parasitic wasps from laying eggs in them.

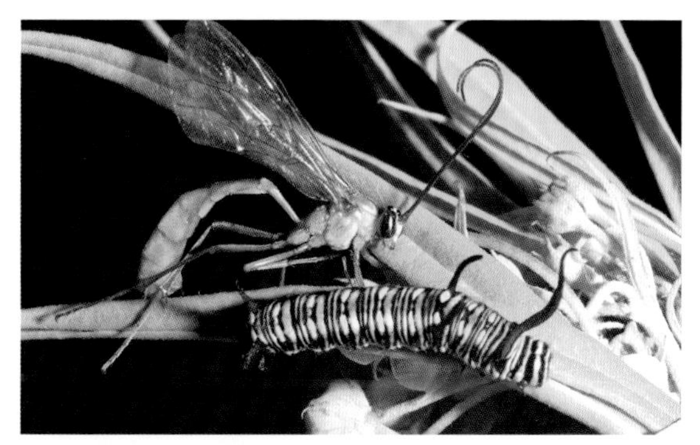

A parasitic wasp lays an egg in a caterpillar.

A caterpillar with the cocoons of parasitic wasp larvae that have emerged from its body

Some caterpillars display false cocoons to deter parasitic wasps from laying their eggs in them.

Eggs with special tricks

Stink bugs lay hard-shelled eggs and often glue them to the substrate. The eggs have a special lid (operculum) that can be opened from the inside, allowing the small nymph to emerge, despite having only sucking mouthparts.

Head lice lay their white eggs (nits) with tough glue on human hair. When nymphs need to emerge, they first swallow air until the lid pops up. Then they force the air through their gut, expel it through the anus and literally pop themselves out of the close-fitting egg pneumatically!

MIND THOSE EGGS!

Insects have developed many strategies to safeguard their eggs during the weeks or months they take to develop and hatch.

Eggs in packets

A common way of protecting eggs is through an egg packet produced by the female's accessory glands, usually while the eggs are being laid. Most roaches produce eggs in an egg packet that is carried in the genital opening until the nymphs hatch; in some species the egg packet is immediately placed in a safe hiding place.

Female roach carrying an egg packet

Mantid nymphs emerge from an egg packet.

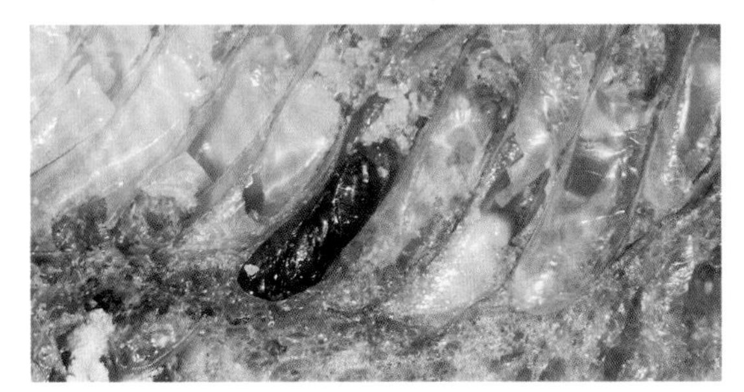

A parasitic wasp develops inside the egg packet of a mantid.

A female katydid uses her long ovipositor to deposit her eggs in the soil.

Female mantids produce egg packets from 'plastic' foam similar to polyurethane foam, which is interspersed at regular intervals with egg chambers, each containing one egg. Eventually the hatching nymphs emerge through a special 'escape route'. The packets are tough and provide excellent insulation as well as protection, and empty packets may last for many months before withering away. One parasitic wasp, however, has developed a long ovipositor to penetrate the packets and parasitise the developing nymphs.

The female grasshopper lays her eggs in soil tunnels that she bores with special auger plates on her abdomen. At the bottom of this tunnel, the female deposits a number of eggs neatly packaged in a 'plastic-foam' parcel, and fills up the hole; however, this does not prevent larvae of blister beetles from finding these eggs and preying on them.

Fascinating fact

In some insects that have access to unlimited supplies of high-protein food, such as blood-sucking tsetse flies and blowflies, the eggs hatch inside the mother and live nymphs or larvae are born. This strategy greatly accelerates their life cycles.

Female blowfly

Father minds the eggs

A very rare case of exclusively male brood care occurs in some water bugs, which carry a whole raft of eggs glued to their back until the eggs hatch. It was originally presumed that these individuals were females, and it took a female entomologist to realise that it is physically impossible for a female to stick the eggs onto her own back. What happens, in fact, is that the female only mates with a male if he submits to having the eggs stuck onto his back. The male, thus burdened, cannot fly and is handicapped in his movements. He will have to faithfully aerate, shuffle and protect the eggs until they hatch and set him free.

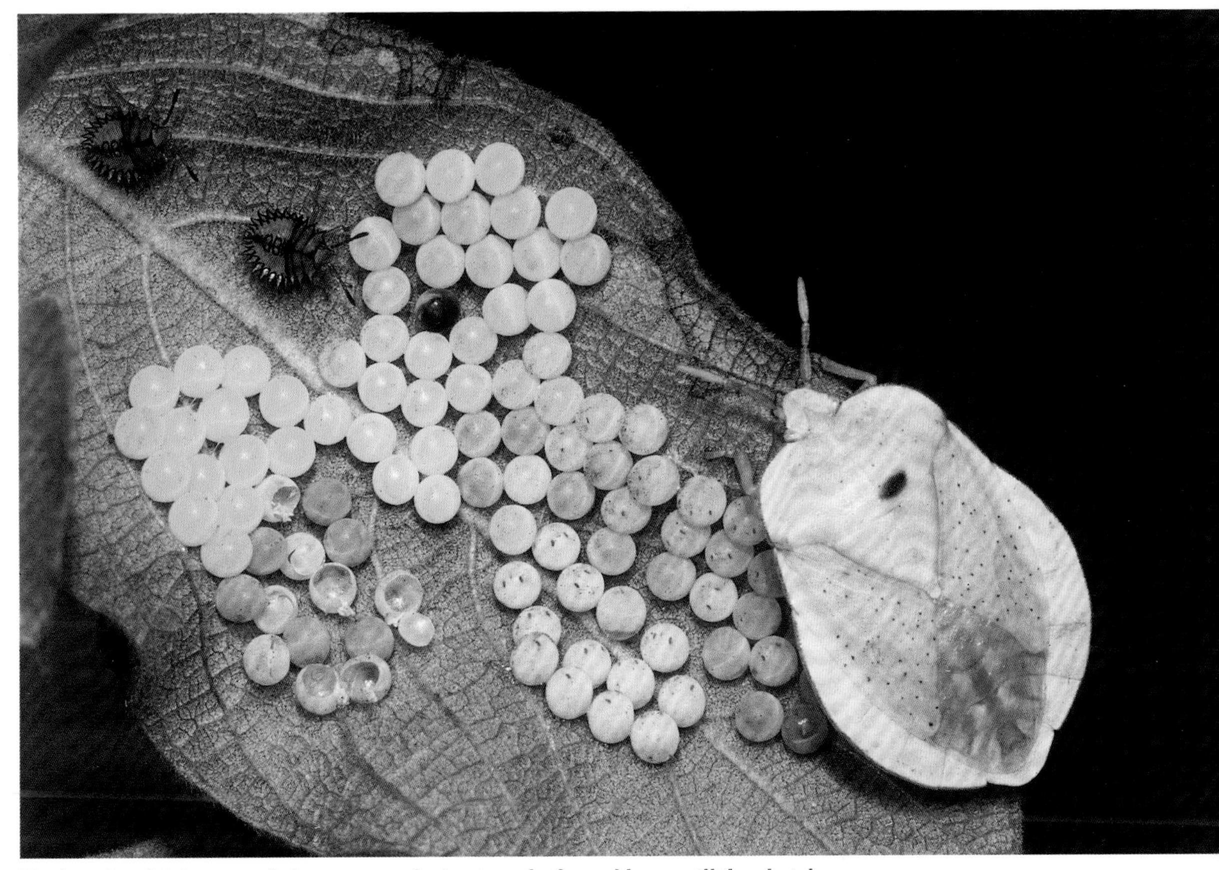

The female stink bug guards her eggs against ants and other robbers until they hatch.

Mother minds the eggs

Some female stink bugs guard their eggs until they hatch. While this strategy is effective against small predators such as ants, small parasitic wasps use the mother as a beacon to find the eggs, which they easily and stealthily parasitise behind her back.

Some wingless roaches not only carry their egg packets, they even carry the hatched nymphs on their undersides for several days. However, the ultimate brood care in roaches occurs in species where hatched nymphs actually re-enter the female and attach themselves to the feeding glands of a 'pseudo placenta'. After growing considerably, they are then literally born again – much like kangaroos emerging from their mother's pouch.

Other groups where mothers actively watch over and protect their eggs are earwigs, web-spinners, some dung beetles and some mantids.

ENDOWMENTS AND INHERITANCE

Many different insects spend considerable time and energy collecting food supplies for their offspring – an activity from which they themselves do not benefit. In addition, the food store invariably attracts robbers, and has to be defended or be hidden at great risk and effort.

All social insects and some solitary insects feed their larvae or nymphs continuously until they reach maturity. In some species this usually means employing sophisticated navigational skills to locate appropriate food sources and to home to the nest.

DESIGNER EGGS

Insects are masterful at protecting their eggs. Mantids, for example, create elongated egg packets on bark, balloon-like packets in grass and foam-type packets on branches, grass or rocks. The balloon structures have a translucent shell, helping to create a hothouse environment for the rapid incubation of the eggs suspended inside. Insects that do not create egg packets use various other means to protect their eggs. Bugs construct glued batches of eggs, mosquitoes build floating egg rafts, and some moths use material from their cocoons to make egg baskets. Lacewings create 'forests' of eggs on long, thin, silken stalks on leaves, probably to place the eggs out of easy reach of ants and other predatory insects.

Balloon-like egg packets

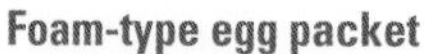

Foam-type egg packet

Moth egg basket made from a pupal cocoon

The green lacewing (below left) lays its eggs on thin silken stalks spun on leaves (below right).

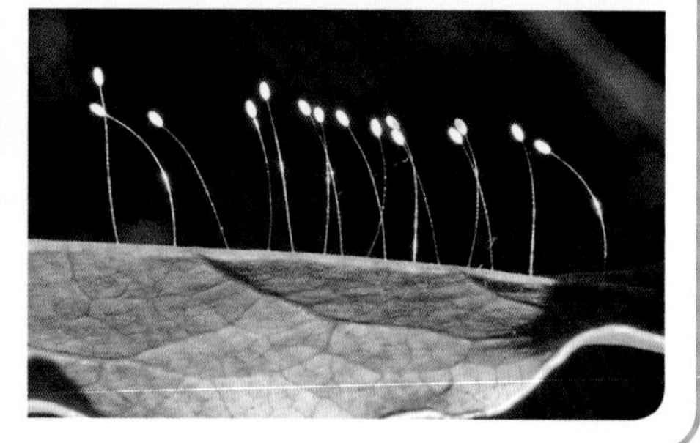

Dung beetles

Some small dung pad beetles lay their eggs directly in a dung pad. Their larvae have only about a week to mature and pupate before their food supply dries out. Other dung beetles, such as the larger, horned dung beetles, for example *Copris* and *Heliocopris* spp., burrow into a dung pad and then dig a tunnel in the soil underneath it, which they provision with dung taken from the pad. Here the female lays her eggs in the dung, and will often stay with her brood until they hatch.

The most striking form of brood care, however, is demonstrated by the ball-rollers, which are mostly diurnal. The male dung beetle shapes a large 'brood ball' from dung and rolls it away with his four hind legs; en route, a female may join him if attracted to his dung offering. Once the pair has buried the dung ball in a subterranean chamber excavated in the soil, the female lays an egg in it and seals the ball with clay. The larva completes its whole growth cycle inside the ball, and pupates there, eventually emerging as a fully grown beetle.

Horned dung beetles lay their eggs in dung balls in a tunnel excavated in the soil under a dung pad.

Ball-rollers cart their food supply of dung a safe distance away before burying it for their brood.

Interesting variations of ball-rolling behaviour occur. Some small ball-rollers (*Sisyphus* spp.) manoeuvre dung balls up grass stems and then cover them in clay. Others (*Sceliages* spp.) feed only on dead millipedes, not dung, and push these forward (instead of rolling them backward, like the ball-rollers do). When the beetle reaches a suitable place, it will dig a tunnel in which to deposit the dead millipede.

Some small dung beetles have learned to become parasitic on larger species, and lay their eggs in their brood balls – or even in their dead millipedes.

Wingless desert dung beetles (*Pachysoma* spp.) occur along the West Coast and in the Namib

A beetle of the *Sceliages* genus pushes a dead millipede.

A small dung beetle parasitises the dead millipede of a *Sceliages* beetle.

A wingless desert dung beetle hauls a dry dung pellet to its burrow.

Desert, where the only dung available consists of bone-dry pellets. These beetles have to cart a fair number of pellets to their burrow.

Because food is scarce, they will even collect leaves as forage, transporting them by pressing the leaves to their abdomen with their hind legs. To feed their larvae adequately on this low-grade food, they need to make repeated foraging runs, which are clearly displayed by the many tracks leading to their tunnels.

They must dig deep tunnels into wet sand layers to moisten the dry foodstuff – a specialised art in the dry sand of the area. The food store eventually becomes infested with fungi, and the dung beetles and their larvae probably live off these, rather than off the dung and leaves.

Tracks in the sand (top) are a sign of the many foraging trips undertaken by the wingless desert dung beetle (centre) to find food, including dead plant matter (above).

Fascinating fact

Female leaf-rolling weevils (of the family Attelabidae) cut leaves in a neat pattern and roll them into solid parcels, still attached to the host plant. One egg is deposited in each parcel, thereby providing the developing larva with both food and protection.

Egg parcel of a leaf-rolling weevil (inset)

Digger wasps

Digger wasps dig tunnels in which they store a food supply of paralysed insect prey for their larvae. Different species specialise in different prey. Most take caterpillars, but various wasps prefer bugs, roaches, grasshoppers, crickets, katydids and even jewel beetles.

The prey is paralysed but not killed, as it is essential that it stays alive for the several weeks it may take the wasp larva to complete its growth. The wasp larva is programmed to feed on the prey in such a way that the prey stays alive for as long as possible.

Digger wasps face challenges during the process of feeding their larvae. Members of their own and other wasp species will try to rob them of their prey, and, once the tunnel is dug, members of their own species will try to open their tunnels, devour the egg, and lay their own eggs on the paralysed prey. Moreover, other parasites, such as velvet ant wasps and bee flies, will also lay their

After paralysing a caterpillar by stinging it, the digger wasp stores it underground as food for its larvae.

A digger wasp steals prey from another member of the species.

Some digger wasps specialise in bugs as prey.

Using a stone, this digger wasp tamps down the soil inside the tunnel entrance to camouflage it and keep out unwanted visitors.

eggs in any provisioned tunnel they find. In an attempt to prevent this, digger wasps camouflage the entrance to their tunnel and tamp down the soil using a rock clamped in their mandibles. This use of a tool is unique among insects (apart from the 'musical instruments' they sometimes construct – see Chapter 7).

Some digger wasps do not simply provision a single nest with adequate food and leave it; they construct a number of nests, and provide each nest with food every day. These wasps have to remember the localities of their hidden nests and, as their various offspring are of different ages, with different food requirements, they have to remember the size and requirements of the larva in each one. These wasps, therefore, need both complex navigational skills and an excellent memory. However, once set, a mother's program cannot be altered.

Every morning, the wasp will visit all her tunnels and open each one for inspection. For the rest of the day she will hunt to provide each nest with what it needs. Should one switch around the occupants of the nests at this stage, the mother will mechanically carry on feeding fully grown pupae and starving young larvae, although she can 'see' that the inhabitants no longer match her feeding efforts. This example illustrates the programmed behaviour displayed by insects, when compared with the more rational behaviour of vertebrates.

Clay wasps

Both mason wasps and potter wasps build clay nests away from the ground, which they provision with prey like the digger wasps do.

The mud nests of mason wasps are built with the entrance usually pointing downward.

Each potter wasp nest contains a single egg.

The wasp transports clay to the building site in dozens of pellets, which she gathers up in her mandibles at a suitable muddy site and moulds it into a clay nest, the shape of which varies according to the species.

In compound nests with several cells, which are added in a continuous process, prey and young larvae, grown wasp larvae and wasp pupae can be found in adjoining cells.

These wasps are also exposed to nest parasitism, particularly by velvet ant wasps and cuckoo wasps.

Spider-hunting wasps

The brood care of the large metallic blue or black spider-hunting wasps is similar to that of digger and clay wasps, but they specialise in spiders as prey.

Fights between spider-hunting wasps and their equally dangerous prey can be spectacular. The wasp must paralyse the spider, thus keeping it alive to be consumed gradually by the wasp larva. Some wasps ensure permanent immobility by also biting off the spider's legs.

The spider-hunting wasp first digs a tunnel and camouflages it, before going hunting. In general, spiders are too heavy to carry in flight, which means that the wasp often has to drag its prey over all kinds of obstacles. Spider-hunting wasps have even been seen to drop their prey into a stream and to propel it across by taking hold of it and fanning themselves forward with their wings.

A spider-hunting wasp drags its prey to its nest, overcoming obstacles along the way.

Leafcutting bees cut leaves in neat semicircles with their scissor-like mandibles. As they cut through the leaf they simultaneously roll up the cut section with their hind legs. The rolled leaves are used as lining in the tunnels of their nests.

Solitary bees

Most bees are not social like the honeybee, but live solitary lives. All of them, however, construct nests with food supplies for their offspring (or at least provide for their offspring by parasitising the supplies of other bees).

Some solitary bees opportunistically make clay nests in pipes (left), small hollow branches (above) or woodborers' tunnels.

Carpenter bees

The large carpenter bee is a common sight in all flowering gardens. Less desirable are the holes they drill into outside timber, such as wooden pergolas. Carpenter bees do not digest wood; they use it to construct brood chambers, which they provision with pollen and honey. Often a number of females may cohabit in one wooden beam, in which case the bees will use and defend a communal entrance. Each female works and cares for her own progeny.

Construction and provisioning of the nest starts with the first cell (comprising pollen, honey and an egg) at the farthest end of the tunnel. As the bee has to keep building up from there, the eggs are programmed to hatch in inverted sequence: the last egg hatches first, with the rest hatching in reverse order. This prevents the first emerging bee from being sealed in by immature siblings.

Foraging toktokkies

One species of toktokkie (*Parastizopus* sp.) found in the Kalahari forages for dead leaves and carries them to a nest in the sand. Male and female toktokkies drag the leaves into the nest at night where they feed them to their larvae. They prefer leaves from *Lebeckia* bushes, as they are high in nitrogen.

Eventually, the first larvae pupate and emerge as adults. They are in no hurry to leave and often stay for two months, feeding on the forage that their parents bring them. One nest can thus include adults from two generations. The beetles also often occupy deserted mouse tunnels, with different families living in branches of the same tunnel.

These interesting 'subsocial' *Parastizopus* beetles house several guests in their nests. One is a smaller toktokkie (*Eremostibes* sp.) and its larvae, which do not contribute to the communal food stores on which they live. Their contribution may possibly lie in their strong defensive secretions which are likely to augment the equally strong-smelling secretions of their hosts.

***Parastizopus* beetle**

NO NERDY MALES WANTED

Males of the foraging toktokkie (*Parastizopus*) are responsible for digging nest tunnels after it has rained. They must be fit and work quickly, as they have to stay ahead of the fast-drying layers of wet sand.

They therefore have to prove their mettle when it comes to mating. To test the 'quality' of a male, the female will lift him with her front legs to 'weigh' him. If he is considered too light, his approaches are rejected, and the female waits for a better proposition.

3

Metamorphosis

Metamorphosis involves the transformation of an insect from egg, via larva and pupa, to adult. This transformation of body form and structure, typical of insects such as beetles, moths and butterflies, only developed late in the evolution of insects. Primitive insects, on the other hand, undergo few changes between emergence from their eggs and adulthood.

Ladybeetle

DRAMATIC TRANSFORMATION

Insects are known for their dramatic physical changes as they grow from hatchlings to adults. However, there are also some obvious advantages to these changes: adults and immatures do not compete for food resources, although they share a habitat, and larvae specialise in feeding and growing, while adults specialise exclusively in reproduction.

The four kinds of metamorphosis

- **Few changes (ametabolous metamorphosis):** This is the most primitive type of development, and we find it only in the bristletails and fish moths, which originated before insects had wings. In these groups, the nymph that emerges from the egg is already equipped with almost all the anatomical structures of the adult in rudimentary form. It moults to grow bigger, but does not change much structurally in the process.

- **From wingless to winged (hemimetabolous metamorphosis):** This development pattern is found among the primitive winged insects, such as booklice, thrips, cockroaches, crickets, grasshoppers, termites, mantids, earwigs, stoneflies, web-spinners and bugs. In general, the nymphs that emerge from the eggs are not only smaller than the adults but also differ significantly in appearance. In particular, the wings that are present in the adult stage are initially completely absent. The nymphs gain additional adult features with each moult – for example, wing buds increase in size with each moult, gradually culminating in the fully winged adult.

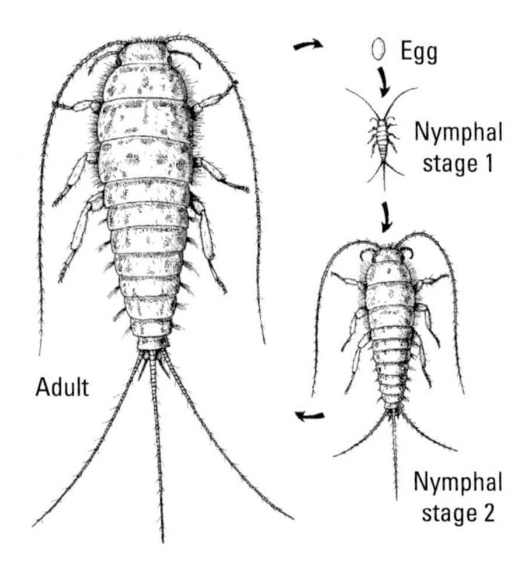

Ametabolous life cycle of a silverfish

On emergence from their eggs, stink bug nymphs (left) do not differ dramatically from the adults (right). They change gradually, through successive moults, until the final adult stage is reached.

A newly emerged adult dragonfly (top) will show adult coloration (above) about two hours into adult life.

Changing lifestyle (paurometabolous metamorphosis): Strictly speaking, this is only a variation of hemimetabolous metamorphosis, but with the difference that the nymphal and adult stages vary considerably. In the last nymphal stage, a growth spurt takes place. This kind of metamorphosis is encountered among some primitive insects where adults and nymphs differ significantly regarding their place of living (habitat) and their activities (ecological niche). Good examples are dragonflies and damselflies, whose nymphs (naiads) live in water. We find a similar situation in the cicadas, whose nymphs live deep underground. There is, however, no pupal stage.

The difference in appearance between a cicada nymph (top) and its adult counterpart (above) is dramatic.

Complete transformation (holometabolous metamorphosis): This kind of development is typical of the highly advanced insects that have a pupal stage in their life cycle. The young stage that emerges from the egg is worm-like and called a larva. This immature stage grows and moults repeatedly, but it remains a larva until it pupates to form a pupa. Pupae are inactive and do not feed. The fully transformed, winged adult insect will emerge from the pupa. Complete metamorphosis is

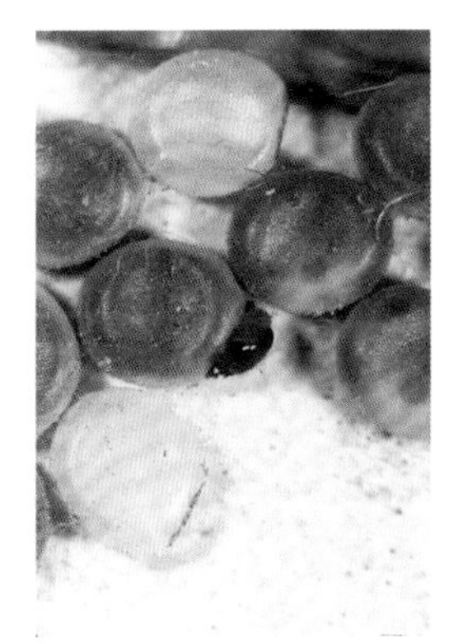

A caterpillar emerges from an egg.

found in some of the smaller orders: alderflies and dobsonflies, lacewings, hanging flies, fleas, and caddisflies. In addition, the four largest and most successful insect orders all undergo a holometabolous metamorphosis: beetles, mosquitoes, midges and flies, moths and butterflies, and wasps, bees and ants.

THE MYSTERY OF THE PUPA

The change that occurs within a pupa is one of the most amazing processes in nature.

Normally, the development of an embryo (embryogeny) is a logical, systematic process. Upon each cell division, neighbouring cells send each other stimulating or suppressing signals that switch parts of the genetic code 'on' or 'off'. In this way, tissues and organs are formed, each with a particular function and in the right place. This is also how a nymph gradually develops into an adult insect.

Inside a pupa, an adult insect has to be created from a larva, whose body parts are quite differently arranged. The larva's digestive system will be of no use to the adult; wings and their muscles and nerves are absent; and the skin is soft and inadequate and lacks hardened plates and hinges. Nothing in the larva will be of benefit to the adult.

Should one cut open a pupal shell after about one quarter of the pupa's development time, one would find a murky white fluid. This is the body fluid in which the living cells that have become detached from the old larval tissues begin the process of turning into adult structures. During this phase, many cells will change position and function. For example, what were muscle cells in the larva may now become part of the adult's reproductive organs. Without hesitation, every cell (and there are millions of them) moves on its own to its new position and role, slotting in with other cells to form a completely new animal. An adult insect emerging from its pupa is quite literally reborn – without following the conventional process of embryogeny.

The tissue in the pupa dissolves, and the cells recombine to form totally different organs and take on different functions in the adult insect.

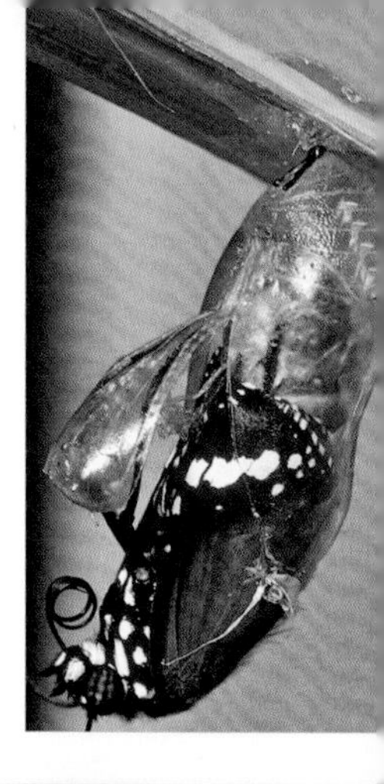

The adult milkweed butterfly (above) after emerging from its pupa (top)

Three kinds of pupae

Three basic kinds of pupae can be distinguished:

- The most common shape of a pupa is a shell within which the wings, legs and feelers are formed close to the body, but separate from it. Such a pupa looks like a pale and partially developed adult. This kind of pupa is generally found among beetles, fleas, lacewings, alderflies, dobsonflies, caddisflies, hanging flies, wasps, bees, ants and some of the more primitive flies, such as the robber flies.
- Moths and butterflies have compact pupae in which the appendages are embedded in the body and are visible on the outside only as grooves (resembling segmentation). In exceptional cases,

Insects in the pupal stage of metamorphosis: rhino beetle pupa (above), snout beetle pupa (left) and fly pupae (below)

The hawk moth's proboscis protrudes from the pupal shell, whereas the wings and feet are embedded.

something may protrude from the pupal surface, like the proboscis in hawk moths.

- Finally, among the more advanced flies such as house flies, no appendages are visible on the pupa at all. The pupal shell is smooth or only slightly segmented, and resembles a cocoon or an egg. The fly develops in the shell, where it is completely detached from the inner wall of its 'home' for the duration of its transformation into an adult.

Many kinds of cocoons

In their final larval stage, many holometabolous insects form a cocoon or shell around themselves, within which the pupa will develop and which will protect it during its transformation.

Moth cocoons

The larvae of most moths spin cocoons of silk; the silkworm (*Bombyx mori*) is a well-known example.

Many moth caterpillars also use objects in their surroundings, such as leaves, twigs or grasses, and spin these together to create a stronger cocoon. The bagworm caterpillar constructs such a cocoon at an early stage, and then drags it along as a protective shelter for most of its larval period.

The defensive hairs of a lappet moth caterpillar have been woven into this cocoon.

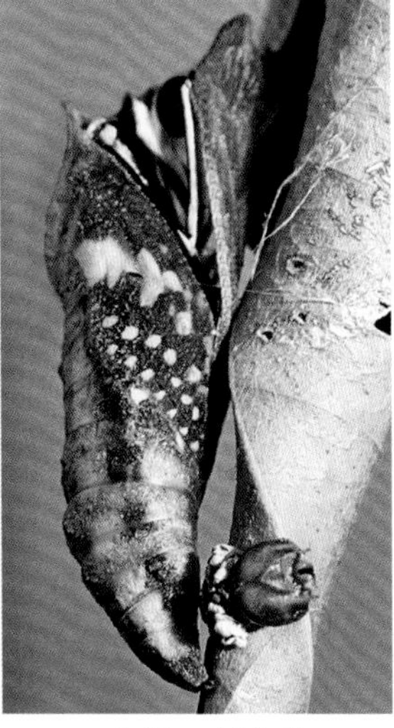
Bagworms have elaborate cocoons (left), which they start carrying around in the larval stage. In contrast, the pupae of butterflies have no covering (right).

Butterflies only spin an attachment pad for the tail of the pupa and a safety girdle to support it. The butterfly pupa then hangs naked from the branch or a rock until the adult emerges.

Those moths that pupate in the soil, such as the emperor moths, make no cocoon whatsoever, and simply pupate in a cavity in the ground.

Wasp, bee and ant cocoons

As a rule, the larvae of wasps, bees and ants also spin silk cocoons in which they pupate. Certain parasitic wasps that parasitise caterpillars spin particularly striking cocoons on the skin of their host.

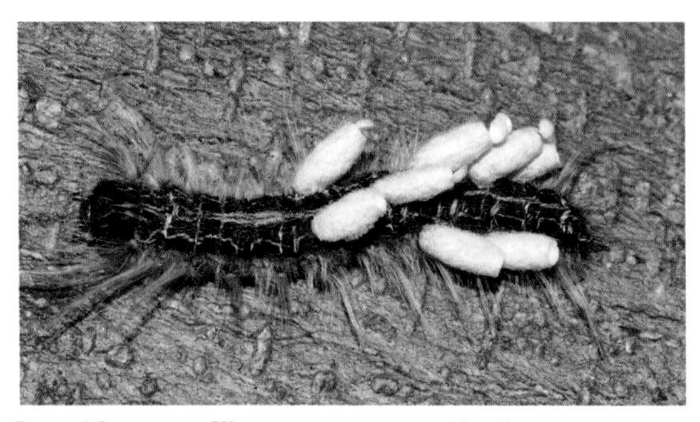
Parasitic wasp silk cocoons on a centipede

The larvae of honeybees and paper wasps spin a thin cocoon inside their cells of wax or paper. The larvae of many kinds of ants also spin cocoons – the 'ant eggs' we frequently see ants carrying around are, in fact, their pupae in cocoons. (The eggs of ants are mostly too small to discern with the naked eye.)

Because bees and wasps generally develop inside cells or tunnels, their pupae are well protected, but most of them, nevertheless, also spin cocoons. Parasitic wasps that parasitise the acraea butterflies develop conspicuous cocoons; when fully grown, the parasite larva leaves the body of the host caterpillar and spins an attractively coloured cocoon at the end of a long silk stalk.

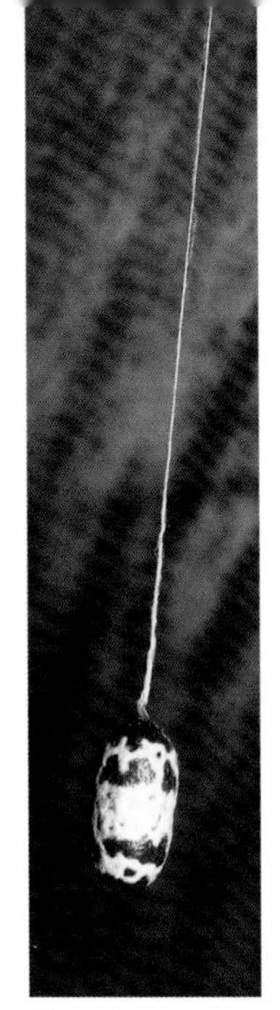
Hanging cocoon of a parasitic wasp

Caddisfly cocoons

Caddisflies have larvae that live under water in elongated little cases they construct by spinning together pieces of gravel or various bits of scrap, similar to the cases of bagworms. The fully grown caddisfly larva either uses the existing case as a cocoon, or builds a special one for the pupal stage.

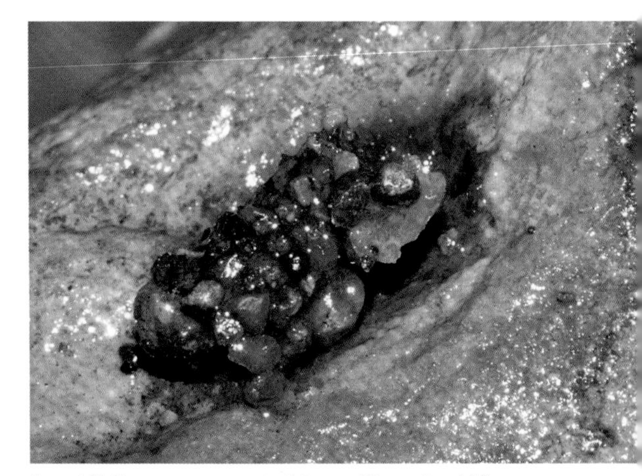
A caddisfly cocoon created from silk and pebbles

Beetles

Although the larvae of beetles are unable to spin silk, many of them do construct cocoons. The larvae of dung beetles use the dung balls that their parents had constructed and sealed with clay, after they had hollowed them out by eating the dung, as their cocoon. Leaf-rolling weevils also use the cocoons their parents had prepared (see page 176). Fruit chafers use their own excrement and glue in their saliva to construct cocoons, into which they incorporate debris from their environment. Those living in birds' nests use feathers, whereas those living in compost use decaying plant material.

Most beetle larvae do not pupate in a cocoon, but directly in the soil or in the place where the larval stages have been feeding – for instance, inside wood, seeds or leaf mines.

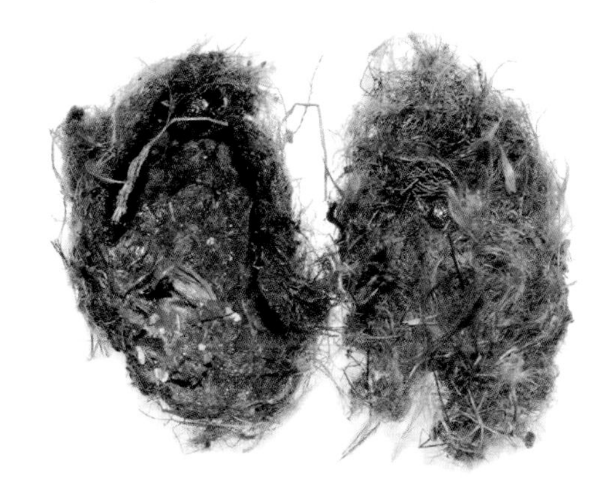

Fruit chafers build cocoons with their own faeces and material found in the larva's environment, including feathers (top) and dead plant material (above).

MYSTERY EGGS

One woodborer in Namibia presented biologists with a riddle. When corkwood trees (*Commiphora* spp.) die and decay, oval, white 'egg shells' of about 30mm in length and 12mm in diameter are often found in the debris. Eventually it was established that the 'shells' are the cocoons of longhorn beetles, the larvae of which have the ability to absorb and secrete lime. These lime shells protect the longhorn pupae against desiccation and against the heat to which they are exposed after the rapid natural decay of the corkwood trees.

Namibian longhorn beetle and its lime cocoon

HOW LONG DO INSECTS LIVE?

It is difficult to infer general rules about the duration of insects' lives. Some have exceptionally long immature stages but live only a short time as adults. In others, the adults live for a very long time, but they have a relatively brief larval stage. Insect larvae and nymphs that have access to an abundance of food, such as leaf feeders and sapsuckers, generally have development cycles ranging from one week to two months. Many insects, such as seed weevils, which are dependent on seasonal phenomena, have a life cycle of exactly one year, to synchronise with the availability of their food.

Long childhoods

Insects that develop in a relatively safe environment, such as woodborers, usually have to deal with a scarcity of nutrients – which means that they can grow only very slowly. Longhorn beetle

An adult click beetle (above) and its extremely hairy larva (right), also known as a 'cut worm'

Antlion larvae build funnel traps in the sand to capture ground-dwelling insects.

larvae, which feed in tunnels that are deep inside dry, dead wood with very little nutritive value, may require 10 years or more before they can pupate. Similarly, the larvae of jewel beetles may require several decades before they can pupate.

In cold areas like Canada, some cicadas have nymphal stages of up to 17 years. In southern Africa, there are some cicadas that require 10 years or more to complete their development. These nymphs live deep underground – as much as a metre below the surface – where they are safe from predators. Here they suck the sap from tree roots, although they lack the heat and oxygen needed for fast metabolism.

The larvae of click beetles may need up to six years to grow to maturity. These larvae live as 'cut worms' in soil or in decomposing wood.

Larger crickets may require up to three years to grow to maturity.

Some insect larvae depend on luck for their food. Antlion larvae, which build funnel traps, may have to wait for months before they can capture anything to eat. A fortunate antlion larva can become fully grown within a couple of weeks, but a less lucky one may need a year or more.

The larvae of longhorn beetles live for many years in wood – dead or alive. Burning dead trees may easily drive these species to extinction.

Fast growers, short lives

A common strategy among small insects with an overabundance of food, but weak defences against their enemies, is to reproduce at a maximal rate. Such groups often complete the whole life cycle in less than a week. These include lice, aphids, many of the flies, and small parasitic wasps that achieve full growth within the parasitised egg of their host.

Among ovoviviparous insects, such as tsetse flies and louse flies, where the larvae hatch inside the body of their mother and are also nourished there, the larvae are sometimes 'born' at such an advanced stage that they can pupate immediately, emerging as adults in approximately a week. In these cases, the free-living larval period spans only a few hours!

The blood-sucking louse fly provides a protein-rich diet for her larvae, which mature internally.

Senior citizens

Termite and ant queens may live two to three decades. A less well-known fact, however, is that adult worker ants can also live for longer than 10 years. Ants have exceptional memories for routes, time and food, and old, experienced workers, which are highly valuable to the colony, frequently take small 'schools' of young workers on training expeditions.

A training expedition led by an old, experienced ant

Some adult toktokkies and weevils can also reach an age of over 20 years. In contrast, adult mayflies mostly die after only a few hours. Many adult moths, as well as adult bot flies, lack any mouthparts and cannot feed or drink, so they live for a few days at most.

TAKING A BREAK

Resting phases are relatively uncommon among vertebrates. Polar bears and other Arctic animals are known for their winter sleep (hibernation) over several months, when their metabolism greatly slows down. Bats hibernate even in temperate climates, and some frogs can survive a long 'drought sleep' underground. Among insects, such resting phases are almost the rule, since few insects can maintain their active life throughout the cycle of the seasons.

There are two types of 'resting coma'. The first is pre-programmed to last for a specific period, and is called diapause. Here the insects enter a pre-progammed resting phase, until they 'awaken' by themselves after a certain span of time and on a specific day. The second is a true resting phase, ending only with the onset of favourable conditions, such as rain, increase in temperature, or the detectable presence of prey or a host. Most insects undergo their resting phase in the egg or pupal stages, and use changes in the length of daylight to 'program' the hibernation.

Locusts time their eggs

Migratory locusts lay their eggs in foam packets some 75mm below the soil surface. The eggs are differently programmed in each packet: some are in diapause and will hatch on a certain day in the coming spring, while the rest are in a 'true' resting phase and will only hatch after it has rained – for which they can wait up to three years. Sometimes there is a third kind of egg that will, for further insurance, skip the first rains and only hatch with the second rains. One reason behind the explosions in locust populations, which lead to swarms, is the simultaneous hatching of all the resting eggs that have accumulated during preceding years.

Fleas wait patiently

Flea larvae feed on shed skin flakes and other organic particles in the homes, nests or roosts of their hosts. When fully grown, they spin cocoons in which they pupate and complete their development to become adult fleas. However, these adult fleas remain inside the cocoons in a resting phase, until vibrations in the substrate awaken them. Then they emerge from the cocoons and search for their hosts to suck their blood. Adult fleas can wait in their cocoons for up to 18 months, which explains why so many fleas may still attack someone who enters a house that has stood vacant for a long time.

Adult fruit chafers patiently wait in their subterranean cocoons, and only emerge when the first spring rains occur.

Butterflies switch off

Most moths and butterflies can produce several generations in a single summer season, so adult moths and butterflies, as well as their caterpillars and pupae, are present throughout summer. In autumn though, one generation of pupae will suddenly enter into hibernation, emerging as adults only in the following spring. The cue for hibernation originates in the mother insect's biochemistry, which responds to changes in the length of daylight, and is relayed to the pupa through the egg and larval stages.

Some moths and butterflies, for example the silk moth (*Bombyx mori*), hibernate as eggs and can be artificially 'awakened' by a physical shock, brief treatment with acid, or sudden cold. These eggs may then hatch in the middle of winter.

Paper wasps overwintering communally in a tree cavity

Some beetles, wasps and flies overwinter in swarms

Some ladybeetles form great swarms in which they hibernate together. The beetles fly from several kilometres away to the highest point on the horizon, where they settle together against a rock. These aggregations represent a survival strategy: ladybeetles are extremely unpalatable. A potential predator may taste one, but will certainly leave the rest alone – which may not be the case if they were sheltering individually.

Paper wasps, which abandon their nests in autumn in order to hibernate elsewhere, aggregate for the same defensive reason. Hundreds of paper wasps originating from a number of different nests hibernate collectively in secluded hollows of cliffs or trees.

The overwintering swarms of blackflies, on the other hand, are probably not defensive but rather as a result of scarce suitable shelter on river banks.

A hibernating aggregation of ladybeetles can be observed every year at the Wonderboom Fort in the Magaliesberg.

Ladybeetles aggregate in a swarm to hibernate.

The rarely seen blue weevil of the Namib Desert

In 1965, the central dunes of the Namib Desert at Gobabeb unexpectedly received good rains of more than 30mm – something that happens only once every four or five years. Within a week the tussocks of dune reed were green, and covered with enormous, powder-blue weevils. At the time, this species of weevil was unknown and had not yet been described; despite intensive insect surveys, not one specimen had been seen during the preceding five years. It became clear that the weevils had been in a resting phase below the sand for at least five years. The resting stage must necessarily have been the pupa, as it was not possible for the larvae of such a large insect to develop so quickly after the rain and before their mass appearance.

DISCOVERING NEW SPECIES

In 1965, after particularly good rains, several weevil and toktokkie species were found in the Namib Desert after an absence of many years; some had never been described. In the desert regions of southern Africa, there are sure to be many more undiscovered insect species that have the ability to survive in a resting phase for many years, appearing only briefly when a rare rain event occurs.

This Namib toktokkie (*Pachynotelus* sp.) emerges only after good rains, a rare occurrence in the desert.

STRANGE PHENOMENA

We usually presuppose a single, unchangeable genetic system that governs the development of a plant or animal, which then determines what the organism will do and what it will look like. However, in insects alternative genetic systems are surprisingly common: within one species, and from the eggs of a single mother, insects can develop that differ drastically from one another. Well-known examples are the social insects with their different castes (workers, soldiers, reproductives) that all develop from identical eggs (see Chapter 10). Among some non-social insects the environment can also have a dramatic impact on what will develop from genetically identical eggs.

The mystery of migratory locusts

Over millennia, vast and devastating swarms of migratory locusts have suddenly and unexpectedly appeared and then inexplicably disappeared. Theories about their origin, destination and whereabouts in years without swarms were legion, and ranged from spontaneous appearance, as if from nowhere, to the existence of hiding places in subterranean caves.

The great locust mystery was only solved in the 1920s, simultaneously by Uvarov, a Russian entomologist who was doing research on desert locusts (*Schistocerca gregaria*), and Faure, a professor of entomology at the University of Pretoria, who was researching brown locusts (*Locustana pardalina*). They discovered that swarming migratory locusts also have a solitary phase, appearing as ordinary grey-green

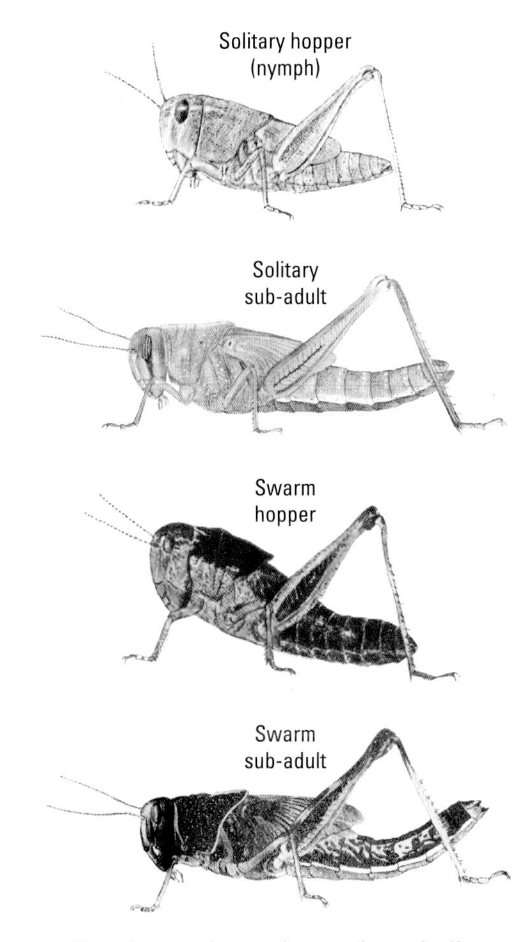

The migratory locust changes dramatically – from a solitary phase to a swarm phase.

Worldwide, 20 species of grasshopper are known to have the ability to transform into migratory locusts.

grasshoppers. Previously, they had been described as a completely different genus from the migratory locusts.

Once these solitary grasshoppers reach a certain 'density' (that is, they meet a member of their own species a certain number of times in one day), their development switches to a 'second genetic programme'. Their wings grow longer, their bodies more slender, and their colour changes markedly. Now, instead of avoiding each other, they congregate in ever-increasing swarms of nymphs (hoppers), which eventually fly away as vast swarms of adults.

Each species of migratory locust has a breeding centre or 'build-up' area, surrounded by an 'outbreak' area that is determined by the prevailing winds of the particular region. When they move away, locust swarms do not set out for a particular destination; rather, the swarm serves as an escape mechanism to relieve overpopulation in their permanent range or breeding centre. Over time, the swarm diminishes as birds and other predators gradually devour the locusts. Some locust swarms may fly out to sea and perish there.

Apart from the brown locusts that build up in the Karoo, in the past South Africa was also regularly invaded by red locusts (*Nomadacris septemfasciata*) that built up in swamps in parts of East Africa.

Polymorphism

Many insects have a permanent array of very different forms, called 'morphs', that co-occur in one population; such species are termed 'polymorphic'. Among the katydids, for example, many species simultaneously have brown and green forms, which, respectively, are camouflaged better in browner or greener vegetation. At different times one form will be preyed upon more than the other, but, in the long run, both forms continue to coexist genetically.

Some butterflies display more pronounced polymorphisms. The females of some swallowtail butterflies (*Papilio* spp.) have an array of genetic forms that differ drastically from each other in colour pattern, and each form mimics a different poisonous butterfly species. Depending on which poisonous butterflies are prevalent in their area, those mimicking females with the most appropriate disguise will be protected from danger.

Green and brown forms of the same species of katydid

COLOUR FORMS AND CAMOUFLAGE

Brush-footed butterflies in South Africa's tropical regions breed throughout the year, but some of them have markedly different summer and winter colour forms. Oddly, the winter forms have much brighter colours.

Grasshoppers and mantids are able to develop camouflage colours that blend in with their background. Similarly, the human louse (*Pediculus humanus*) takes on different colours when infesting different human races.

The winter colour form (left) and summer colour form (right) of the same species of Nymphalidae

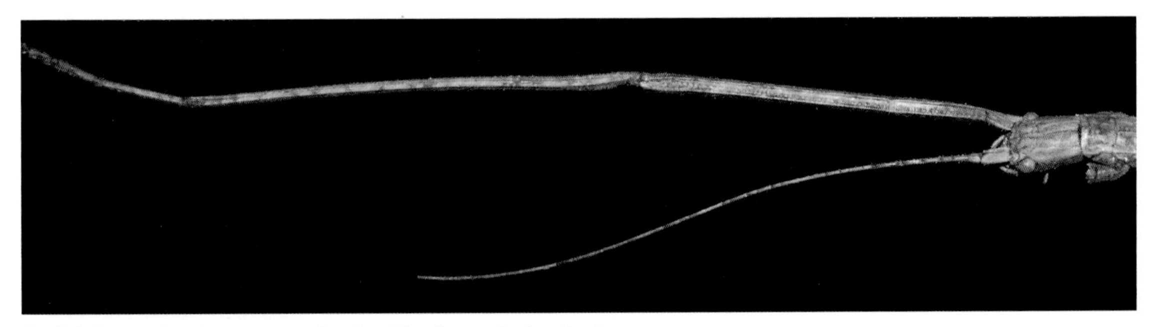

A stick insect that has grown a leg (top) in place of a lost feeler

Growing younger!

One of the strangest phenomena in all of nature is the ability of some insects to develop 'in reverse' and in effect 'grow younger'.

Termites are one example. The requirements of a termite colony may suddenly change, resulting in inappropriate ratios between numbers of workers and soldiers. The termite colony, however, can remedy this: by manipulating their food and hormones, the members of one caste can begin to moult 'regressively' and become undifferentiated nymphs, which can then moult 'forward' to become a different caste!

In honeybees (*Apis mellifera*), workers pass through age-related phases. In the first phase, they develop glands to provide royal jelly to young larvae and queen bee larvae. Later, these glands degenerate, and wax glands develop instead to produce wax for building honeycombs. After this phase, when the bee becomes a fieldworker, these glands also degenerate (see Chapter 10). Should a hive, however, lose too many of its younger workers, the old fieldworker bees are able to regress to working inside the hive, even regaining the glands they had in their youth!

HEALING WOUNDS

If an insect is injured or damaged at the nymphal or larval stage, it is generally able to repair the damage through subsequent moults. Adult insects, on the other hand, are only able to seal their wounds.

Stick insects can regrow a lost limb through subsequent moults. Strangely, they are only programmed to grow back legs – should they lose a feeler, for instance, a leg is regrown in its place!

CANNIBALISM FOR SUSTAINABILITY

Although armoured crickets occur in extreme abundance in arid regions in summer, they cannot last through the long, dry winter. As a survival strategy, these otherwise herbivorous crickets start eating each other. A few will simply start nibbling on one of their companions, from the legs upward, with the victim still alive and (ineffectually) kicking during the attack. Soon after, the feeders will consume one of their cannibal mates – including its still undigested stomach contents! This rather gruesome strategy enables about 10 per cent of the population to make it through winter. Without cannibalism, the whole population would otherwise perish.

Armoured ground crickets feed on one of their own species.

Movement

Insects live in every imaginable habitat on earth – in the air, in water, underground, in wood, on plants and even in other animals. Most insects rely on their six legs and four wings to get around, but some have developed an ingenious array of mechanical and hydraulic mechanisms to help them move about.

Katydid

INSECT RULES FOR WALKING

The standard leg rhythm of insects, such as beetles and cockroaches, is as follows:

- Always lift only one leg of a pair at a time.
- Lift a leg only when the one right behind it is on the ground.

Applying these simple 'rules' means that three legs are placed on the ground at any one time: two legs (fore- and hind legs) on one side and one (middle leg) on the other.

Long-legged Namib toktokkie

A MANY-LEGGED GAIT

Equestrians know the rhythms and sequences a horse uses to put its feet on the ground in order to walk, trot, canter, gallop or jump. In insects, things are considerably more complex, since they have six legs.

Only four legs at work

Insects that have modified front legs for grasping walk only on their four hind legs and have the same gait options as a four-legged animal. Pond skaters, mantids, some assassin bugs and mantidflies are all insects that do not use their front legs when walking.

The mantidfly uses its four hindmost legs for walking; its front legs have been modified for grasping.

Dung beetle with short middle legs

On the other hand, grasshoppers and other jumping insects, like fleas, do not use their hind legs for walking. They will either keep their hind legs retracted, or use them only occasionally to nudge themselves forward.

Mosquitoes keep their long hind legs in the air, and generally do not walk much.

In some of the large dung beetles, like *Pachylomerus femoralis*, the front and hind legs are specialised for walking – the middle legs are reduced and mainly used when rolling a dung ball. The middle legs of the giant wingless dung beetle (*Scarabaeus cancer*) from Angola are so reduced that they do not even touch the ground.

More than six legs

Although insects have a maximum of six legs, the larvae of moths and butterflies have sucker-like 'false legs' (prolegs) on their abdomens to help them cling to plants and move about. These caterpillars usually have five pairs of abdominal 'legs', but some, like the loopers, have only two functional pairs. Looper caterpillars, also called inchworms, measuring-worms or geometrids, alternately hunch themselves up and stretch out again, while they change the grip between their six thoracic legs and their four abdominal 'legs'. These movements are achieved hydraulically, not by muscle power; a looper caterpillar will lose the ability to walk if it had a puncture wound.

The larvae of hanging flies and sawflies have eight pairs of abdominal prolegs similar to those of moth and butterfly larvae.

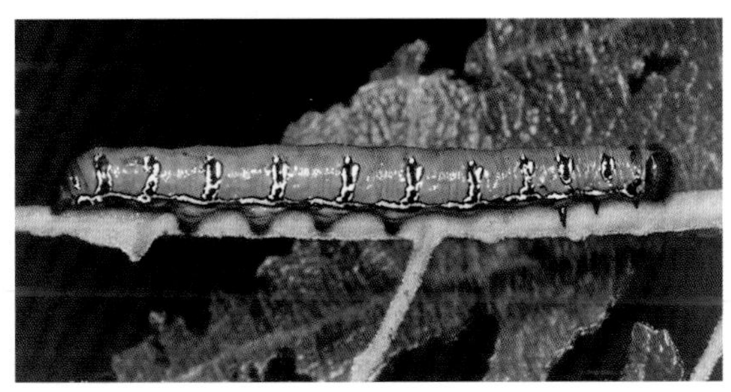

Caterpillar with five pairs of prolegs on the abdomen

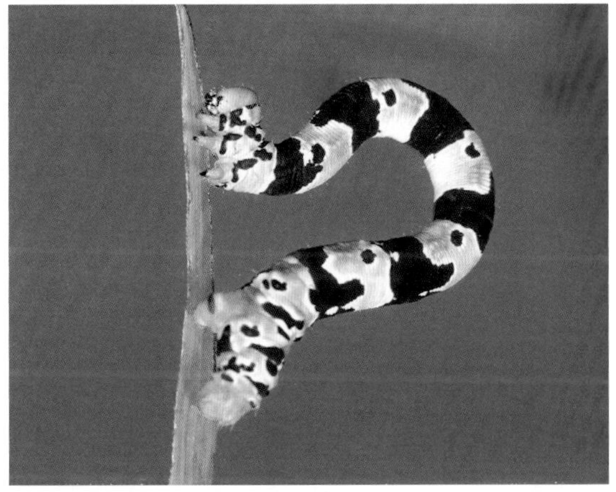

A looper caterpillar employs its two pairs of abdominal prolegs to move itself forward.

THE HIGH JUMP AND THE LONG JUMP

A number of different insects, in several orders, have developed special jumping legs – usually to escape from danger. The legs adapted for jumping are always the hind legs, which are closest to the insect's centre of gravity. Groups that jump include almost all crickets and grasshoppers and many plant bugs, such as lantern bugs, treehoppers and leafhoppers. Among the beetles,

On Marion Island a species of moth has lost its wings and developed jumping legs like those of a cricket.

The hind legs of grasshoppers are used only for jumping.

Leafhoppers (top) and flea beetles (above) have hind legs that are adapted for jumping to escape from would-be predators.

tumbling beetles and flea beetles are particularly expert jumpers. Bristletails jump by forcefully bucking their bodies; many caterpillars do the same to escape danger, but their jumping abilities are not very impressive.

Champion jumpers

A human flea (*Pulex irritans*) is only 2mm long, but easily jumps 200mm high and 300mm horizontally. After each jump, the flea will start running, because it cannot immediately jump again. The flea's specialised jumping mechanism limits it to one jump at a time.

The joints of the jumping legs have a built-in cushion of resilin, the most elastic substance found in nature. When ready to leap, the flea gradually compresses the resilin cushions with its strong leg muscles. A type of trigger mechanism then releases the leg joint, the cushion straightens the leg, and with all the energy built up in the resilin and the muscles, the flea is propelled ahead at 20G – much like a crossbow is operated. Flea beetles and some other kinds of jumping insects may have similar resilin jumping mechanisms.

Hydraulic jumping

Fruit fly maggots desperately seek out shade if placed in the sun. They do not have legs, but propel themselves forward with impressive leaps through the air. To achieve this feat, the maggot pulls its body into a bow shape and then increases the pressure in its dorsal blood vessels to suddenly straighten it out.

The larvae of the jumping-bean moth (*Emporia melanobasis*) develop inside hard seeds such as those of the tamboti. To get out of the sun, these larvae use the same mechanism as fruit fly maggots – they 'jump' inside the hollowed-out seed, taking the seed with them.

Australian 'bull ants' can jump by pressing their mandibles to the ground and then forcefully opening them – this behaviour has, however, not yet been observed in any of our local ant species.

A jumping mechanism in their hind legs helps fleas leap up to 200mm in the air.

Fruit fly maggot prepares to jump.

THE POWERFUL JOLTING OF CLICK BEETLES

Click beetles have a unique jumping mechanism that is so forceful, they stand a good chance of escaping the muzzle or beak of a predator when putting it into action. The thorax of a click beetle hinges up and down against the hind body at an angle of 45°. The beetle has a strong peg below and behind the thorax that fits in between two round knobs on the base of the hind body. By pushing this peg against one of the knobs with all its might and then suddenly slipping it into the groove between the knobs, the click beetle jerks its body so powerfully that it shoots upwards, with an acceleration of about 380G, achieving a height several times its own body length.

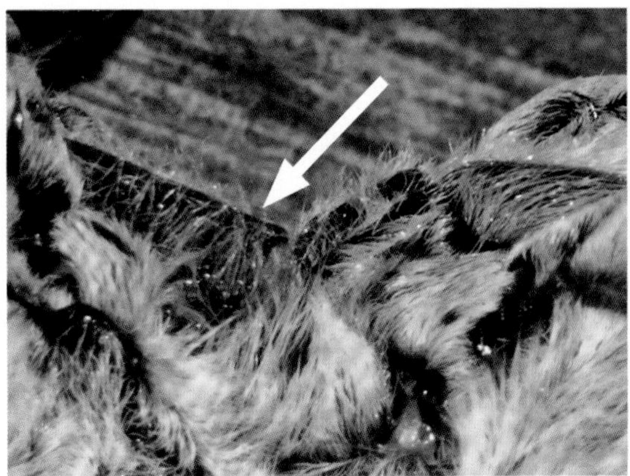

Like all of the approximately 700 species of click beetle in southern Africa, this species raises the peg in its thorax (left) and then snaps it back into place (right). This movement is accompanied by a loud click and a violent upward jerk of the body.

Should the click beetle land on its back, like the species shown here, it cannot right itself, given its torpedo-like body and short legs (above). Instead, it has to use its 'clicking' mechanism to regain its footing (right).

WATER SPORTS

Insects such as water striders and pond skaters exploit the surface tension of water and move around on its surface like terrestrial insects would on solid ground. Unique adaptations for locomotion are found in insects living under water.

Oars and paddles

The hind legs of predaceous water beetles are modified into long, flat 'oars', with swimming bristles on the foot segments that open up with the back stroke of the leg to increase the surface area. Boatmen and backswimmers have similar 'rowing oars'. All these insects have lost the ability to walk on dry land where they scuttle around helplessly. The four hind legs of whirligigs have been modified into short swimming paddles, which function equally well when they are swimming around on top of the water surface or diving below water.

The hind legs of predaceous water beetles are modified to function like oars or paddles.

STRANGE BUT TRUE

Many insects that live under water are poor swimmers and prefer walking around on the bottom substrate and on water plants. Some examples are giant water bugs, water scorpions, and the larvae of alderflies, dobsonflies, predaceous water beetles and whirligigs.

Giant water bug

Jet propulsion

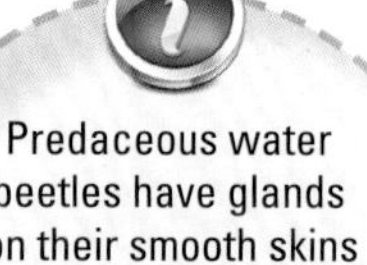

Predaceous water beetles have glands on their smooth skins that continuously secrete an emulgent, leaving them unaffected by water friction, like a well-waxed surfboard.

The most unusual mechanism for underwater movement is the jet propulsion of the nymphs (naiads) of dragonflies, which suck up water into their strongly muscular rectum, then eject this water with such force that the insect is propelled forward. Their breathing gills are conveniently placed inside the rectum, so that they can simultaneously get rid of carbon dioxide and take up oxygen. Alternatively, the naiads walk about under water and on water plants, as they also have six normal walking legs.

Wriggling like an eel

The aquatic larvae of mosquitoes and midges move around in the water by writhing like eels. Mosquito larvae are equipped with swimming brushes to get around. Mosquito pupae, too, are able to swim; they use flaps at the end of the abdomen to paddle in the water – an exceptional achievement for a pupa. Like all maggots, bloodworms – the small, red maggots of midges – are legless. They also move by wriggling.

Bloodworms (above) move by wriggling. For other insects, at times, immobility is the best strategy. Snout beetles (left), for example, fool predators by acting dead.

Stick insects' wings are usually folded and hidden, but the loud rattle made by opening them can scare a predator.

Soap boats

As children, we used to propel a small paper boat by fastening a piece of soap to its end. The soap then breaks the surface tension of the water, causing the boat to sail in the opposite direction. For this very purpose, a weevil that lives on rushes growing in water has a gland that secretes an emulgent on its abdomen. Should it fall in the water, the weevil is propelled forward until it reaches a host plant again.

AERODYNAMICS

All adult insects – except for bristletails and fish moths – were originally equipped with four wings. Many insects have subsequently lost their wings, due to lifestyles in which flight has become pointless. However, those with functioning wings have developed a diversity of flying techniques.

Windmill wings

The large wings of butterflies and most moths operate more or less like the sails of an old-fashioned windmill or a sailboat. A wing beat simply displaces air – enabling the butterfly or moth to 'row' through the air.

Many insects that mainly fly with their hind wings, such as cockroaches, crickets, grasshoppers, mantids and stick insects, have broad, fan-like flight wings, and use this method of flying. It demands little energy, but does not achieve great speed.

The aerofoils of beetles

The forewings of beetles are hard sheaths that are kept still in flight. Initially, it was assumed that these forewings were just an impediment during flight, but later it was discovered that they function as an aerofoil, and their presence partly counters some of the turbulence created by the hind wings. In fact, some beetles, like tiger beetles and jewel beetles, can fly exceptionally fast and effectively. On the other hand, slow-flying beetles, for example blister beetles and dung beetles, can manoeuvre their wings to enable them to land with a great deal of accuracy.

The forewings of beetles, such as this blister beetle, are motionless when the insect is in flight.

Flies have modified hind wings, known as halteres, which are used to optimise the movement of the forewings during flight (far left). Syrphid flies are able to hover in one spot (left).

Fast flyers

The front margin of an insect's wing is stiff, whereas the vane is elastic. Therefore, the wing itself undulates through its up-and-down movement, lifting the insect upward and propelling it forward. In insects with two pairs of wings, turbulence develops between the fore- and hind wings at high speeds, making the hind wings relatively ineffective. Hence, some of the fastest flyers, such as flies, have lost one of

The hawk moth's fore- and hind wings are coupled together by a rigid hook and rod, thus forming a single 'pair' of functional wings.

Some flies, for example the bee fly and hover fly, not only fly fast but can also hover.

The fore- and hind wings of a bee are coupled into a single unit by small hooks.

their pairs of wings. Their hind wings have been reduced to sensory organs (halteres) – small club-shaped structures behind the forewings – which appear to have a purely sensory function to measure airflow and turbulence, thereby ensuring optimal movement of the forewings.

Fast-flying moths, such as the hawk moth, as well as virtually all wasps and bees couple their fore- and hind wings with small hooks – or a rigid spine and hook in the moths – which enables them to beat all four wings as if they were just a single pair. This method of flying is also used by cicadas.

HOW DO MOSQUITOES BUZZ?

The characteristic buzzing of mosquitoes results from their exceedingly rapid wing beat: up to 1,000 beats per second. Since no muscles can contract and relax at such a rate, mosquitoes have elastic plates on the thorax onto which the wings hinge, and these plates develop an oscillation that needs only intermittent muscle action to keep it going.

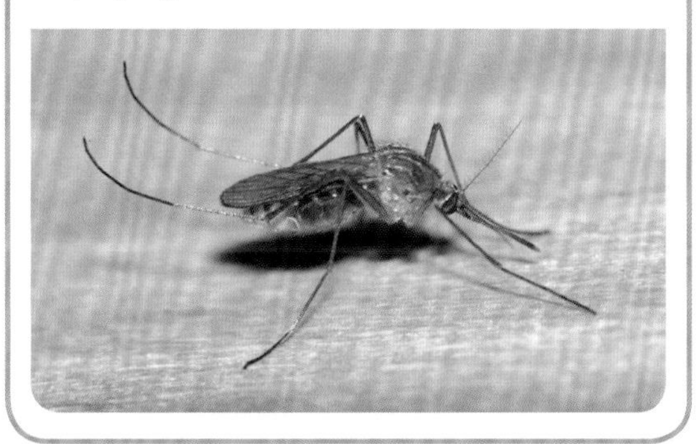

Fascinating fact

Some very tiny fairy-fly parasitic wasps, less than half a millimetre in length, have wings that consist of only a miniscule rod bearing long hair. The aerodynamics of these 'bottlebrushes' is still a mystery.

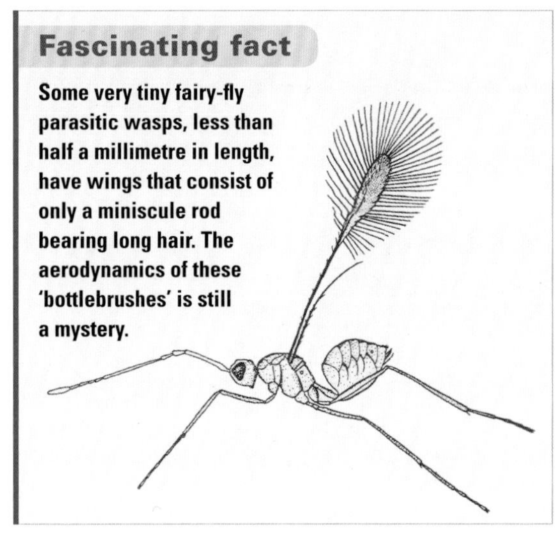

Wingless flight

Several small insect larvae, such as the larvae of bagworms and the nymphs of scale insects, spin silken threads to float away on air currents. Small spiders also disperse in this manner. Also referred to as aeroplankton, these larvae and nymphs can be found up to 10,000 metres high and can be carried right across the oceans by jet streams. Since they have no control over the direction the wind is taking them, only a few fortunate ones land on a suitable host plant. Females compensate for this loss by producing large numbers of offspring.

STRANGE WAYS OF MOVING ABOUT

To escape danger, reach food and survive in harsh environments, some insects have developed highly unconventional ways of moving about.

Surviving the desert

In the shifting dunes of the Namib Desert, the surface temperature can reach 70°C. No insect can survive this temperature, and several species have special adaptations for digging tunnels in the sand to escape the heat. Where the sand is hard, or where loose sand is relatively stable and compact, for example in the early morning, insects

A desert-dwelling *Lepidochora* toktokkie 'swims' into loose sand.

are able to dig tunnels. However, those insects that are forced to live on loose sand must be able to 'swim' into the sand to escape the sun. Several Namib toktokkies, such as the blade-shaped *Lepidochora* species, have special adaptations to do this.

The larvae of antlions make their funnel-shaped pits by crawling backwards into loose sand and flicking it out with their flat heads.

In other sandy regions, some fish moths and the larvae of many beetles are also equipped to wriggle their way into loose sand.

Going into free fall

Most insects are too small to come to harm by falling – their air resistance is too high and terminal velocity too low. Leaf-feeding insects do not hesitate to fall from a tree in order to escape danger, and many insects, when attacked in the air, simply close their wings and fall to the ground. Owlet moths, which have ears to detect the sonar of bats, often use this method when they hear a bat.

Hitchhiking

Hitchhiking among insects is more common than we think.

Unable to fly against the desert wind, small flies in the Namib Desert travel for free on flightless dung beetles to find their favourite food source, dung, which their hosts are more adept at locating.

The winged females of the fig wasp carry their flightless males to new figs. By contrast, the winged males of velvet ant wasps are known to carry their wingless females around.

Flies catch a ride on a wingless Namib dung beetle.

Twisted-wing parasites and bee lice use flowers as stopovers to climb from one wasp or bee to another, thereby hitching a ride to a different nest or hive.

All parasitic insects, like fleas and lice, naturally hitchhike on their hosts to reach other hosts of the same species. Insects, in turn, play host to a multitude of parasitic mites that hitchhike on them to get access to the host's offspring or other members of the same species.

The agents of diseases transmitted by insects – from viruses in plants to parasites such as liver flukes – not only use insects as a form of transport, but also use them as intermediate or secondary hosts.

BETTER ON THE BACK

When removed from the compost in which it lives, the white grub of the fruit chafer flips onto its back and moves away to find shelter with quick, undulating movements: in this way it can move much faster than would have been possible with its short legs.

HANGING ON TIGHTLY

Attached to the extremity of most insects' feet (tarsi) is a pair of claws, with a spongy cushion between the claws. On the underside of the foot segments, various kinds of hair (some sensitive to vibrations or smell) are found.

Flies walk on windowpanes

Some insects, such as flies, are able to walk upside down on a glass pane. However, their feet are not sticky nor do they have any suckers: the secret lies in the microscopic structure of the hairs on the underside of their feet. These very fine hairs, which can penetrate the glass at molecular level, function like Velcro fasteners.

Geckos also have such micro-hairs and can cling to seemingly impossible surfaces.

Trapped by a mantid

The front legs of mantids and some other predatory insects are modified in such a way that the upper and lower parts of the legs clamp onto one another like a trap, complete with barbs on the inside to prevent prey from escaping. Similarly, the legs of lice are modified to clamp onto the hairs or feathers of the host: the single-segmented foot (tarsus) folds against the lower leg (tibia). The claws of each louse species are exactly adapted to the nature and shape of the hairs or feathers of its specific host. Interestingly, the claws of the human head louse (*Pediculus humanus*) found on various human races differ slightly to fit the different types of human hair more precisely.

These legs aren't made for walking

The legs of adult damselflies and dragonflies are orientated forward, and together they form a basket with which insect prey can be caught on the wing. These insects also use their legs for sitting or clinging to perches, but not for walking.

Mantids grab their prey with their modified front legs.

The legs of damselflies (above) and dragonflies are not used for walking.

A fly clings upside down to a pane of glass.

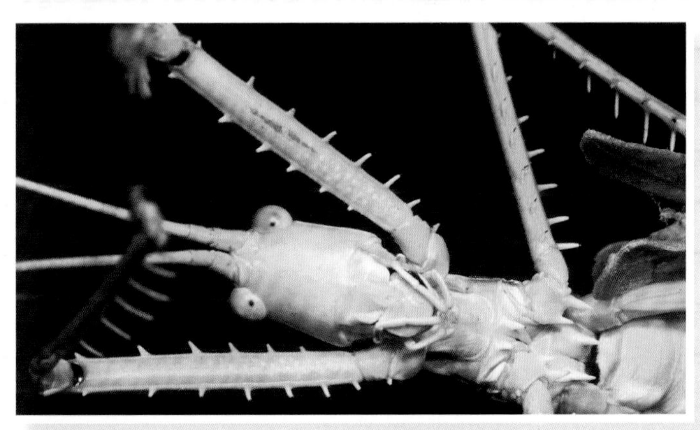

Formidable spikes occur on the legs of a predatory katydid.

IT'S A PLAGUE!

The synchronised directional movement of large swarms of insects is an impressive sight. There are diverse reasons for these mass migrations, but they are not always understood. While the functions of the swarm movements of bees and red driver ants, and of the mating swarms of, for example, midges, drones and cockchafers (see Chapter 2) are clear, there is no obvious explanation for the sporadic swarming of dragonflies, which are sometimes observed migrating in one direction, far away from any water source. We also do not know which of the many nocturnal flying insects migrate in swarms.

A migrating colony of red driver ants

Migratory locusts

The transformation of locusts from the solitary phase to the gregarious (swarming) phase was explained in Chapter 3. Once hopper bands form, they tend to move upwind and stay together, providing one common direction for the whole swarm. Flying swarms, on the other hand, mostly move with the wind, so that areas likely to be invaded by the swarms can be predicted from the prevailing seasonal winds. For example, red locusts originating in East Africa will move more or less southwards or south-eastwards, reaching mainly KwaZulu-Natal and the Eastern Cape. Brown locusts that start swarming in the Northern Cape will invade the northern provinces and the Free State.

Armies of caterpillars

Outbreaks of armyworm caterpillars (*Spodoptera* sp.) are dramatic and can destroy grazing and crops as effectively as locust swarms do.

Similar to the hoppers of locusts, armyworm caterpillars feed upwind and devour whatever lies in their way. They pupate in the soil, and their moths emerge during the night. Although the flying moths are seldom seen, from light trap catches it seems that they attain great densities at times, and that they possibly fly in swarms.

Caterpillar trains

The caterpillars of the moth family Thaumetopoeidae, commonly called processionary caterpillars, typically are hairy and live together in large groups, moving from tree to tree. Such 'caterpillar trains' can grow as long as 20m, as each caterpillar joins up with a train, and smaller trains join up with each other. While walking, each caterpillar spins a thin thread of silk, so that the procession leaves behind a track of silken threads. Eventually, they pupate together in a large bag enclosed in several layers of silk – as many as 600 pupae have been found in a single bag. Although the amount of silk in such a bag is considerable, it cannot be used commercially because of the stinging hairs of the caterpillars which are woven into it.

Some people mistakenly believe that white butterflies (*Belenois aurota*) are the adults of armyworms.

Armyworm caterpillars eat all vegetation in their path.

Clever constructions

Second only to humans in their ability to change their environment, insects use all sorts of natural resources to construct their nests.

Termite heap

ARCHITECTS AND ENGINEERS

Many insect nests are underground. In particular, the nests and tunnels constructed by ants and termites are mainly subterranean, with the structures visible above ground constituting just a minor part of the nest.

However, there are many other burrowing insects, including earwigs, most crickets, some root-feeding plant bugs, more than half of the larvae of beetles, and a number of beetle adults (such as dung beetles). Some insects also burrow underground for their pupal stage, for example thrips and several moths and flies.

Insects digging in loose sand have to overcome special challenges. Low temperature and high humidity cause grains of sand to bond better, and therefore insects tunnel in dune sand mostly at night or during the early hours of the morning.

Excavated earth piled around an ant nest entrance

Building an ant palace

Most types of ants build nests underground and then carry the excavated earth to the surface. Some distribute the excavated earth in the area, and others pile it up loosely around the nest entrance, where eventually it will be eroded away by wind and rain.

Every species has its own characteristic nest design. Normally these nests consist of storage space for food, holding rooms for the brood, and storage areas for refuse. The nest is designed to regulate temperature and the circulation of fresh air by, for example, selectively opening or closing surface ducts that are in shaded or hot, sunny areas. There are as few as possible of these openings as each requires protection by guard ants. Some ants build vertical shafts that end in a maze of concentric circles, of which only the innermost passages lead back to the nesting rooms. The reason for this construction could possibly be to divert rainwater and to mislead hostile invaders.

THE FATE OF THE FILLER ANT

One type of diurnal ant seals the nest's vertical entrance shaft at night and reopens it the following morning. To accomplish this, at least one ant must fill the hole from above with small stones while others brace the plug from below, effectively shutting out the 'filler ant'. This ant seldom survives its nocturnal exposure.

An ant filling the nest entrance with stones

NEST DESIGNS

There are three distinct termite nest designs with significant constructions above ground:

- Above their actual nests, small harvester termites (*Trinervitermes* spp.) build dome-like nests with thousands of clay rooms used purely for storage of hay.
- Some fungus-growing termites (*Odontotermes* spp.) build short chimneys protruding from a clay foundation. The clay 'floor' is the product of deeply excavated soil, and the chimneys serve to extract hot air from the nest (see Chapter 9), although they do not lead directly into any populated area in the nest.
- Another genus of fungus-growing termites (*Macrotermes* spp.) build towers that can reach a height of several metres and serve as the air-conditioning systems or 'lungs' of large underground colonies. The towers themselves are uninhabited.

Visible in the distance are multiple dome-like mounds created by harvester termites.

Carbon dioxide from fungus-growing termites' nests is expelled through chimneys, keeping the nests from overheating.

Termite clay castles

Like ants, termites dig out complex nests underground. They also sometimes build complex structures above ground by gluing the excavated grains of soil together with their saliva. Such constructions may contain several tonnes of clay, made weatherproof by the saliva.

A cooling tower created by fungus-growing termites leans towards the noon sun.

Fungus-growing termites harvest food under the cover of a thin layer of mud.

They also build temporary clay roofs over dead plant matter that they are harvesting. Termites live and work underground, and their tunnels stretch over hundreds of metres, leading to food sources and, usually, also to subterranean water sources.

Cricket clarinet

Mole crickets tunnel under grass, where they and their nymphs feed on roots. The adult mole cricket can fly, which it does mainly at night. The male constructs its tunnel so that it has one or two flared openings at the soil surface and a spherical cavity below. When the cricket stridulates, it positions itself at a strategic point in the tunnel where the sound is amplified by the cavity, like in a clarinet.

Male mole cricket

Fascinating fact

Spider-hunting wasps, digger wasps and leafcutting bees build clay funnel entrances to deflect parasites and robbers away from their underground tunnels. They may also build decoy entrances that lead nowhere.

Clay funnel entrances to tunnels are built to keep out unwanted visitors.

THE RIGHT EQUIPMENT

Insects that burrow in loose sand have to overcome special challenges requiring unique solutions and species-specific adaptations.

Sand-tunnelling beetles, such as the wingless dung beetles (*Pachysoma* spp.) found in the Namib and West Coast dune regions, are equipped with special sand brushes on their legs, while predatory dune crickets (*Comicus* spp.) have beautifully branched 'sand shoes' to facilitate digging in and jumping on loose sand.

Most of these species make their tunnels at night or during the early hours of the morning, when low temperatures and high humidity cause the sand grains to bond better, making it possible for them to burrow into their subterranean abode.

As the sand surface heats up during the course of the morning, the tunnel entrances collapse, effectively camouflaging these retreats during the daytime.

Sand brushes on the legs of a dung beetle

Dune crickets have 'sand shoes'.

CHOOSING THE RIGHT MATERIALS

Some insects engage in clay 'masonry' or 'pottery' to build their entire nests. Others use plant material for this purpose.

Mud nests of potter and mason wasps

Potter wasps gather balls of mud in their mandibles and carry them to their chosen building site. Using only their mandibles, the wasps glue their nests together with clay mixed with saliva.

Potter and mason wasps have their own, distinct nest designs. The clay 'pots' built by these wasps each contain a single egg, laid by the female, and are stocked with food for the larvae and pupae that will develop inside.

Certain mason wasps build their nests under rock ledges or roof eaves. The nest consists of a group of clay cells, with new cells added progressively as soon as the previous one has been fully provisioned.

A mason wasp builds its nest with mud that it carries in its mandibles.

Paper nests

Like other species of social wasps, paper wasps construct their nests from plant fibre. Using their mandibles they shave bark fibre from plants, mix it with saliva and chew it to a pulp. This 'papier-mâché' is then worked into the fine adjoining hexagonal tubes or cells of the nest.

The queen paper wasp provides each cell with an egg, and the workers feed the developing larvae continuously until they pupate. The pupae develop in the cell and hatch as adults. The cells are cleaned out and then reused.

Cocktail ants (*Crematogaster* spp.) also make their dark brown tree nests from pulped bark. On the inside, the nest consists of thousands of small cells, enclosed in an outer layer of 'cardboard' that is adjusted as the nest expands.

Paper wasp nest with larval cells under construction (right) and sealed pupal cells (left and at the rear)

Paper wasp larvae beg for food like nestlings.

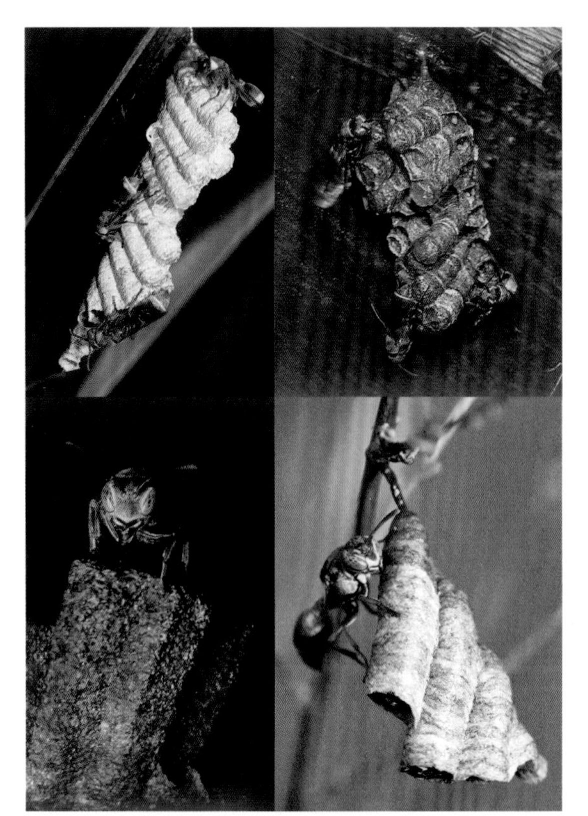

Although designs are species-specific, all paper wasp nests hang upside down from a single stem. Cells range from round to hexagonal, and colour depends on the plant fibres available in the vicinity.

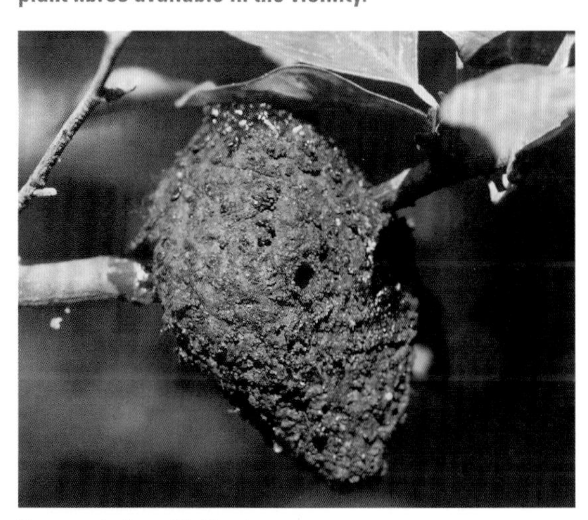

Tree nest of cocktail ants

Resin glue

Some flowers reward pollinating bees with resin rather than with nectar. The honeybee (*Apis mellifera*) mixes resin with wax to create propolis, a dark 'glue' used to seal off nest entrances and exits.

Mopane bees (*Meliponula* spp.) build beautiful translucent resin funnels at the entrance to their nest, most probably to keep ants out.

Carder bees weave exceptional cotton nests from plume seeds and other fine fibres. Leaf-rolling weevils make equally well-engineered leaf parcels for their larvae and pupae. (See Chapter 2.)

Resin glue produced by honeybees on a hive (left) and a funnel entrance made from resin by mopane bees (right)

GLANDULAR SECRETIONS

Insects also build permanent housing structures using a variety of glandular secretions.

Beeswax combs

Honeybee workers have special wax glands on the underside of their abdomen, in between segments. The wax is produced in thin, transparent sheets, which are collected by other worker bees, kneaded in their mandibles, and then shaped into the well-known hexagonal cells of honeycombs. Although wax is a soft, malleable material that will melt at 70°C, these combs are strong enough to bear the weight of the honey, even though the combs may reach a length of up to a metre.

HONEYBEE CELL DESIGNS

Honeybees build three types of cells.

- They build normal cells in which the young bees are reared and pupate. These are also used as storage cells for honey or pollen.
- During spring, they build a number of combs with larger cells, in which the queen lays male eggs that will develop into drones.
- When needed, bees will build a few independently hanging queen cells, in which new queens are bred. These cells are large, vertical and cigar-shaped.

'Normal' honeybee cells (below), larger cells for housing male eggs (below right), and hanging queen cell (top right)

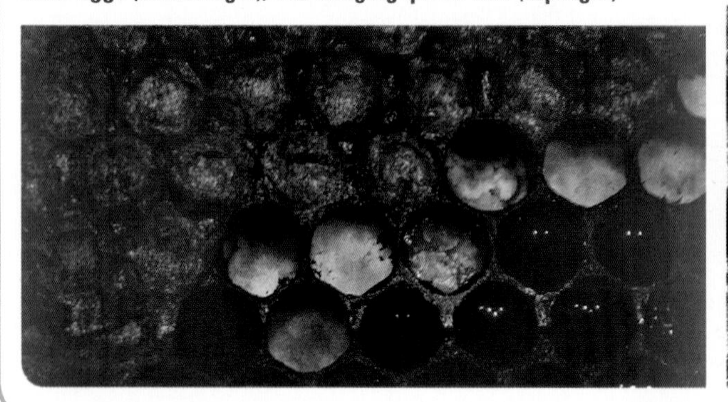

Fascinating fact

The ideal temperature in a honeybee nest is close to 37°C. Bees regulate the temperature in the nest by fanning their wings and evaporating water on their tongues.

Silk structures

A variety of insects have the ability to produce silk. Most of them, for example antlions, parasitic wasps, moths and fleas, use silk only to spin cocoons in which they pupate.

Weaver ants (*Oecophylla longinoda*) that occur along the tropical coast of KwaZulu-Natal build nests by pulling leaves together. Often long chains of workers work co-operatively, pulling at each other's legs. Once the leaves are in position, the ants use some of their own fully grown larvae to produce silk (normally the larvae would use the silk to spin their own cocoons), which they then use to weave the leaves together. Eventually a nest is constructed of several layers of leaves spun together, in which the whole colony lives.

Weaver ants use their larvae's silk to spin together a nest of leaves.

Web-spinners of the Embiidae family produce silk from glands on their thickened front legs and not from their saliva glands. This enables them to spin a web, called a 'gallery', under which they live communally and which serves to protect them against predators.

Bagworms and some other moth caterpillars create silk structures – these provide the larvae with full-time protection, eventually serving as cocoons in which they can pupate. (See Chapters 2 and 3.)

Some moth caterpillars and booklice that live on bark cover their entire host tree in a protective tent of silk.

The water-dwelling larvae of caddisflies construct silk cocoons incorporating stones, twigs and leaves, which provide protection and also serve as silk sieves to capture food from the water.

Wax or lacquer homes

Scale insects, such as soft scales, giant scales and armoured scales, have 'shells' that are not truly part of their bodies; instead, these structures are tiny 'homes' of wax or lacquer, secreted by the insect using special glands. These 'shells' are continually enlarged, from when the small nymph first settles on the plant, until the adult female lays eggs under the protective cover of her shell.

PROTECTION IN PLANTS

Woodborers and seed weevils automatically acquire a tunnel or protective home as they burrow into their food source. Many insects, however, live in plants without feeding on them. Others force the plants to produce special growths (galls), which they then use as protective homes as well as their food supply.

Carpenter bee tunnelling into wood

Carpenter and tunnelling bees

Carpenter bees bore tunnels into wood or reeds for nesting purposes, not to eat the wood. Some species concentrate on hollow reeds, in which they bore lateral entry holes.

Many bee species, for example leafcutting bees, do not bore their own tunnels but depend on second-hand tunnels, such as those that woodborers have vacated. They constantly scout for any open tunnel into which they can carry food for their larvae and then seal with leaves or clay.

Leaf miners

Many of the smaller plant-eating insects have larvae small enough to feed exclusively between the top and bottom epidermal layers of a leaf. They use the leaf itself as a home, and eventually as a cocoon for their pupae. The pattern of their tunnelling is visible from the outside, and each pattern is characteristic of a different species of leaf miner.

Insect groups that mine in leaves include a number of beetles, of which the larvae of certain

Horned soft scale

Giant scale with her offspring

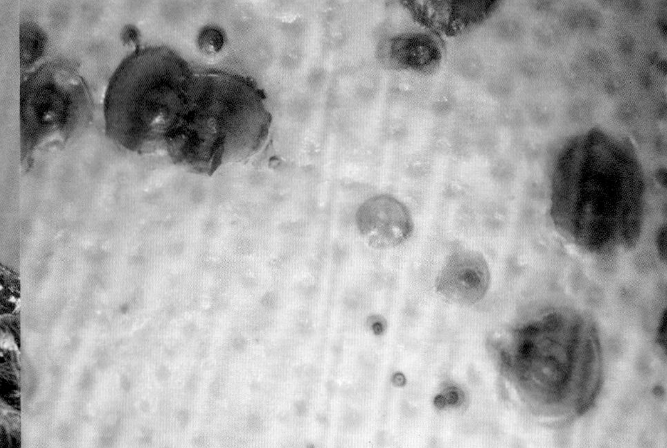

Female armoured scales under their hard shells

Some jewel beetle larvae feed between the top and bottom epidermal layers of a leaf.

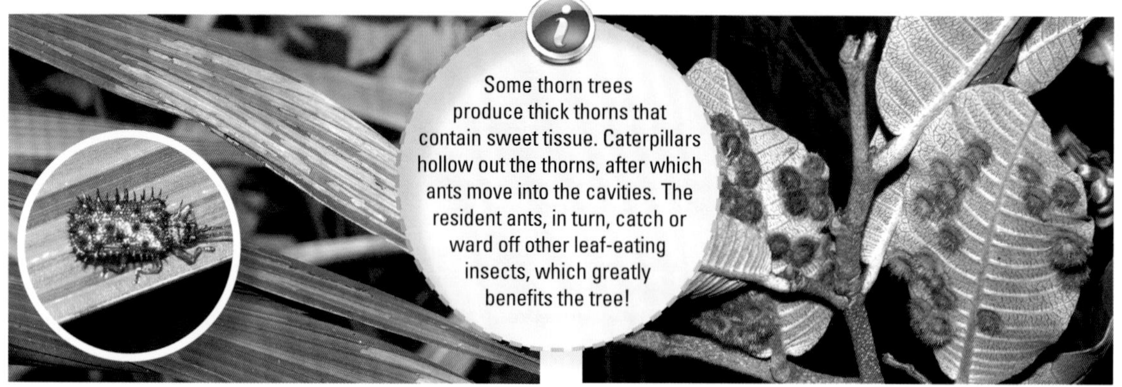

Some thorn trees produce thick thorns that contain sweet tissue. Caterpillars hollow out the thorns, after which ants move into the cavities. The resident ants, in turn, catch or ward off other leaf-eating insects, which greatly benefits the tree!

Leaves damaged by the larvae of spiny leaf beetles (inset)

Seed tissue formed on leaves by gall wasp larvae

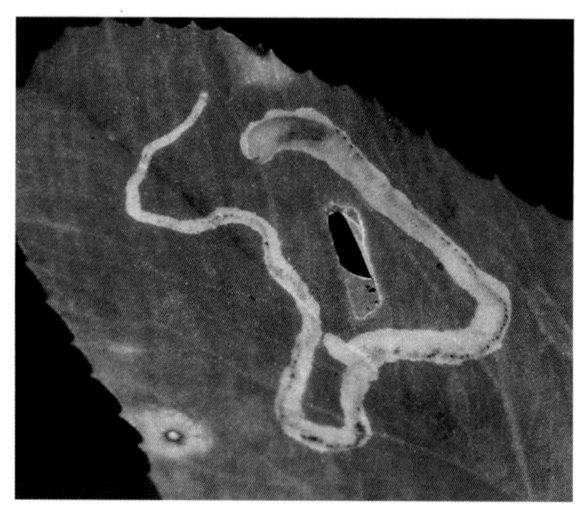

The larvae of leaf miner flies chew 'mines' or channels through leaves.

small jewel beetles and hedgehog beetles are probably best known. Leaf miner flies, many of which are agricultural pests, as well as leaf miner moths, for example Nepticulidae and several other smaller moth families, are also common.

Gall formers

Several insect groups have developed the ability to form galls on plants. The insect secretes chemicals that manipulate the plant's physiology, causing growths that supply the insect with shelter and food. The chemicals stimulate plants to produce strange tissue types in all the wrong places, for example seed tissue on the stem or on leaves, or growths of the same tissue, such as nodules on leaves.

Gall nodules on the leaves of a coral tree

Gall formers are widespread among the insects. Groups specialising in this lifestyle include certain booklice, lace bugs, psyllas, aphids, thrips, jewel beetles, longhorns, weevils, gall midges, leaf miner flies, leaf roller moths and gall wasps (in several families of the small parasitic wasps).

Light and sight

Insects use light primarily for gathering information. They often find food and mating partners by sight, and their eyes warn them of approaching danger. Besides these straightforward uses, insects' remarkable compound and simple eyes also serve as navigation tools, compasses, chronometers and calendars.

Assassin bug

SIMPLE EYES

Many insects have small eyes (ocelli) comprising a single lens, situated on the forehead between the two large compound eyes. The ocelli may be three simple eyes in a triangle, or two simple eyes, side by side. They do not 'see', but they register light intensity (thus serving as a 'clock') and the extent of daylight (thus serving as a 'calendar' through the seasons).

In many orders, families are found with or without simple eyes, and in some orders, such as the beetles, simple eyes are absent altogether. Where the ocelli are missing, the compound eyes have taken over the function of timekeeping.

Flies program their eggs

In cold climates, female flies lay eggs in late summer, which develop into maggots and eventually pupae that hibernate in diapause. The eggs are 'programmed' by the extent of daylight that the female has measured with her simple eyes, causing the pupae to hatch on a particular day in the following spring.

The three simple eyes of a seed bug

The term 'diapause' refers to a fixed period of decreased metabolism and suspended growth in insects and some other animals, especially when conditions are unfavourable, such as during very cold winters or dry summers.

ALARM CLOCKS

Insects, like all animals (including humans), have 'built-in clocks', which more or less keep going in a 24-hour cycle of active and passive metabolism. Simply put, the observed light period resets this clock every day; in insects, this is done by the ocelli.

In mayflies and stoneflies, the nymphs themselves have simple eyes. Depending on environmental conditions, it may take several years for them to develop under water, but by using their simple eyes they can determine the most suitable season and time for synchronised emergence.

COMPOUND EYES

The compound eyes of insects are amazing organs. Their convex surface consists of hundreds or even thousands of densely packed small lenses, behind each of which is a cone-shaped eyelet. Each facet or eyelet has its own 'retinal' tissue and nerve supply. The visual fields of the individual eyelets overlap widely. The picture seen by the insect is, therefore, probably something like a hologram: three-dimensional vision, often with a visual field of nearly 300 degrees!

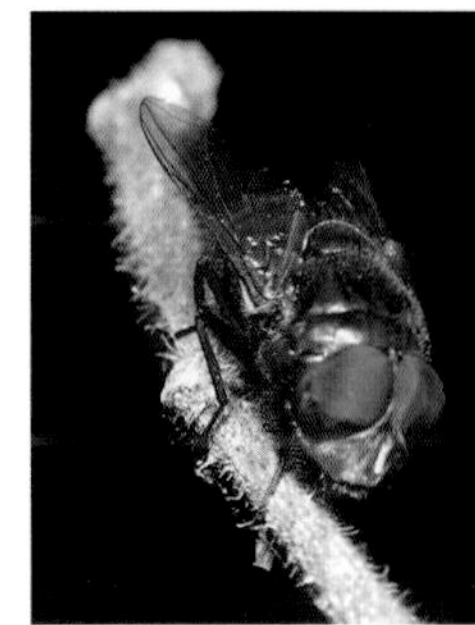

Large compound eyes of a fly

Each of the two large compound eyes of dragonflies (left and above) contains approximately 26,000 eyelets.

The artificial horizon of dragonflies

Pilots use an instrument called an 'artificial horizon' to work out the position of the plane relative to the horizon. Most flying insects keep level simply by orientating themselves in relation to the brightest light from above and least light from below. This technique generally works well, but not when they fly over water, as the bright reflection of the sun or the moon on the surface of the water causes the insects to become disoriented.

Dragonflies, which habitually fly over water, have developed an orientation mechanism that protects them from being misled by bright reflections from below. They have evolved a special line of eye facets across the middle of their eyes, which they keep directed at the greatest contrast between light and dark (the horizon).

Another mechanism helps to align the body and head of the dragonfly when it flies at an angle. Tiny hairs at the back of the head and at the front of the thorax provide the dragonfly with information about the position of its head, making sure the head is kept level when it banks.

Speed vision

The eyes of humans are lazy or 'slow', and can only distinguish between different sequential images at a rate of about 12 images per second. Our eyes have to 'reset' between pictures, otherwise the images will blur. The illusion of continuous motion in films and video games relies on this slow response of our eyes.

Relative to their size, insects and their prey move very fast. If they had eyes like ours, they would only see flickering images. Predators such as dragonflies and robber flies have eyes that can 'reset' so fast that they can identify 200 separate images per second!

Near-sighted and far-sighted

Eye lenses of insects are fixed, and since few insects need to see beyond more than a few metres, their focal depth is limited. There are exceptions though.

Dragonflies can see very well for up to 40m, and pollinators such as bees and fruit chafers can also distinguish flowers at distances of tens of metres. Insects that navigate according to celestial bodies must have sharp enough infinity focus – at least on the upper part of their eyes – to navigate accurately.

Selective vision

Similar to the selective smelling abilities of insects, it makes sense for insects to see only certain things in their environment. For instance, honeybees cannot see any difference between a square and a triangle. They can, however, immediately distinguish a radial pattern comprising 15 or 17 arms. The reason is obvious: for a bee, geometric patterns are meaningless but radial patterns that distinguish flower species are highly significant.

Butterflies, with their bright species-specific colour patterns have eyes that are more attuned to the colours and patterns of mating partners of their own species. Artificial models that exaggerate these colours and patterns (while keeping them recognisable) will attract more mating partners than the real thing.

Visual display showpieces

Visual displays, when involved in mating selection, may result in absurdly enhanced showpieces. Males of peacocks, fighting fish and whydah birds are prime examples. In insects such 'display' structures are found in males of king crickets, rhino beetles and some fruit chafers.

Stalk-eyed flies have ended up with a truly bizarre anatomy, due to male competition in which the male flies face each other and 'see eye to eye'. The male with the widest eyes automatically wins the contest and the loser moves away. Through this selection, the eyes of species of the Diopsidae family have therefore moved further and further apart, so that now they are burdened with what must be the maximum bearable width! This 'wide head' trait is not carried on the male sex gene only; females are saddled with equally wide heads.

Display horn on the head of a male fruit chafer

Male stalk-eyed flies 'outstare' each other.

COLOUR VISION

Colour vision in insects may differ greatly from the colour spectrum humans can see. Some are colour blind, some see short wavelengths (ultraviolet) way beyond our range of vision and others see long waves (infrared) that are invisible to us.

Flowers attract pollinators with colours, ultraviolet light and patterns often invisible to humans.

Seeing red

Infrared is associated with heat, but some insects see this wavelength as a colour (see Chapter 9).

Almost all adult butterflies are pollinators. They have a long proboscis with which to suck nectar, and their colour vision ranges from yellow and orange to red and purple. Flowers that specialise in pollination by butterflies open in the day, are usually in the red part of the colour spectrum, and have deep calyxes. Yellow flowers aim for the maximum variety of pollinators and attract butterflies, flies, beetles, wasps and bees. Bees, on the other hand, are able to see ultraviolet patterns on flowers that guide them to the pollen.

Night vision

The moon and stars radiate relatively high levels of ultraviolet light. Nocturnal insects such as moths see well in the ultraviolet range but are otherwise mostly colour blind, especially for yellow and red. Flowers that open only at night and depend on pollination by moths are usually white or light purple, as these colours reflect ultraviolet well.

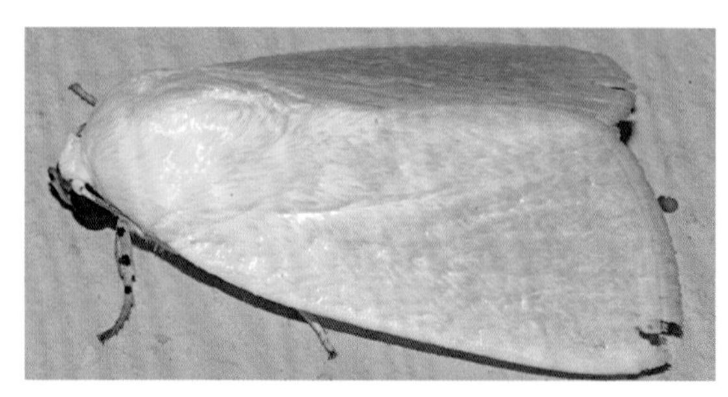

Night-flying moths are mostly white (top) or have metallic gold reflectors (above).

The night-flying hawk moth has a long proboscis for extracting nectar from white flowers with deep calyxes.

Outside lights with a yellow glow will not attract or disorient nocturnal insects, and are therefore ideal for streetlights and other outdoor illumination. Ultraviolet lamps, on the other hand, are used specifically to attract night-flying insects.

Fleas can 'see' such short wavelengths that they can even detect X-rays!

Warning colours and mimics

An interesting side effect of differential colour vision is the phenomenon of poisonous or venomous animals displaying warning (aposematic) colours. In nature, the 'universal code' for danger is black, combined with white, yellow, orange or red. The choice of colour tells us who the main predators are. If the predators are vertebrates like birds, which

Warning colours of a ground beetle

see colour, the potential prey will display black with red and yellow. If, however, the main predators are reptiles and arthropods, which are mostly colour blind, the potential prey will display black and white for maximum contrast.

Many poisonous or venomous animals mimic each other to mutually strengthen their message to predators, a phenomenon known as Müllerian mimicry. For this reason, all flat beetles have the same colour pattern, as do all velvet ant wasps and all reds.

In the natural world, black, in combination with white, yellow, orange or red, signifies danger.

TWO TYPES OF MIMICRY

Müllerian mimicry is a form of imitation in which poisonous or venomous species that share common predators mimic each other, which they do by displaying similar warning signals such as the same colour patterns. These signals protect both species, as predators that have learned to avoid one of the species will avoid the other too. Batesian mimicry is a mechanism whereby harmless species imitate the appearance of poisonous or venomous ones as a way of deterring predators and thereby protecting themselves.

Müllerian mimics: Butterfly reds are all poisonous, and mimic each other to reinforce warning signals sent to predators.

Batesian mimics: Some harmless beetles (below) mimic the colours of venomous velvet ant wasps (bottom) to trick predators into avoiding them.

MIMICKING FOR PROTECTION

Harmless visual mimics of poisonous or venomous insects must not only look like the insects they are imitating, they must also occur in the same habitat and move like their models. The mimicry affords both the model and the mimic protection from predation. The success of the imitation must be credited to the predator's discriminatory abilities, not the mimic itself, as the latter has no control over its appearance and has no idea what it looks like. Examples of poisonous or venomous insects and their mimics appear below.

Model	Mimic
 **Flat beetle** Protection: poison, reinforced by mutual benefits of Müllerian mimicry for species	**Clerid beetle**;  **Moth**;  **CMR beetle** 
 **CMR beetle** Protection: poison; colour warns predators of toxicity	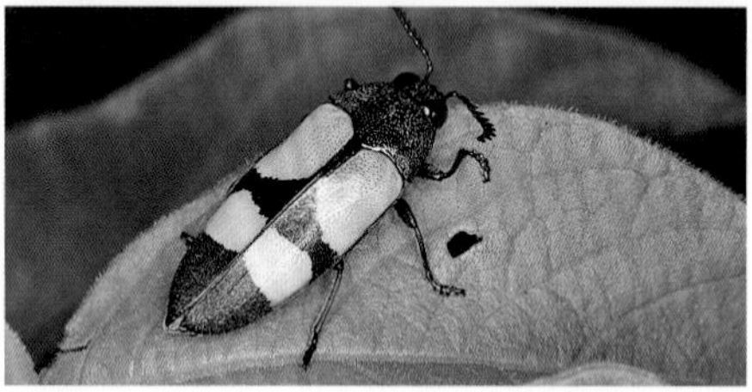 **Meloid-mimicking jewel beetle**
 **Honeybee** Protection: venomous sting	 **Hover fly**
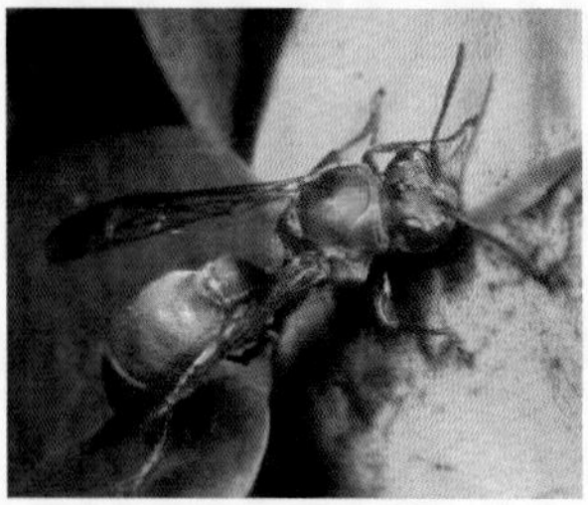 **Paper wasp** Protection: venomous sting	**Conopid fly**;  **Mantispid** 

Fascinating fact

Large black and white carpenter bees with venomous stings (below left) are mimicked by equally large robber flies (below right), which also prey on carpenter bees! They can often be seen hanging around the nests of these bees.

CAMOUFLAGE

Warning colours (and the mimicry thereof) are the exception among insects. Most insects are harmless and try to be as invisible as possible. For this purpose, they often mimic the shapes and colours of their background surprisingly well.

Getting covered

Caterpillars use bags and cocoons as both camouflage and protective armour. A number of insects, however, cover themselves with debris from their surroundings for camouflage only.

The larvae of hanging flies use debris for camouflage as they stalk their prey on plants, and so do the larvae of lacewings, which add the carcasses of their sucked-out prey to the detritus on their backs.

Some assassin bugs that hunt in humus have special glue on their integument, which collects any debris in their surroundings.

Larvae of fool's gold beetles have a special barbed fork on their tail, which they use to collect their shed skins and excrement. This fork, with its accumulated debris, is curved over the body to shade and hide the larva.

Other leaf beetle larvae cover themselves with sticky slime and faeces to appear as unappetising and unrecognisable as possible.

A hanging fly larva covered in debris to camouflage itself (left), and with debris removed (right)

Fool's gold beetle larva with an 'umbrella' of its own shed skin, collected on its barbed tail fork

PLANT MIMICS

As most insects are plant feeders, it stands to reason that they need to mimic the vegetation in their immediate environment to camouflage themselves if they want to avoid attack from predators and parasites. Examples of insects and the plants they mimic are shown below.

Plant matter being mimicked	Mimics
Grasses For an insect to conceal itself in grass, an elongated body with similar dimensions to a blade of grass is necessary. Grasses are imitated by many groups, including mantids (top right and bottom right), bugs (top far right), crickets (bottom centre) and grasshoppers (bottom far right).	    
Bark and lichens Many nocturnal insects, such as moths (right) and bark mantids (far right), hide on bark in the daytime, instinctively selecting backgrounds that most closely resemble their colours, patterns and textures.	 

Leaves Leaf mimics are common, particularly among katydids (right) and leafhoppers (far right). Because of their shape, these insects make natural leaf mimics – provided they are the right shade of green.		
Thorns Thorns on host plants are suitable models for small insects such as giant scales (right) and treehoppers (far right).		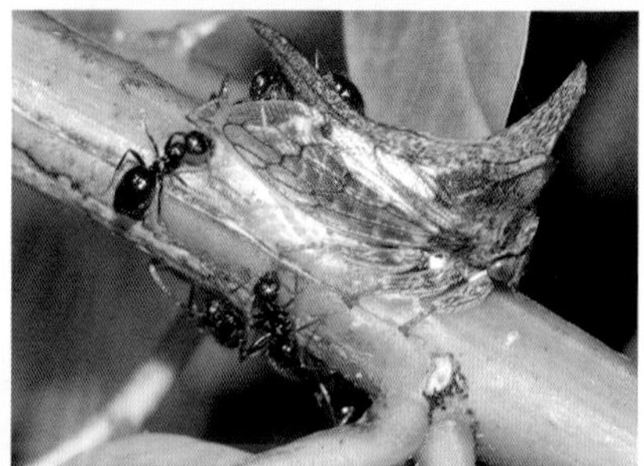
Sticks and branches Lantern bugs (right) grow preposterous extensions to resemble a twig, whereas stick insects (far right) are natural twig mimics.		
Leaf litter Many ground-dwelling insects take on the appearance of the surrounding leaf litter. Insects that resemble dead leaves or twigs include butterflies (right) and moths (far right).		

IS THAT A ROCK?

Grasshoppers living in barren deserts have nothing to mimic but bare rock, which they do extremely well.

HOW LOW CAN YOU GO?

Some insects demean themselves to the extent that they even mimic the droppings of their enemies! The caterpillars of the citrus swallowtail (*Papilio demodocus*) mimic bird droppings on leaves, complete with a characteristic white blotch. Only in the later stages, when the caterpillars grow to an unrealistic size, do they switch to mimicking leaves with chew marks. The caterpillars of tussock moths as well as various jewel beetles and clerid beetles also mimic bird droppings.

The first two larval instars of the citrus swallowtail caterpillar (above) and clerid beetles (below) mimic bird droppings.

Dummy eyespots and feelers on the hind wings of a blue butterfly prevent a predator from attacking its head.

DISRUPTIVE FORM AND ILLUSION

A common technique employed by insects to deceive predators is a misleading, disruptive colour pattern. Another common defence mechanism is the use of body poses that render the insect unrecognisable.

Butterflies with false 'heads'

Blues sitting with wings in a folded position often have noticeable eyespots and mobile 'feelers' on the rear ends of their wings. Butterflies are most vulnerable to attack in a sitting position, and the many specimens we see with the false 'head' missing from their wings (bitten out by birds or other small predators) testify to the effectiveness of this ruse.

Changing form

The contortionist sitting pose of longhorn antlions and some moths may serve to confuse predators. Absurd growths on nymphs of lantern bugs are examples of form disruption.

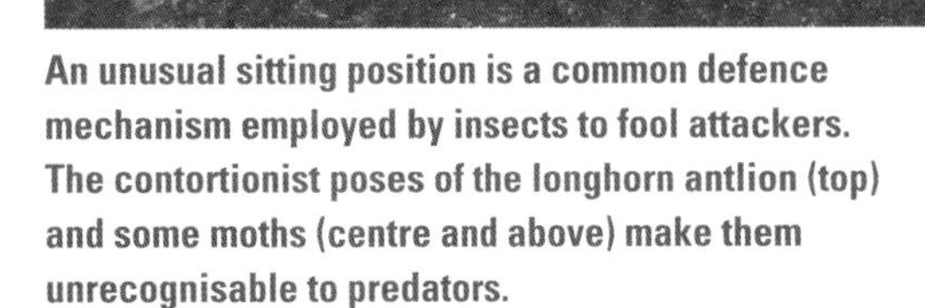

An unusual sitting position is a common defence mechanism employed by insects to fool attackers. The contortionist poses of the longhorn antlion (top) and some moths (centre and above) make them unrecognisable to predators.

Confusing colours

Many plant bugs, grasshoppers and moths have cryptically coloured forewings, but brightly coloured hind wings. To frighten a potential predator, the bright hind wings are suddenly exposed and flashed during the escape bid – only to be hidden again when the insect settles. The predator, still looking for a bright object, is often fooled. The bright 'horns' of the citrus swallowtail caterpillar, which can be displayed to deter predators and then retracted, may also serve to disorient would-be attackers.

The term 'cryptic' is used to refer to the markings or coloration that serve to mimic or camouflage an animal in its natural habitat.

A cryptically coloured grasshopper may distract and confuse a predator by suddenly flashing its coloured hind wings during a short escape flight.

Frightening predators away

Emperor moths have developed two large eyespots on their hind wings. Suddenly exposed when the wings are opened, they resemble the large bifocal eyes of a predator, such as a cat, owl or falcon. All small predators will quickly back off at such a sight. Some owlet moths have similar eyespots on their forewings, but these are not as effective, as they cannot be hidden and unexpectedly exposed. Eyespots are also found on many caterpillars.

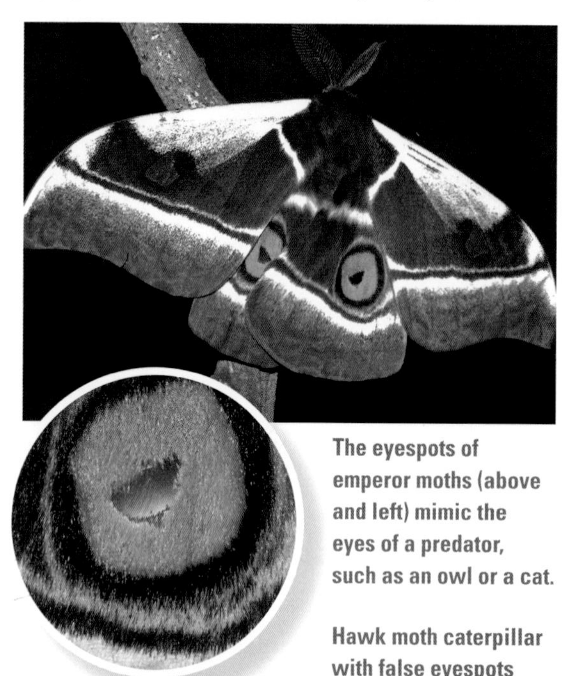

The eyespots of emperor moths (above and left) mimic the eyes of a predator, such as an owl or a cat.

Hawk moth caterpillar with false eyespots

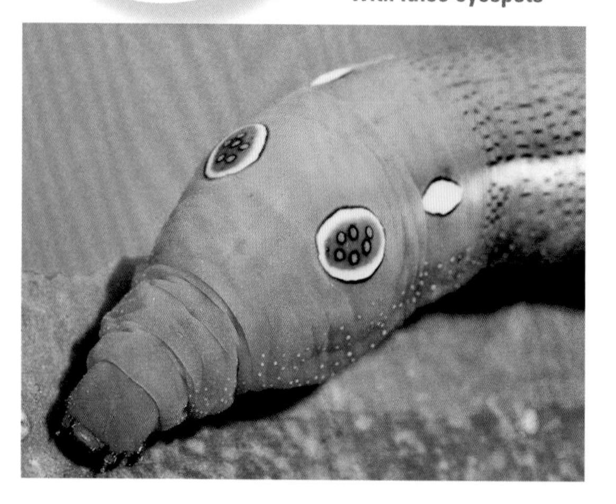

NAVIGATING BY THE SUN AND THE MOON

While many nesting insects rely on their memory to find their nests, most of them also use the sun, moon or stars for navigation. These insects include bees, wasps, dung beetles, social toktokkies (*Parastizopus*) and harvester termites. Insects active by day navigate by taking bearings relative to the sun. Nocturnal insects navigate by the moon or the brightest star.

Honeybees are expert navigators

When a worker honeybee flies out to forage for nectar and pollen, she explores erratically, not in a straight line. The bee curves, circles, flies at an angle and interrupts her flight to inspect flowers, without any fixed pattern. When she finds a worthwhile stand of flowers, she fills either her crop with nectar or her pollen baskets with pollen, or both, before making a 'bee line' back to the hive.

Considering that an exploration like this could take hours and cover more than a kilometre, homing straight back to the nest requires incredible navigational skills. It means that the bee has calculated her position throughout her erratic flight, factoring in changes in the position of the sun and the impact of wind gusts.

Bees can also guide themselves home on overcast days. Because their eyes can distinguish between polarised and unpolarised light, they can determine the position of the sun despite cloud cover. In addition, they have a backup system for navigation on very cloudy days, or in the dark. They can detect the earth's magnetic field, which they can employ as a means of navigation (like a magnetic compass).

Back in the nest, the worker bee 'tells' her colleagues about her find, and where it is located, by doing a 'dance' in the pitch dark, while the other bees follow the action with their feelers. The bee does the dance repeatedly, running in a straight line on the vertical comb and waggling her abdomen, before returning to the base.

An Austrian zoologist, Karl von Frisch, was the first person to understand the 'language' and meaning of the bees' dance. He worked out that the linear direction of the dance accords with an

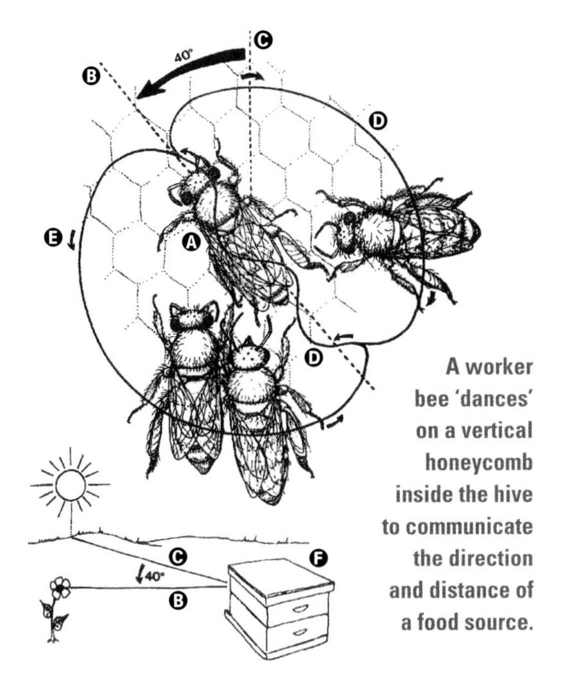

A worker bee 'dances' on a vertical honeycomb inside the hive to communicate the direction and distance of a food source.

A Dancing bee
B Direction of food source
C Direction of the sun
D Waggle lines, indicating distance
E Direction of the dance
F Hive

angle relative to the sun (represented by gravity in the dance). The waggles indicate distance: the fewer waggles, the further away the food source is. A tail wind is danced, indicating a 'shorter distance'; a head wind dance, conversely, describes the route to a location that is further away. This is remarkable since the bee would have experienced the opposite on its 'bee line' back to the nest.

Bees 'reading' the dance will now fly out to investigate. Every bee returning with a worthwhile load will repeat the dance, recruiting more workers. Unsuccessful workers will not perform the dance upon their return. In this way, the optimal work force for every harvest is recruited.

BEE ROBOTS

Many experiments support Von Frisch's discovery of the meaning of the bee dance. Some work was even done using mechanical dancing 'bee robots'. Today, we know that bees develop 'dialects', and can misinterpret the dance of bees from another region!

Fascinating fact

Despite the brain of a honeybee being smaller than the head of a pin, it reliably does the work of many navigational instruments, including a chronometer, gyroscope, compass, theodolite, sextant and navigational computer!

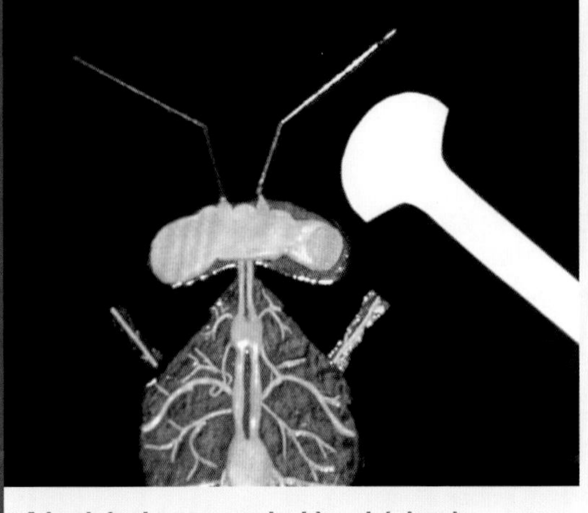

A bee's brain compared with a pin's head

When scouts find a new nesting site, they will return to the hive and dance for hours, continuously changing the angle of their dance to align it with the movement of the sun outside. They sometimes dance throughout the night, maintaining the correct angle in relation to the sun (which, at night, is below the horizon). At dawn, the bees' dance will perfectly correspond with the position of the rising sun. A spectator bee, using the same instinctive arithmetic, will find the correct route in the morning, even though it may have 'read' the dance at midnight!

Dung beetles watch the sun

Ball-rolling dung beetles also use sun compass navigation to stay on track. Although they do not have to aim for a specific nesting site, they have to try to move in a straight line. The object of their ball rolling is to get their loot away as far as possible from thieves and competition in the shortest possible time, an attempt that would be futile if they were to move in circles.

A dung beetle rolls a dung ball along a straight line, using the sun as a means of navigation.

Once the ball has been formed, the beetle takes a sun bearing and then doggedly sticks to it, over all obstacles in his way.

Wingless species of West Coast and Namib dung beetles (*Pachysoma* spp.) dig tunnels to which they have to carry several small dung pellets or pieces of plant litter (see Chapter 2). As scent markers and landmarks would be useless in the shifting sand, they certainly navigate by the sun, and quite accurately so. Recently it was found that nocturnal ball-rollers use the Milky Way for navigation.

INSECTS RESPOND TO LIGHT

Night-flying insects use the brightest celestial body by which to navigate, and try to follow a straight line. Usually they fixate on a bright star and then fly at an angle smaller than 90 degrees to the star. From a celestial light source, light beams are, for all practical purposes, parallel and the flight path will be straight. However, when the insect encounters a brighter (artificial) light source on earth and navigates according to this source, the fixed flying angle will inevitably spiral the insect towards the source.

Virtually all night-flying insects are 'attracted' to lights in this way. Because they see mainly ultraviolet light, ultraviolet lights appear brighter to them. Once near the this light source, it seems so bright to them that they switch to 'daylight' behaviour and go to sleep.

Some diurnal insects, however, are roused from sleep, and are then attracted by the lights. Among these are cicadas and flies.

Mantids, like geckos, learn to move closer to lights at night, where they can hunt sleeping prey.

Flight path of an insect guided by celestial light (left) and by artificial light (right)

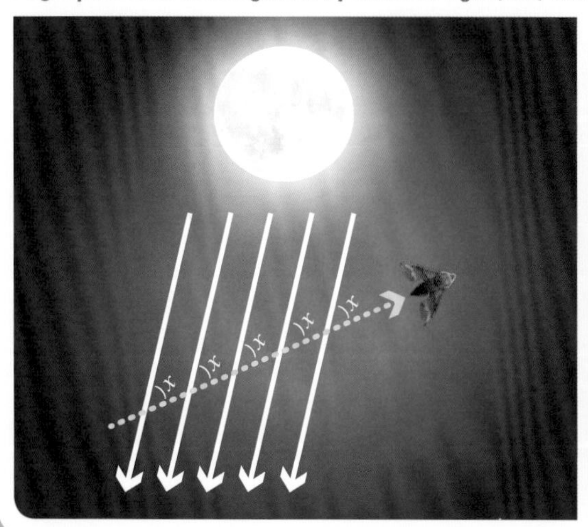

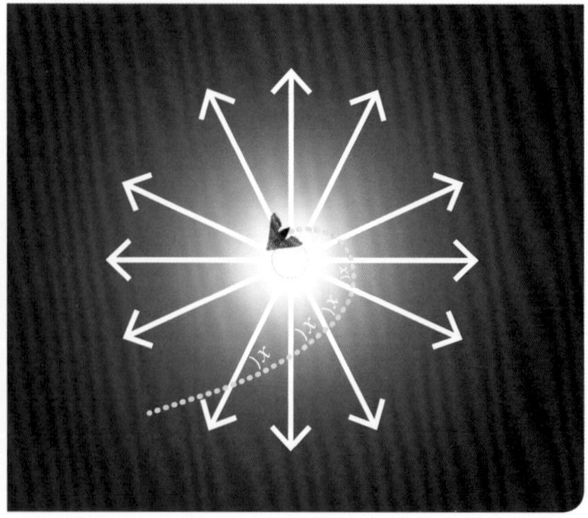

ANTS LAY TRAILS

Ants commonly use scent trails to mark their routes to and from their nests (see Chapter 8). Although scouts often use sun compass navigation, they cannot tell other workers where a food source is, other than by laying a scent trail or physically leading them to it.

Bees and wasps use landmarks

Apart from the parasitic groups, virtually all bees and wasps construct nests to which they return repeatedly. Most of them have a keen memory of the landmarks close to their nest. Honeybees also memorise the objects near their nest entrance to facilitate navigation of the last few metres.

A simple, classical experiment demonstrates this practice of 'landmark homing'. While a digger wasp is in its tunnel, place some highly visible landmarks around it, such as yellow blocks. After the wasp has inspected the area and left, shift these objects so that the nest entrance is now behind one of the blocks and only a few centimetres 'out of position' in relation to the blocks. Upon its return, the wasp will not be able to find its nest, and will keep searching for the entrance relative to the yellow markers.

MARVELLOUS FIREFLIES

In South Africa, fireflies are the only light-producing insects. In other parts of the world, light-producing click beetles and maggots of midges also occur.

The light of fireflies is a marvel of nature and, like photosynthesis, it has only recently been fully analysed. The light organ underneath the tip of the abdomen has a 'mirror' consisting of highly reflective air-filled cells. The actual light is triggered by nerve endings initiating a chemical enzyme reaction that generates light and can, therefore, be switched on and off by nerve impulse. The light-producing reaction is extremely efficient: while filament globes produce about 7 per cent light and 93 per cent heat from the energy they consume, fireflies produce cold light, with no measurable heat loss.

Fireflies are predators, feeding mainly on snails and slugs. They are poisonous and their light advertises their inedibility, like warning colours. Therefore, even their larvae glow.

Adult fireflies use their light for sexual attraction. Most species have winged males and wingless females ('glow worms'). Males fly around at night flashing their species-specific code, searching for females with their large, ventrally placed eyes. Females ready to mate will raise their tails and flash back, whereupon the male will land and mate with her. Some female glow worms answer and attract male fireflies of species other than their own, only to devour them when they land. Once satiated they will answer and attract males of their own species with their own species' code.

A wingless female firefly (glow worm)

The firefly's light advertises its inedibility to predators.

Fascinating fact

In some tropical firefly species, both sexes are winged, and they often aggregate in mating swarms on specific trees. The entire firefly-covered tree then flashes in synchrony – a truly spectacular sight!

BLIND INSECTS

All blind insects have lost their eyes because of a lifestyle in which eyes have become redundant.

Most blind insects, such as lice and fleas, are parasites that do not use their sight to find their hosts, although fleas have light-sensitive 'eyespots' and can tell light from dark.

Immobile insects that live in protective structures are also blind. They include the females of scale insects; armoured scales and mealy bugs; bagworms and other bag-living lepidopterans; fig wasp males; and termites (barring the reproducers and the workers of some harvester termites).

Insects living in caves usually lose their pigmentation and eyesight. Such 'troglodytes' are common in the northern hemisphere, but are very rare in southern Africa. Best known are blind fish moths found in caves and in ant and termite nests.

The magnified head of a flea. Although blind, fleas can distinguish between light and dark.

Workers and soldiers of most termite species live in perpetual darkness and do not need to see.

Scale insects are motionless and do not require sight.

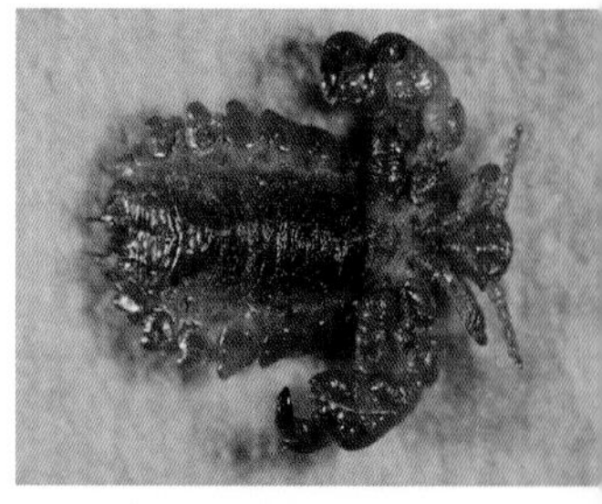

Like all sitting parasites, lice are blind.

7

Sound and hearing

Woolly chafer

Sound is used as an energy-efficient means of communication throughout the animal kingdom, and insects are no exception. They excel in the diverse ways in which they produce and detect sound and the variety of uses they have found for it.

SOUND IN SEXUAL ATTRACTION

Most sounds produced by insects serve to attract a mating partner. A handy characteristic of sound is that combinations of pitch and rhythm allow for an endless variation of songs, each of which is restricted to one species only. Similar to a single telephone line that can simultaneously transmit hundreds of conversations (converted to different frequencies), the night air can carry the songs of hundreds of different crickets, frogs, katydids and nocturnal birds, without any confusion among the many listeners that are able to recognise the sounds made by members of their own species. The sounds insects produce are, in fact, sometimes the most reliable identification feature, and the accurate classification of crickets is largely based on their species-specific sound codes.

Mosquitoes do not buzz for nothing

Mosquitoes are a species-rich group of insects, and at any one given location, easily a dozen different species may be present. These species frequently share the hosts available in their area by seemingly working in shifts. The mosquitoes biting you early in the morning will probably differ from the species that bit you at midnight or early in the evening.

Female mosquitoes make their characteristic buzzing sound by rapidly vibrating their wings for a purpose. Males have to recognise the females of their own species in the dark. The females of each species therefore have a different 'wing pitch', which changes after they have had a blood meal and are ready for mating.

The male choirs of crickets

The singing sex in crickets is the male; female crickets can make only a very faint sound, and then only when mating. Male crickets chirp or stridulate by rubbing the front edges of their forewings against each other, while the wings are raised slightly in the shape of a parabolic reflector. This amplifies and directs the sound, making it difficult to locate a cricket when it turns around while chirping.

THE THERMOMETER CRICKET

The chirping rhythm of the common garden cricket is so closely associated with temperature (the colder, the slower the rhythm) that the species is also known as the thermometer cricket. The number of cricket chirps per minute can be used to estimate the ambient air temperature in degrees centigrade.

Common garden cricket

Cricket species recognise their kin based on their song, which differs from species to species in frequency, rhythm and sound quality. Since crickets are cold-blooded, their rhythm picks up pace when the environment gets warmer, and the females adapt their hearing accordingly. However, if the male and female are kept at different temperatures, the female will fail to recognise the song of her male.

Most crickets use their wings as parabolic sound amplifiers, but the wings of armoured ground crickets are reduced to stubs, with the exclusive purpose of producing sounds. The thoracic plate that covers the wing stubs has a parabolic shape and when lifted serves as a sound amplifier.

The uncontested masters of sound amplification are the tree crickets (*Oecanthus* spp.). They cut a hole in a leaf and use their legs to fold the leaf into the shape of a large parabolic reflector, which is their sound amplifier. Those that live in grass bend grass blades for the same purpose. In this way, the sound can be increased by a factor of 500.

These behavioural patterns are all the more astonishing when one takes into consideration that the male crickets have no way of hearing the result of their clever tricks, as the amplified sound is only audible half a kilometre away from the source!

Fascinating fact

The mole cricket builds an underground tunnel with a sound chamber close to the entrance which has trumpet-shaped openings, amplifying the sound dramatically (see Chapter 5).

A fiddle-bow on the hind leg

The males of most species of grasshopper also chirp, but in their case the male rubs a rough area on the inner side of his hind leg over the front of his forewing. While the large grey rain locust (*Lamarckiana* spp.) makes a remarkably loud and persistent rattling noise at night, most other locusts and grasshoppers stridulate by day.

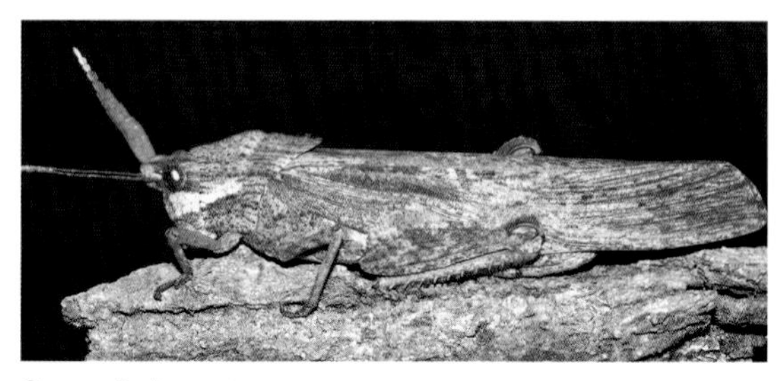

Grey rain locust

The armoured ground cricket's thoracic plate performs a dual role when it comes to creating sound: it covers the insect's sound-producing wing stubs and when lifted also functions as a parabolic amplifier.

The male grasshopper chirps by rubbing the inside of his hind leg over the edge of his forewing.

An unusual variation of stridulation with the hind legs is found in bladder grasshoppers. The stridulating apparatus of the male bladder grasshopper is located on the hind legs and on the sides of the abdomen, where it is discernible as a row of little knobs. While the female has a normal abdomen, the male's abdomen is transparent, enormously enlarged and filled with air, with the intestines lying in a narrow strip along the bottom. This hollow abdomen serves as a resonance box, similar to the body of a drum or violin, which greatly amplifies the sound of his stridulation.

The stridulating apparatus of the male bladder grasshopper appears as a little row of knobs on the side of the hollow abdomen.

Bladder grasshoppers are found all along our coastline – from the cold west coast to the tropical east coast. Depending on the climate, the various species are either diurnal or nocturnal.

Cicadas, the champions of loudness

When it comes to noise, the only insect that can outdo the bladder grasshopper is the cicada.

The cicada male, with its shrill and incessant call, produces the loudest sound any insect can make. The mechanism employed to produce this noise is rather unusual: it consists of a gently convex plate at the base of the abdomen that is buckled inward by a muscle – much like making a dent in the lid of a metal tin. The arched plate, known as a tymbal, bounces back to its original position under power of its own elasticity, and is then buckled inward again through contraction of the internal muscle. Each time the plate is indented and bounces back a clicking sound is produced. The speed at which this happens is accelerated until the arched plate starts oscillating and has to be buckled only occasionally using muscle power. The plate soon oscillates at hundreds of rounds per second, producing a shrill, high-pitched note.

The male cicada's vibrating membranes are located at the side of his abdomen, which is hollow like that of the bladder grasshoppers. In addition, the sound-producing organ has a hinged lid that can be manipulated to muffle or direct the sound.

The vibrating membranes of a male cicada

The male cicada is the loudest and shrillest of all insects.

Parasitic male cicadas hide close to a singing male to intercept females attracted by his song.

The phenomenon of parasitic males is common among cicadas. These males are mute and do not spend any of their own energy on singing, but rather hide behind the branch on which a singing male is sitting. Up to three or four mute parasitic males may hide close to a singing male, where they try to intercept females attracted by the singing male. They apparently succeed often enough to make this kind of cheating a popular strategy.

Similar behaviour is found among many other kinds of insects, such as crickets and grasshoppers, where the males make a sound to attract females.

THE CANTOR EFFECT

Another interesting phenomenon is the 'cantor effect', which can be observed among frogs, crickets and other singing creatures. The loudest singer starts up first, with the rest of the choir falling in with their songs. The moment the 'cantor' stops singing, the rest also abruptly keep quiet. Any sound louder than the voice of the cantor (like a jet plane passing overhead) will stop both the cantor and the rest of the choir from singing for a while.

Knock knock, who's there?

Our region boasts a great diversity of toktokkies. Both sexes of many of these species locate each other by making tapping sounds with their abdomen on the ground. As with crickets, the sounds they make are species specific, and, since half a dozen different toktokkies can coexist in the same area, the tapping rhythms can become rather complicated. The tapping codes of some toktokkie species include rolls that are so fast that the beetle appears to blur while tapping.

Using these tapping sounds, the male and female toktokkies move closer towards each other. Their feet feel the vibrations in the ground, and they can even 'hear' the direction by sensing the infinitesimal delay between one foot and the other. Because solid matter is a better conductor of sound than air, these wingless beetles can locate each other over astonishing distances.

Toktokkies that use the tapping strategy are found even in the sand dunes of the Kalahari. Through their tapping, they compact the sand to such an extent that they can produce a loud and clear knocking sound.

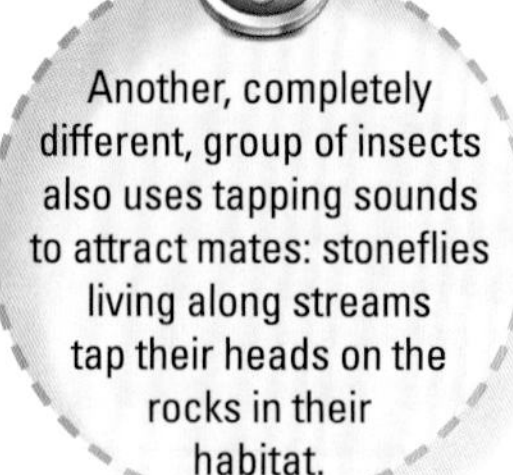

Another, completely different, group of insects also uses tapping sounds to attract mates: stoneflies living along streams tap their heads on the rocks in their habitat.

One smaller species, living on the soft crests of sand dunes, has adopted a different, unique way of producing its species-specific call. This toktokkie swings its feelers around at such a stupendous rate that they start humming.

Fascinating fact

Many night-flying moths and beetles have developed a woolly covering because it absorbs sound. These insects are, therefore, not so easily detected by bats using sonar sound.

Night-flying moth with its woolly fur

SOUND AND SELF-DEFENCE

For many animals, sound has an important function as an early warning against approaching danger; in insects, sound is used with remarkable versatility for both passive and active defence.

The ultrasonic detectors of moths

Although they cannot make any sounds, many kinds of owlet moths have large hearing apparatuses at the sides of the thorax. The purpose of these 'moth ears' is to listen for the echolocation signals emitted by bats, and the hearing organs are, indeed, sensitive to nothing but the ultrasonic frequencies produced by foraging bats.

An owlet moth hearing an approaching bat will take evasive action, displaying all the skill of a fighter pilot. If the bat is still some distance away, the moth will bank to the side or perform a rolling manoeuvre. If the bat is closing in, the moth may even power dive into the ground at full speed. However, bats have also learnt to expect certain manoeuvres from moths, and intercept them with remarkable dexterity.

DEMONSTRATING THE DIFFERENCE

The difference between moths that can hear bat calls and those that cannot is easily demonstrated at an outside light where a number of moths have settled. Tinkle a bunch of keys close to them, and some of the moths will immediately fall to the ground. These moths have 'ears', but not those that remained sitting at the light. A bunch of keys produces 'white noise' with sufficient overtones that correspond to bat sonar.

False alarm of the death's-head moth

The death's-head moth is a very large, impressive hawk moth with the unusual ability to squeak through its proboscis. Insects do not have lungs, and the moth produces this sound by drawing air

The owlet moth's hearing organ is geared specifically for detecting sounds emitted by bats.

Death's-head moth

INSECTS WITH WIND INSTRUMENTS

In southern Africa, the death's-head moth is the only insect that uses its proboscis like a wind instrument to make a noise – sucking in and expelling air from its gut to produce its characteristic high-pitched squeaking notes. Some cockroach species found in Madagascar also use air to create sound. They do so by whistling or hissing through their spiracles (lateral breathing openings).

The short proboscis of a death's-head moth

into its stomach and forcing it out again over a vibrating flap near the opening of the proboscis, like a ventriloquist.

The purpose of this peculiar squeaking is remarkable. Death's-head moths frequently enter the hives of honeybees to steal honey. Their squeaking sounds exactly like the piping alarm signals of the queen bee, and causes the worker bees to 'freeze'. This, in turn, enables the death's-head moth to enter and exit the hive with impunity.

Alarm chirping

Various dung beetles, longhorn beetles and velvet ant wasps chirp rhythmically in stressful situations, for example when held between the fingers. This sound is similar across a range of insects that call when distressed. As these insects are all solitary, the sound is not intended as a warning aimed at other members of their species. Furthermore, the beetles do not have specific defence mechanisms, so the chirping cannot serve as a warning to would-be predators. The explanation for this phenomenon probably lies in the fact that the main predators of these insects are birds, and generally, birds instinctively regurgitate food in reaction to the high-pitched cheeping of their nestlings. So, when a bird catches such an insect and the insect chirps in its beak, the chirping sound is directly and loudly relayed through its beak and skull to its ears, with the result that it will instinctively spit out its prey. This trick must work often enough for evolution to have selected the same chirping distress sound among all these unrelated insects.

Many longhorn beetles chirp when in distress.

Most dung beetle species chirp when attacked, and their sounds are remarkably similar.

Beetles make their chirping sound by scraping a rough part of the exoskeleton over a 'file' between the thorax and hind body. One can see when some beetles utter their chirping sound: they rhythmically rub the thorax up and down against the hind body.

NOISY WINGS

When some insects fly, a loud rattling of their wings can be heard. In grasshoppers, this sound, combined with the confusing effect of bright colours on their hind wings, serves to frighten potential predators. The confusion is reinforced when both the colours and sound suddenly disappear the moment the grasshopper lands.

In other insects, such as the spider-hunting wasps, the purpose of the continuous, loud rattling of the wings is still unknown.

SOCIAL FUNCTIONS OF SOUND

Sound functions as a medium of communication in all groups of social insects. Because a message communicated via sound can immediately be sensed throughout the nest, this method has an advantage over chemical communication.

Bee sense

When a swarm of bees becomes agitated or aggressive, the bees create a characteristic buzzing sound with their wings. (Apparently bees also convey more subtle messages by buzzing their wings.)

To investigate the behaviour of bees, a group of American researchers built a mechanical-electronic bee, capable of dancing on a comb like a real bee (see Chapter 6). The researchers found that the bees did not pay much attention to the artificial bee, until they made the robot bee buzz. The bees then paid more attention to the dancing and buzzing robot, but still much less than they would have paid to the dancing and buzzing of a real bee. The researchers concluded that the robot bee probably did not buzz enough 'sense'!

When bees want to rear a new queen, they rear several at the same time. The first queen to emerge from her cell begins to chirp or pipe and the other queens respond with the same sound. This sound causes the worker bees to become passive – probably to prevent them from taking part in the ensuing fights. The queens find each other by the sound they make, and then fight to the death until only one victor remains. Even queens that have not yet emerged from their cells cannot help piping an answer, and are stung to death in their cells.

Death-watch beetles, which burrow into wood, make a knocking sound without any provocation. Perhaps their knocking helps them to orientate themselves, so that they do not tunnel into each other's burrows.

Termite soldiers raise the alarm

When a nest of the large fungus-growing termites (*Macrotermes* spp.) is disturbed, a rustling sound can be clearly heard, even outside the nest. Soldier termites create this sound by rapidly tapping their jaws on the ground. The sound spreads like lightning and is repeated by other soldiers. Within seconds the whole nest, over its range of hundreds of metres of tunnels, is put on a high state of alert.

Marching music in Matabele ants

Bands of Matabele ants (*Megaponera* sp.) that are out on a termite raid stridulate audibly while they are walking in file. They create the sound by rubbing spines, located on the stalk between the thorax and abdomen, against the thorax.

Matabele ants use sound to maintain contact.

This sound appears to keep the Matabele ants in contact with one another and to synchronise their actions. After an attack on termites, they maintain complete silence for a while before again making a great noise on the way home. Several ant species, such as stink-ants (*Streblognathus* sp.), stridulate when they are threatened. However, the function of these sounds is not well understood.

INSECT HEARING ORGANS

- As sound is nothing but vibration, any hairs with nerve endings at their base can serve as a hearing organ on an insect. Special long hairs on the feelers most often serve this purpose.

Long bristles on feelers of male midges and mosquitoes serve as sound receptors.

'Ear' of a grasshopper on the front of the abdomen

- In many insects specialised 'ears' are found, which consist of tympanic membranes (eardrums). In the case of moths and locusts such 'ears' are located on the front sides of the abdomen.
- In crickets, 'eardrums' are located on the front of the forelegs, which can be placed well apart for stereo listening.
- Toktokkies (and probably most insects) can feel vibrations or sound in the substrate through their feet. Parasitic wasps are particularly sensitive and can hear woodborers feeding inside wood.

Eardrums on the forelegs of a cricket

Smells and smelling

Smell is the identification of airborne molecules. We use moist mucous membranes in our noses to trap and identify such molecules while breathing. Reptiles use their tongues, which they flick into the air and then push into the Jacobson's organ in their palate. This scent organ, known as the vomeronasal organ, is also found in mammals and amphibians.

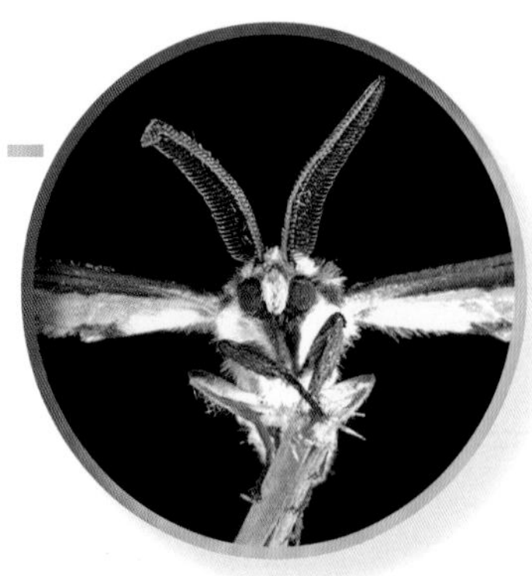

Enlarged feelers of a male moth

SPECIALISED SENSE OF SMELL

Insects smell by means of thousands of small pits on their feelers, or on their feet. Feelers with enlarged surface areas, such as those of some male moths or the bulbous antennae of dung beetles, which can fan open like pages of a book, are evidence of a powerful sense of smell in these insects.

As with other senses in insects, the sense of smell is specialised: it tends to be limited to a few smells only, but with uncanny acuity. A male emperor moth can identify the presence of his mate with only a few molecules of her alluring smell (pheromone) in the air. He can also determine the direction from which the smell is coming by comparing its intensity on his left and right antennae!

Although insects mostly use smell to search for food and a mate, they also regularly employ it for a variety of other functions: self-defence, individual identification, orientation and even as a component of 'language'!

> A male emperor moth's acute sense of smell is comparable to the ability to taste a grain of sugar in the water of a swimming pool.

SMELLING FOOD

Most adult insects find their food by smell. Larvae usually lack feelers and depend on their parents to deposit them on or at the appropriate food supply.

The flying 'truffle dog'

Truffles are mushroom-like fungi that grow underground, often as deep as a metre. Truffles are a sought-after delicacy in Europe, and dogs and pigs have been trained for centuries to smell out these treasures. Some species of a beetle family closely related to dung beetles, the Bolboceratidae, breed only on truffles. These peculiar, round beetles must, therefore, be able to trace truffles much as a truffle dog does – even from the air above the vegetation layer as they fly overhead. It's their massive bulbous and layered antennae that enable these beetles to accomplish this astounding feat of smell.

Dung beetles 'pinch their noses'

Dung beetles and their close relatives form the second largest group of beetles, with an estimated 2,500 species found in southern Africa. As adults, they are characteristically solidly built, and their

Beetles that specialise in truffles use their bulbous antennae to locate these underground delicacies.

Scarabaeus rubripennis **(left) feeding on insect carrion**

Unlike most dung beetles, fruit chafers prefer nectar.

The millipede dung beetle is a specialist feeder, taking sustenance from dead millipedes.

DESERT FEAST

Dung beetles are not the only insects with a nose for decomposition – all carrion insects and blowflies rely on their keen sense of smell to find food. In the desert, even vegetarian darkling beetles and millipedes are attracted to such nutritious food sources as decaying carcasses.

Darkling beetles making a meal of a dead locust in the Namib Desert

larvae all look like the C-shaped grubs commonly found in compost heaps. The most distinctive feature shared by all dung beetles is their club-shaped antennae, of which the segments can be compressed into a ball or fanned open to sense odours. While the beetles are in flight, the clubs on the feelers act as their 'nose', enabling them to detect fresh manure from hundreds of metres away. However, when the beetles land on the dung and get to work inside it, they have to protect these sensitive organs against overload. They therefore close them into airtight balls – the equivalent of humans pinching their noses.

Not all scarabs feed on dung. Fruit chafers feed on nectar, ripe fruit and sap flows on trees. Millipede dung beetles specialise in dead millipedes. Some species, such as *Scarabaeus rubripennis*, feed on carrion. All of them, however, depend on their keen sense of smell to trace their food.

Smelling the prey

Predators and parasites often use their sense of smell to find their prey or host. None demonstrates this better than the parasitic wasp that parasitises larvae of woodborers. The female wasp runs over dead tree trunks, using her sensitive feet to listen for gnawing sounds from within the wood. When she hears a borer, the wasp starts playing her feelers over the wood. Not only can she smell the species of her host, but she can also tell whether this host is already parasitised or is, in fact, still available! Then she drills through as much as 20mm of wood, and accurately deposits her egg on the hapless woodborer. The wasp larva gradually devours the woodborer larva, but, before the final kill, graciously allows it to tunnel close to the surface of the wood. This enables the wasp that hatches from its pupa to make its way out of the wood.

See Chapter 6 for information about how flowering plants also use colour and shape as strategies to attract specific insect species.

The perfume industry of flowers

Flowering plants attract insect pollinators to achieve cross-pollination with other flowers of their own species. The more specific a flowering plant is in attracting certain insect species, the better the chance that these insects will transport pollen to another flower of the same species. One way to achieve specific attraction is by emitting a specific smell. The wonderful variety of smells that different flowers produce (and on which much of the perfume industry is based) derives from these efforts by plants to attract specific pollinators.

The odour of rotting flesh emitted by carrion flowers of the genus *Stapelia* attracts flies and blowflies.

Most flowers reward pollinating insects with sweet nectar, but carrion flowers (*Stapelia* spp.) produce the smell of rotting flesh, and combine this with petals that realistically mimic decomposing meat, sometimes even with replicas of 'maggots'! This ploy misleads flies and blowflies so effectively that they often deposit maggots on the flowers. In their frantic efforts to get at the 'meat', the insects pick up pollen that will fertilise the next flower as they continue on their futile quest.

Some assassin bugs secrete a substance that attracts ants, and which intoxicates and disables them as the bug eats them. The relatively slow assassin bug can thus capture and eat its otherwise much faster ant prey at leisure.

Bedbugs find us by smell

Blood-sucking parasites that feed on humans, including fleas, lice, mosquitoes and bedbugs, use mainly their sense of smell to locate us. In addition to detecting our body heat, they can all also pick up the carbon dioxide concentrations we generate around our bodies. (To the human nose, carbon dioxide is odourless.)

Bedbugs that specialise in humans can tell us from other creatures by smell. In Vietnam, the Americans conducted an experiment using bedbugs in electronically rigged cages as early warning systems for enemy movements. The cages, fitted with tiny radio transmitters, were hidden in the jungle, and as soon as the bugs detected human smell, they would excitedly run around, thereby triggering the radio transmitter.

SEALING IN THE SMELL

The antlion larva doesn't use a sense of smell to find its food, although it has to conceal its own odour from potential prey. To trap ants and other small insects, the antlion larva burrows backwards into loose sand, which it then flips out with its flat head to make a funnel trap. The larva waits at the bottom of the funnel for prey to tumble in. This may happen at intervals of weeks or even months. As soon as prey falls in and tries to scramble out of the funnel, the antlion bombards it with sand grains shot from the top of its flat head. When the prey is thoroughly tripped up, the antlion lunges out to grab it with its large pincers, injects the prey with enzymes and sucks out the contents of its digested body, using the same hollow pincers in reverse.

However, ants have a very keen sense of smell, so the antlion cannot afford to give off any trace of odour, as it will chase away its prey. Thus, both its mouth and anus are completely sealed by skin. Eating is managed only through the hollow pincers, while waste products accumulate in the sealed rectum, until the antlion sheds its skin. The accumulated excreta are then left behind with the skin, and the antlion must dig a new, clean funnel. Eventually the antlion pupates underground, and the winged, night-flying adult emerges.

Antlion larva with flat head and sealed mouth and anus

Winged, night-flying antlion (adult)

Pincers of the antlion

ODOUR AS SELF-DEFENCE

Like plants, many insects defend themselves from predators with odious, poisonous or unpalatable chemicals, whether sequestered from their host plant or self-made. Inedible insects also use smell to advertise their unpalatability.

Citronella oil: the citrus swallowtail's insect repellent

Because most insects are herbivorous, plants have tried throughout evolution to develop defensive chemicals against these foragers. The tens of thousands of chemicals that have evolved in this way constitute nature's rich pharmacy, from which we have borrowed most of our medicines, insecticides and insect repellents.

Plants benefit from discouraging female insects from laying any eggs on them at all, so they use smell to advertise their defensive chemistry at a distance. The characteristic smells of citrus, blue gum, pine and herbs are well-known examples. These aromas usually arise from volatile oils, which evaporate when exposed to the air, like the citronella oil of citrus. For a time (on the geological timescale), these chemicals may confer immunity to attack, but eventually some insects become resistant to the repellent. Such insects benefit in two ways: the smell of the host plant makes it easily traceable and competition for food is minimised as the host plant repels other competitors.

The benefit to the resistant insect can go one step further. For example, the large, beautiful indigenous citrus swallowtail (*Papilio demodocus*) originally developed on indigenous plants that just happened to also use citronella oil as their defence mechanism. Although both male and female butterflies visit flowers for sustenance in summer, once fertilised the female loses complete interest in all but one smell: citronella. So, when citrus was introduced to Africa, the butterflies readily switched to this new host, laying their eggs on its leaves. Unexpectedly, citrus farmers were confronted by a new pest.

The larva of the citrus swallowtail does not digest the citronella oil; instead, it converts it to a concentrated defensive secretion of its own. Glands are situated on protrusible tubes (osmeteria), which are located behind its head. When the larva is attacked, the tubes release a powerful smell while simultaneously flashing a red warning colour. The host plant contributes to this defence free of charge!

Fascinating fact

Recently it has been found that some plants pick up the smell of caterpillars feeding on them, and then mass-produce the caterpillars' chemical smell. This overpowering 'caterpillar' smell attracts parasite wasps from far and wide, and they soon rid the plant of its pests!

Parasite wasps are attracted by plants on which caterpillars feed.

Reflex bleeding as a defence

Stink locusts all have poisons in their haemolymph to repel predators. To impress a would-be predator with this fact, the stink locust has to get the foul-tasting and foul-smelling blood to the surface of its body before it is eaten. This process is called reflex bleeding and involves bursting a thin skin membrane in a joint and using blood pressure to expel a quantity of blood. We also find this defence mechanism in armoured crickets, blister beetles, ladybeetles and even tiger moths.

Bubbling air through the blood to create froth increases the surface area and smell of the exposed blood. This improvement on reflex bleeding is found in the red stink locust (*Dictyophorus spumans*) and some tiger moths.

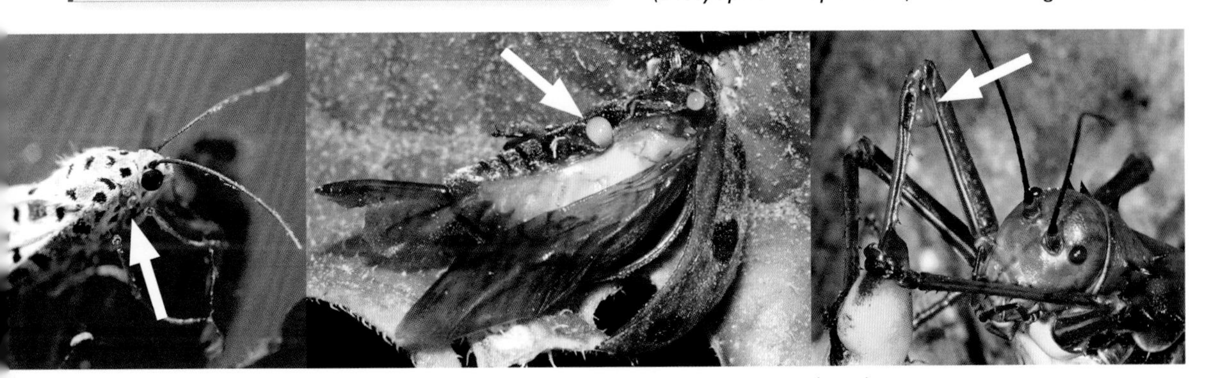

Reflex bleeding in a tiger moth (left), ladybeetle (centre) and armoured cricket (right)

Blood froth produced by a stink locust (top) and a tiger moth (above)

The green stink locust can squirt its repulsive smelling blood over a distance of half a metre.

A SOPHISTICATED DEFENCE MECHANISM

One of the most specialised defence mechanisms involving smell can be found in insects that have developed specific glands for this purpose. These glands produce odious secretions that deter potential attackers. Insects that use this technique include virtually all bugs, all carabid beetles, some darkling beetles (for example *Gonopus* spp.), the stink-ant and the Matabele ant.

Darkling beetle (*Gonopus* sp.)

Other insects, such as some stick insects and green stink locusts, have evolved an even more effective defence mechanism – they can squirt their reflex bleeding at enemies over a fair distance.

SEXUAL ATTRACTION

In insects, the sexes mostly find each other by smell. The advantage of this is that an endless number of organic chemicals (and their combinations) can be created so that each species can have its own specific smell that will attract a mate from the same species at a distance. As males are usually smaller and more mobile (and, indeed, more expendable) than females, they usually do the travelling, lured by the smell, or pheromone (a chemical substance produced and secreted externally to elicit a reaction from members of the same species) produced by the female. In green lacewings, however, the males produce the pheromone. Most insects with odious defensive secretions also use these for the purpose of sexual attraction.

'Radio signals' of termites

When Eugène Marais wrote his book *The soul of the white ant* in the early 1920s, he observed how the female reproductive shed her wings and raised her abdomen, which quickly attracted a male. The male also shed his wings and followed her closely in her search for a suitable nest. Together, they then started tunnelling to establish a new termite colony.

Marais quite rightly deduced that the female was able to send a signal to the male in the darkness of night without any visual aids. He thought the most feasible explanation for this was that she transmitted 'radio signals'. (At the time radio was still a new and fascinating invention.) Later he speculated that the female transmits a type of smell signal. Decades later, pheromones and their surprising range were discovered. Unwittingly, Marais had made one of the first behavioural observations of the role of pheromones in an insect.

Chafers with wingless females

On many of southern Africa's mountain ranges, we find species of a peculiar group of fruit chafers with wingless, clumsy and rounded females. Males are fully winged and active flyers, often adorned with horns on the head, and always with exceptionally large antennal clubs.

This genus (*Ichnestoma*) contains distinct isolated species that survive on mountain peaks, as the females cannot fly. After the first spring rains, males and females emerge from the soil. Females walk to the nearest suitable grass tussock

A male fruit chafer, with large antennal clubs, alights near a wingless female fruit chafer.

DEPENDENT ON PHEROMONES

Besides fruit chafers and termites, other insect groups in which wingless females depend completely on their pheromones to attract males are army ants (*Dorylus* spp.), bagworms, velvet ant wasps, some cockroaches, mantids and web-spinners.

Most night-flying moths are also totally dependent on pheromones to find their mates. Male emperor moths have an uncanny sense of smell for this purpose. Many female moths, such as some Noctuidae, have special 'hairbrushes' to spread the smell from their pheromone glands for better effect.

Army ant swarm, including large winged males

Bagworm cocoon in which wingless females live

and dig into the soil. Males fly about, smelling for females that have secreted pheromones. They land close to these females and mate with them, after which the females lay their eggs at the roots of grass growing in the leached sand on the mountain top. Larvae seem to feed on these grass roots and pupate in the sand, from where the new generation of males and females will emerge.

Among fruit chafers with fully winged females, the males also often smell to find the females, evidenced by the fact that males often have much larger antennal clubs than females do.

'Restaurant' rendezvous

Many insects follow the smell of their food (or their larvae's food) to achieve a rendezvous with the opposite sex. Near a carcass, blowfly males aggregate even before the first females arrive. These males have no interest in the carcass but know that females will come to oviposit. Similarly, females of dung beetles are attracted to the dung balls the males are trundling along. The females favour those males with the most impressive 'wheels', and latch on to them.

Male fruit chafers fight off other males at a sap flow.

Gathering near a food source, such as a smelly carcass, male blowflies lie in wait for females.

Trees with wounds created by borers, for instance, may contract bacterial infections, causing the wound to 'fester' and ferment. The sap flowing from such wounds is much sought after by fruit chafers, and males try to monopolise the sap flows by fighting off other males. These efforts are not so much to feed themselves, as there is usually ample sap to go around, but to monopolise the females that will predictably be attracted to the aromatic food source (see Chapter 2).

Any food concentration with an identifiable smell can serve as a venue for a mating rendezvous, but will also attract parasites and predators. A flowering tree or shrub, for example, may serve as the rendezvous for a multitude of beetles, bees, wasps and butterflies. On a compost heap, we find not only aggregations of chafers and fruit chafers, but also patrolling male scoliid wasps that are waiting to intercept female wasps of their species. These, in turn, come to lay eggs on larvae of chafers in the compost.

Aggregating pheromones

Some insects prefer to aggregate with large numbers of their own species, and so they produce a smell to attract each other. Cockroaches often produce such an aggregating pheromone, which may be useful for both attracting a mate and facilitating the exchange of gut flora, which they do by eating each other's droppings.

Ambrosia beetles secrete an aggregating pheromone in the interest of maintaining genetic diversity of their gene pool, and also to support their fungal culture. Ambrosia beetles often aggregate in large colonies under tree bark, where they make their characteristic black tunnels. The timber is infected with special fungi, of which the beetles carry spores in special pouches. Both adults and larvae then feed on fungi, rather than on wood, much as fungus-growing termites do.

THE USE OF SMELL IN SOCIAL INSECTS

Each individual colony of termites, bees, wasps and ants has its own characteristic smell by which members of the colony recognise each other and identify foreigners. In all social insects, sex pheromones also facilitate mating. These uses of smell, however, are only the start of something much more complex. In social colonies or 'superorganisms', smell acts as a kind of 'language' of communication between individuals.

Guard bees distinguish between nest companions and potential thieves by means of smell.

Bees communicate by smell

Bees have good eyesight and a keen sense of smell. When they return from the discovery of a worthwhile harvest, they dance to convey route instructions to their comrades (see Chapter 6). While dancing, they also communicate the specific smell for which the foragers should search.

Guard bees are always found at the entrance to colonies, checking every new arrival for the colony's smell or 'password'. Foreigners are repelled or attacked. This precaution is necessary, as there are colonies that specialise in stealing honey from other bee colonies.

When bees arrive home from a harvesting foray they are only cursorily inspected by the guards, given that they are obviously heavily laden and fly slowly and laboriously. 'Professional' thieving bees mimic this way of flying, even though they are not laden with supplies, and thus manage to get past the guards. A while later, when the thieves emerge fully laden, they get away easily because the guards ignore bees that exit the hive.

> The pheromone that drives bees to aggressive frenzy is found in nail varnish remover.

Worker bees also have a special scent gland (Nasanof gland) in front of their last abdominal segment, which they can evert to produce an aggregating pheromone that keeps migrating bees together. When a nest is disturbed or a new nesting site is occupied, bees fan air over their everted Nasanof glands to rally lost and confused bees to the nest entrance.

The specific nest odour of bees is also used outside the hive to 'peg off claims'. Like many mammals, bees mark a territory with their scent markers. In their case, the territory pertains to a harvest: the bees will monopolise a stand of flowers for their colony using their smell, and attack transgressors from other colonies. When food is scarce or the rewards are great, such as a honey spill, these fights may escalate into proper warfare between hives. These battles may end with the complete destruction and plundering of one colony, and aggression among the bees becomes so rampant that they will attack and sting everything in the vicinity that moves.

VENOMOUS BEES

The smell of bee venom is so strong that even the primitive nose of a human can detect it. To bees, this smell serves as an aggression pheromone. A beehive can be driven to aggressive frenzy by simply releasing this pheromone in a nest. This reaction to smell also explains why other bees always sting at the same spot at which the first bee stung.

Smell in ant colonies

Because many ants are active at night, and worker ants do not fly, smell plays a vitally important role in ants' reproduction and the protection of their nests. Winged reproductives that fly out on nuptial flights find each other through the female's sex pheromone. Each nest also develops an individual

Ants use their antennae to smell their way along a pheromone scent trail between their nest and their food source.

nest odour, and some species have a special guard caste. Members of this caste block the entrance to the nest with their heads and only allow workers in after having smelled them with their antennae. Territorial wars, similar to those among bees, break out among ants and can be just as destructive. Ants, however, use their odour for far more than this.

The neat roads or highways along which ants move between their nest and the food they harvest are paved with odour. A scout that finds a worthwhile source of food will lay an odour trail on the return journey to the nest. It finds its way back to the nest using a combination of light compass navigation and memory of landmarks, much as wasps and bees do (see Chapter 6). The scout lays the odour trail by using a special gland on the tip of the abdomen that produces a 'route pheromone', and at regular intervals it will touch the substrate with its abdomen. When the scout returns to the nest, workers are immediately alerted to the new food discovery by the smell of the route pheromone. They smell the food on the scout, and then set out along the odour trail.

All workers who manage to collect more booty will lay a route trail on top of the old one on their way back, strengthening the trail and recruiting more workers. When the source is depleted, workers will stop marking the trail on their return journey and the route will evaporate. Thus, the route pheromone not only marks the route, but also elegantly recruits and regulates the optimal number of workers for every harvest.

Unfortunately, route pheromones also have their disadvantages. Unlike the dance language of bees, they can be obliterated by wind and rain, and large animals can trample them. When a route is disrupted or destroyed, ants will start searching for it until they find it again, and then restore the odour trail where it was damaged.

A worse disadvantage of odour trails is that nest parasites and other enemies of ants soon latch on to them and find the ant nest. Since every ant species has a characteristic odour trail, the hundreds of species of beetle, fly, butterfly, fish moth and other arthropods that parasitise ant nests all use route pheromone trails to lead them to the nest of the particular host species they need.

THE SMELL OF DEATH

A curious application of odour in ant colonies is the 'death smell'. All large assemblages of individuals are prone to the epidemic spread of diseases, and must therefore maintain strict hygiene. Dying ants produce a 'death smell' long before they putrefy, and this smell stimulates their comrades to swiftly dispatch the carcass. This smell is so convincing that workers will promptly dismember any ant that has been treated with this death smell, in spite of its very lively behaviour and active protestations!

Adaptations to heat and cold

Female mosquito

Insects are generally called cold-blooded, but this term is misleading. The term 'ectothermic' is more correct, as it implies that the body temperature of insects is controlled by the temperature of the environment in which they find themselves, and that their body temperature could be colder or warmer than the approximately 37°C found in endothermic animals (mammals and birds). However, these terms do not tell the whole story. Insects and other ectothermic animals can and do regulate their body temperature to a surprising extent, but their techniques differ from those of endothermic animals.

CONTROL OF BODY TEMPERATURE

We regulate our body temperature through increased metabolic activity, which raises temperature, or through evaporation during perspiration and breathing, which decreases temperature. Insects do not have these mechanisms at their disposal, but they are able to use a surprising number of strategies to keep their body temperature close to 40°C.

Namib toktokkies regulate heat

On the dunes and sand flats of the Namib Desert, there is no shelter that provides protection against the noon sun. The air temperature in the shade seldom rises above (a safe) 40°C, but shade is a scarce commodity. In direct sunshine, the surface temperature of the sand can easily reach 75°C. The air just above the surface is almost as hot, but 20mm above the sand the temperature may only be as high as 45°C.

Developing long legs is one adaptation some day-living toktokkies have made to survive these conditions. In the mornings and evenings, when the air temperature is low and the toktokkies want to draw heat from the warm sand, they bend their legs. During midday and the afternoon, the toktokkies keep their legs stretched out, so that their bodies move up to 20mm above the deadly hot sand surface.

Some toktokkies have developed extremely long legs to escape the lethal surface temperatures of desert sand.

Another adaptation, particularly in toktokkies of the Namib Desert, is their white shell, which serves to reflect heat rays. During midday and in the afternoon, the toktokkies move about, keeping their head low and their white backside to the sun. Conversely, when they want to warm up in the morning and the evening, they turn their black head and thorax towards the sun.

Even the black toktokkies running around during the day in the Namib have a sophisticated

Some Namib toktokkies have developed white shells to reflect the heat.

The shell of some black toktokkies in the Namib Desert has a microtexture that helps with selective absorption and reflection of different light wavelengths.

temperature control: the microtexture of their shell absorbs red light and deflects other wavelengths. Therefore, the toktokkies absorb more radiation in the morning and the evening (when the light is relatively more reddish) and less around midday.

Using muscles to warm up

When we are very cold, we start shivering, which means that our muscles contract involuntarily. This activity generates heat in the human body.

Insects do the same with their strong flight muscles. One may often see moths and mantids resting on walls in the vicinity of electric lights at night, vibrating their wings without actually flying. Even day-flying insects commonly vibrate their wings, causing the temperature of their body and their flight muscles to increase to the 35°C or more that is required for flight.

To incubate their eggs, female European bumblebees generate heat in the same way – by shivering their flight muscles. Similarly, honeybees in a hive can increase their body temperature through contractions of their flight muscles, with the added advantage of increasing the temperature of the whole hive.

Fascinating fact

Males monopolising females in the barren Namib confer a rather useful fringe benefit on the females – they serve as temporary umbrellas against the sun, allowing the females to forage for longer periods.

A male Namib toktokkie (*Onymacris* sp.) monopolising a female

Cooling off

Besides removing themselves from the heat, most insects cannot do much to cool off. Owing to their small volume, sweating would cause them to lose all their body moisture within seconds. There are, however, two exceptions. Blood-sucking insects and plant sap-sucking insects absorb an overabundance of water in their food and then have to get rid of the excess liquid. Such insects can, therefore, cool themselves with the water they excrete – something that becomes necessary when they are exposed to direct sunlight while they are sucking and are unable to move to a cool spot.

A blood-sucking fly covers itself with its own watery excretion to cool itself off.

Sitting on the stoep

A well-designed veranda will allow you to sit in a sunny or a shady spot by simply moving your chair – and you can spend a comfortable day there. Almost all insects use this very technique to regulate their heat. Caterpillars and other leaf feeders simply position themselves on one or the other side of a leaf. Similarly, insects foraging on the ground under plants can move to sunny or shady spots as required.

Caterpillars can regulate their body heat by sitting in the sun or escaping into the shade.

An unusual variation of this form of temperature regulation occurs in ectothermic animals. When scorpions and reptiles contract a bacterial disease, they are known to intentionally expose themselves to too much heat, thereby developing a 'fever' to combat the germs causing the disease. Similar to endothermic animals, these animals will try to regulate their fever to keep it just below a temperature lethal to themselves. Such 'behaviour fever' probably also occurs in other ectothermic animals, including insects.

RESISTANCE TO HEAT AND COLD

Few animals can survive a body temperature in excess of 45°C for any length of time, and the absolute upper limit lies at around 60°C. Insects resistant to extreme cold are found only in the polar regions, where they survive extreme cold because of the anti-freezing effect of substances dissolved in their body fluids. In only a limited part of our region does the mercury drop to a few degrees below freezing for any length of time.

The hottest insects

Body temperature measurements of insects found in the Namib Desert have shown that their behaviour keeps them just below their lethal upper temperature limit. This seems to be a general tendency, and can be explained by the fact that at high temperatures, insects are at their fastest and most active, and thus have the best opportunities for getting food and mates and the best chances of evading enemies.

Jewel beetles can tolerate high body temperatures.

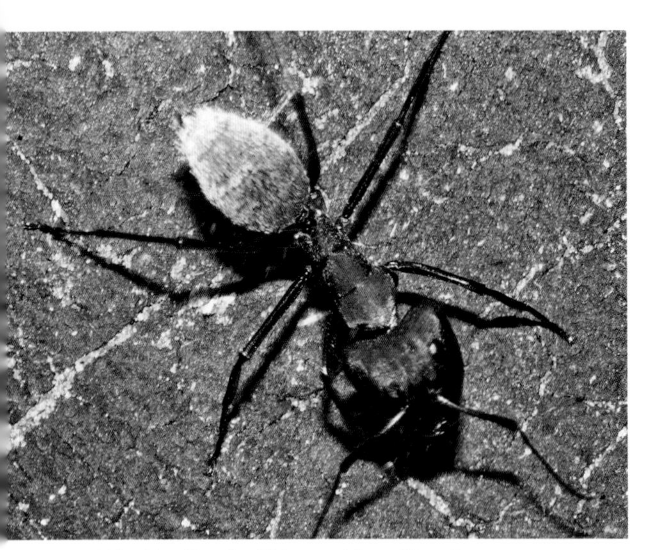

Like Namib toktokkies and jewel beetles, ants are extremely active in very hot environments, such as the Namib Desert.

It follows, therefore, that those insects that are exposed to the highest temperatures are also some of the fastest, including some of the Namib toktokkies, ants and jewel beetles. All these insects prefer a body temperature slightly above 40°C.

The coolest insects

Insects generally become cold tolerant by losing body water and, in doing so, 'drying themselves out'. The less water the insect has, the higher the concentration of solubles in its body fluids, and therefore the lower the temperature at which the water in its body will freeze. Freezing is deadly to cells, because ice crystals destroy cell membranes and cell structures. In their 'dehydrated' phases, insects are passive and have to enter a stage of rest or diapause (see Chapter 3).

There are, however, insects that remain active at temperatures below freezing. Such insects have special substances in their haemolymph, much like the antifreeze used in the radiator of a motorcar. In southern Africa, such an adaptation makes sense only among the high-altitude inhabitants of the Cape and Maluti mountains, but it is the rule among insects, such as weevils, found on the sub-Antarctic Marion Island.

MANIPULATING ENVIRONMENTAL TEMPERATURE

All social insects have the ability to keep the temperature of their nests remarkably constant.

Air-conditioning a honeybee hive

One of the functions of the nest workers in a honeybee hive is the ventilation of the hive and the regulation of its temperature to keep it constant – at approximately 35°C. The mechanism used to convert nectar to honey influences the cooling process in the hive. To condense nectar to form honey, the bees hold the nectar on their tongues and fan it with their wings, so that excess water in the nectar evaporates. This process of evaporation cools the air inside the hive.

Close to the entrance to the hive, some bees fan stale air to the outside and fresh air inwards. If the outside air is too warm, the bees evaporate more water from their tongues. If it is too cold, they generate heat by shivering their flight muscles.

For the process of cooling by evaporation, the bees have to carry water to the hive. Most bees seen at watering points are fetching water for this purpose. In the Kalahari and Namib deserts, bees are even reported to store an emergency supply of water in honeycombs.

Climate control in a termite nest

Termites and ants living in subterranean nests mostly control airflow and nest climate by means of a range of tunnel openings, some in warm, exposed areas, others in cool, shaded spots. They selectively open or close their tunnels to achieve the desired airflow and temperatures.

The air circulation in the nest of fungus-growing termites is driven by the fungus garden, where the rapid growth of fungi generates temperatures often in excess of 40°C, similar to the heat in a compost heap. This warm air rises in the large central chimney. At night, the air cools off and sinks down into the network of tunnels close to the surface.

By day, cool air descends only in the shaded part of the nest. While the air is descending close to the surface, carbon dioxide and oxygen are exchanged through the thin, porous layer of clay. The result is

Fascinating fact

Of all ectothermic animals, fungus-growing termites have the most advanced climate control system. They build enormous clay towers above the ground, which are exclusively for the purpose of air-conditioning, and are largely uninhabited.

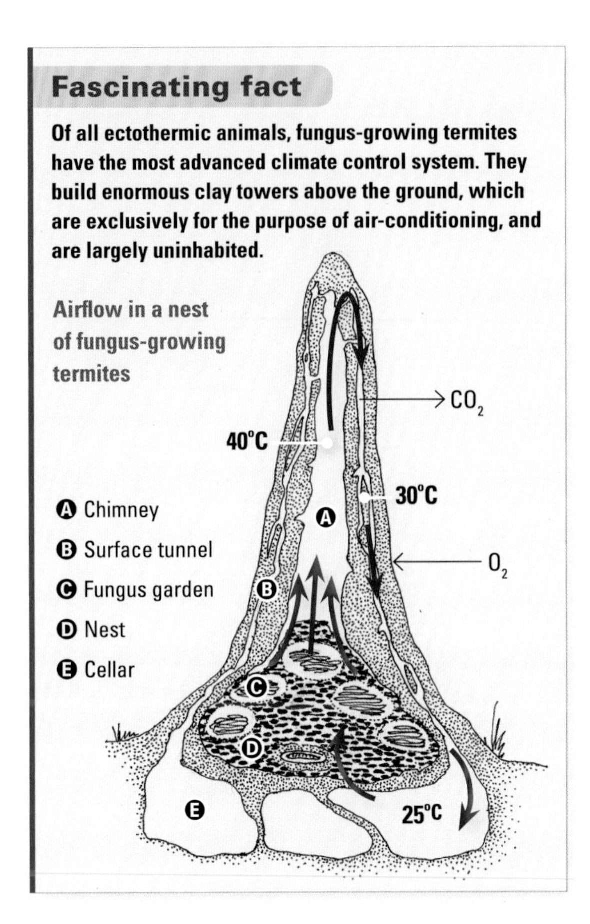

cool, oxygen-rich air in the bottom chambers of the nest, where it is also moistened to almost 100 per cent relative humidity. The fungus gardens and the large chimney create an upwards draught, and the cool, moist and oxygen-rich air is sucked into the inhabited chambers just beneath the fungus garden. The only thing left for the termites to do to regulate a constant temperature is to selectively open or close the small circulation tunnels.

USING HEAT SENSORS TO FIND FOOD

Insects can sense heat and cold, and can adapt themselves accordingly. Some even have special heat sensors to tell the difference between warm and cold objects at a distance.

Jewel beetles can 'see' sick plants

It is possible to take aerial photographs of plantations or cultivated fields with infrared film or sensors, which make plants with microbial diseases clearly visible. This is because these plants are warmer than healthy plants, exactly like an animal with a fever.

Similarly, jewel beetles can sense the heat differences in plants at a distance, and can therefore distinguish ailing trees or branches from healthy ones long before any obvious signs of disease are visible. Many jewel beetles lay their eggs exclusively on plants that are still alive (and contain sap), but which are about to die and so are unable to defend themselves with sap flow or resin against invading insects. Infestation by jewel beetles is a foolproof indication that the tree or branch is sick and has been in the process of dying.

Parasites respond to heat

Fleas, bedbugs and mosquitoes, all specialist bloodsuckers of warm-blooded animals, are attracted to a heat source. These parasites can detect infrared radiation (heat) at a distance to find their prey, besides also making use of scent, carbon dioxide concentrations and vibrations caused by movement.

Although no commercial parasite traps utilise heat or infrared radiation, it is, in principle, a possibility. Inmates in prisons used to catch bedbugs by standing a torch on matchsticks and shining its light onto the floor. Bedbugs are attracted to the warm crevice between the torchlight and the floor, regardless of the fact that they normally hide from light.

Jewel beetles lay their eggs on ailing plants, which they identify with heat (infrared) detectors.

10

Superorganisms

Driver ants

In some insect species, individuals have formed such close-knit units that they can no longer live as single organisms. In his classic work, *The soul of the white ant*, Eugène Marais saw this phenomenon as a kind of 'soul shift' from the individual to the group. Such social communities are now referred to as superorganisms.

SOCIAL COMMUNITIES

Swarms or flocks of insects should not be confused with superorganisms. Mating (see Chapter 2), migration (see Chapter 4) and defensive or hunting behaviours (see Chapter 3) all constitute reasons for insects to aggregate, but without their having to forego their own individuality and reproduction.

Superorganisms consist of individuals that specialise in different service roles, which require them to sacrifice their own reproduction and even their lives. They do not mature to adults, although they receive extended brood care (see Chapter 2). However, some species that engage in extended brood care, such as the *Parastizopus* beetles found in the Kalahari, may display all the characteristics of a superorganism, except that individuals eventually leave the nest and breed on their own.

True social organisations or superorganisms have developed in only four insect groups: termites, paper wasps, bees and ants. In these groups, we find sterile castes that never reproduce or leave the colony.

These superorganisms may originate in two ways: one way is demonstrated by termites and the other by the hymenopterans – wasps, bees and ants.

TERMITES

Termite colonies consist of roughly equal numbers of males and females. However, the only individuals that can reproduce are the founding pair ('queen' and 'king'). All workers and soldiers are sexually underdeveloped males or females and are permanently infertile. The founding pair has to feed and raise their first generation of offspring themselves, using mainly their own fat reserves. In the process, they also suppress the sexual development in these first workers with hormones that they secrete, which then get passed on from one individual to another. Workers raise further progeny similarly, except for a select group that are fed differently to mature into winged and fertile adults with eyes, wings and reproductive organs. These are the 'fliers' that will leave the colony on their nuptial flights to mate and start new colonies. In termites, sterile castes are thus formed according to a selective 'favouritism' – the inverse of the selective slavery imposed by parents on most of their offspring in favour of the small group that is raised to reproduce.

Colony life cycle

Termite colonies start when winged males and females fly away to found their own colony. After a flight of anything from a few to hundreds of metres,

Winged termites are the only fertile and reproductive individuals produced by the colony.

Termite queen attended to by workers

Termite soldiers with large mandibles

the female will land, break off her wings along a special suture and spread pheromones to attract a male (see Chapter 8). The male who finds her will also shed his wings and follow her to where she starts tunnelling. Together they will dig the first nest chamber and mate for the first time. Mating does not occur unless both of them have flown from their nest, and shed their wings. This prevents reproductives from mating inside their own nests.

The female grows enormously fat and lays up to 10,000 eggs per day – the equivalent of her own weight. The male mates with her several times a day to fertilise all the eggs. Workers are kept continuously busy, feeding the pair, grooming and cooling the queen and moving eggs to nursery chambers. Together the male and female will raise the first generation of workers, after which they stop working for the rest of their lives (up to 30 years).

The population of workers increases steadily and the nest is extended. Later, some nymphs are

Termite soldier with a nasus for spraying a toxic 'glue'

stimulated by food and hormones to develop into soldiers. In some species, soldiers have large mandibles and in others, they are armed with a nasus that can squirt a poisonous sticky fluid.

When a termite colony has died, its clay nest may be re-colonised by a new founding pair; in this way, the same nest may remain occupied for centuries.

When the workers in a colony have increased to the point where they have been able to gather a food surplus, a number of nymphs are fed on a diet that will turn them into winged adults. On a spring day, generally late in the afternoon after rain, the winged termites will fly out from all the nests of a particular termite species in an area. These are the males and females that will start new colonies as 'kings' and 'queens'.

When a queen dies, she can be replaced by a number of smaller 'reserve queens' bred straight from nymphs in the nest. These never reach full size, and three or four are needed to replace the original queen. This process can be repeated once, but then, for unknown reasons, the colony 'ages' and dies out, giving it a maximum life span of 60–90 years.

Castes

Most termite colonies have three castes: workers, reproductives and (one or two types of) soldiers. Fungus growers (*Macrotermes* spp.) have 'major' and 'minor' soldiers that are distinctly different in size. All termite castes genetically consist of approximately equal numbers of males and females.

Fascinating fact

Large harvester termite workers (*Hodotermes* sp.) are pigmented and have eyes (unique among termites). They often work in daylight on overcast days, foraging and cutting grass stalks.

Large harvester termites forage in daylight.

Feeding

All termites are decomposers that live off dead plant material. Some have specialised micro-organisms in their gut, which can break down plant fibre, and they digest the wood into which they have burrowed. These micro-organisms are closely related to those located in the gut of cockroaches, which is one reason why termites are believed to descend directly from roaches.

Two unrelated termite groups, large harvesters and small harvesters, snip off dry grass stems and carry these to their nests. There they store the grass and eventually consume it. The small harvesters also use this grass to insulate their domed nests, some of which are used exclusively as storage sheds and are not inhabited.

Another group, the fungus growers, have evolved over millions of years to cultivate fungi. They collect crumbs of wood chiselled off dead tree trunks or roots. These crumbs are bonded with saliva to create multi-storied structures in the nest, which are then seeded with fungal spores and watered. The termites also treat the fungi chemically to limit growth to small 'buttons', which serve as food for the colony. When fungus gardens have been depleted, they are deposited outside the nest. Here 'fairy rings' of mushrooms may appear, serving as a source of fungal spores for the next seeding.

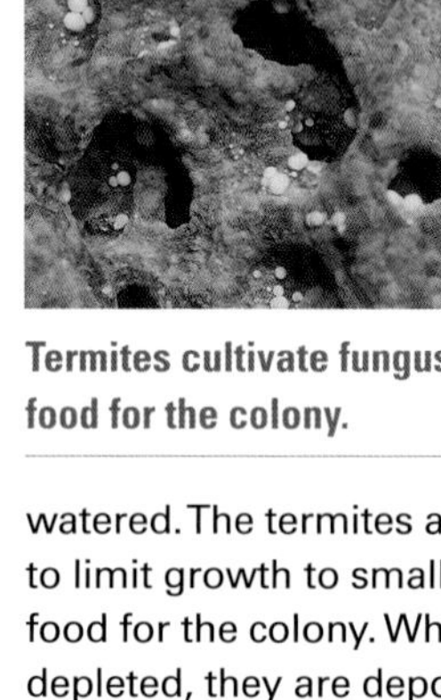

See Chapter 5 to find out more about the different kinds and shapes of nests built by termites.

Multi-storied fungus gardens in a termite nest

Termites cultivate fungus 'buttons' in the gardens as food for the colony.

Natural enemies

Ants are termites' most important enemies. Most ants will attack termites opportunistically – but only when the termites are feeding and working far away from their nests. Some ant species, however, such as the Matabele ants (*Megaponera analis*), are specialist termite predators and execute organised raids on the termites' working sites. In addition, several mammals feed on termites, with the aardvark, pangolin and aardwolf being the most specialised.

Inside their nests, termites have hundreds of parasitic arthropod species that feed either on the termites and their brood or on their food stocks. These are mostly beetles, fish moths and flies, but spiders, millipedes, centipedes and woodlice are also well represented.

When termite nuptial flights occur, a great variety of normally non-termite-eating species (including humans) will share in this highly nutritious bonanza. Many smaller insectivorous birds and mammals are dependent on the nutritional boost of termite flights to accumulate enough energy to breed. Without this protein boost, they can survive but not reproduce. However, even pelicans, kudu, impala and lions have been observed feeding on flying termites.

PAPER WASPS

Paper wasps are from the order Hymenoptera. In this particular order, more than 10 groups of independent superorganisms have evolved, while in all other insect orders only one has evolved: termites, from the Isoptera order.

THE 'FAIRY CIRCLES' OF THE NAMIB

The bare circular patches appearing in the short-lived grass cover that sprouts after rare rainfall events in the Namib Desert are an intriguing natural phenomenon. The patches are created by colonies of the sand termite (*Psammotermes* sp.), which build their nests from sand and excrement in a dune slope, a few metres outside and below the 'fairy circles', and about a metre underground. The cleared circles are exposed to wind erosion, and soon become depressions. Any follow-up rain collects in these depressions, which causes a chain of events.

Firstly the sand below the depression becomes deeply saturated, creating a water reservoir for the termite colony. Secondly, the moisture allows larger perennial grasses to grow around the depression.

After the short-lived seasonal grasses have been depleted by the termite foragers or blown away by the wind, the longer-lived grasses will serve as food for the colony for months to come. Water penetration in the circles is subsequently enhanced by scorpions, beetles, spiders and even vertebrates, which prefer the moist patches for their tunnelling activities.

The renowned 'fairy circles' in the Namib Desert are caused by sand termites.

The theory about the prevalence of superorganisms in Hymenoptera is based on their unique genetic system. Females in this order all have a normal double (or diploid) set of chromosomes. Males, however, have a single (or haploid) set. Any fertilised egg becomes diploid and female, while unfertilised eggs remain haploid and become male. The consequence of this peculiar system is that females will replicate their own genes more successfully by producing siblings (enhancing their mothers' breeding success) than by producing their own offspring (achieving their own breeding success). The female workers in hymenopteran social colonies do exactly this, and sociality is believed to be so common in this order because it makes evolutionary and genetic sense.

Colony life cycle

A colony of paper wasps starts in spring when a single fertilised female awakens from a winter diapause and starts constructing her nest. She scrapes fibres off plants and chews them, mixing them with saliva to form a pulp, which she then shapes into hexagonal paper cells. Nests vary between species, but always consist of open hexagonal paper cells that are reusable. In each cell, she deposits a fertilised egg. She feeds the hatched larvae with pre-masticated caterpillars, while she nourishes herself with nectar and water.

Eventually, the first larvae are fully grown and pupate in their cells after having spun flimsy cocoons. Female wasps hatch from the pupae; they are, however, unable to mate, since no males are around in summer when they emerge. The founder wasp becomes a dominant queen, intimidating her daughters and spending all her energy on laying eggs fertilised with her stored sperm. All her offspring grow into female workers that have to care for more offspring.

In autumn, the queen runs out of stored sperm and starts laying unfertilised eggs. These develop into males, and then the colony breaks up as males and females of various colonies find each other and mate. Large hive beetles (*Oplostomus* sp.) usually attack deserted nests and devour any remaining brood.

In winter, mated female paper wasps form hibernating swarms in protected cavities for the same reasons ladybeetles seek communal protection (see Chapter 3). In spring, they split up, each to start a new colony.

Castes

Paper wasps have only two castes: the reproductive caste (males and queen) and the non-reproductive caste (female workers). The last generation of these will become the next generation of queens.

As the venomous stings of all females are without barbs, they can be used repeatedly, and these females therefore double as efficient soldiers.

Males never form part of the social colony and appear for a short free-living life in autumn only.

The founder queen of a paper wasp colony

Female paper wasp workers

A large hive beetle raids the nest of a paper wasp.

Feeding

Paper wasp larvae need protein (usually masticated caterpillars) to grow, while adult wasps can make do with nectar and water. Interestingly, the larvae are able to secrete saliva on which adults are very keen; the larvae seem to bribe workers with this saliva to feed them in return.

Natural enemies

Apart from large hive beetles, ants are the chief attackers of paper wasp nests. Since paper wasps do not store food, and their nests are exposed to weather, they have no specialist nest parasites. Workers are mainly exposed to predation by birds, spiders, mantids and other predators while out foraging for food.

HONEYBEES

The social system of honeybees is similar to that of wasps, except that bee colonies are perennial and males are present throughout summer. The female workers furthermore differ in appearance from the queen, and are sterile. All transitions – from completely solitary to fully social – occur in the bee family, Apidae, making it the best family for studying the evolution of sociality.

Colony life cycle

A hive cannot start with a solitary queen, since she lacks mouthparts, a honey crop and pollen baskets, and cannot forage at all. The queen of a hive produces a hormone that the workers lick and circulate to all colony members, together with the communal nectar food that is continuously passed on from mouth to mouth. The sharing of the hormone in the hive plays a role in preventing replacement queens from being bred.

If a swarm becomes too big, or the queen too feeble to provide all workers with adequate queen pheromone, some workers that have not received this hormone will start building queen cells in which to raise queens. To achieve this, the normal larvae in

Fascinating fact

Rock art paintings provide early evidence of organised honey harvesting, and honeycombs are a recurring theme in many of these paintings found in southern Africa. Some, dated at 20,000 years old, even depict the use of smoke to pacify bees.

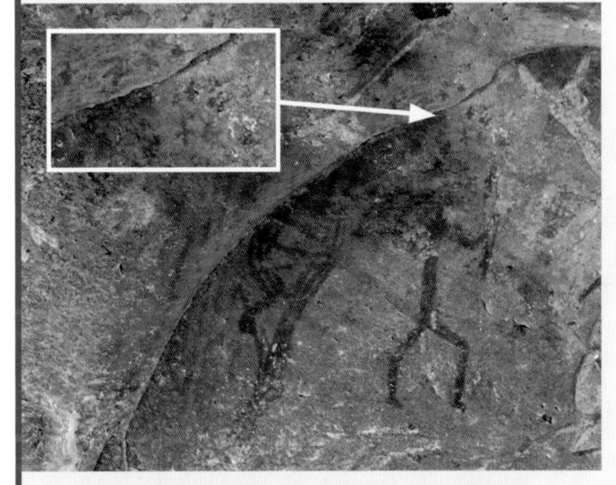

Rock art painting of a bee hunter from Eland Cave in the Drakensberg, with bees faintly visible at the top right.

Migrating honeybees camp in swarms in trees while scouts look for a nesting site.

these cells are fed only royal jelly. This causes them to grow into fully developed, fertile queens, without the anatomical peculiarities of a worker.

Queens are considerably larger than workers. When several are bred simultaneously, they eliminate each other in lethal duels until only one survives (see Chapter 7). The surviving queen will leave the nest on a nuptial flight and return to the nest with her sperm container (spermatheca) loaded with a supply of sperm that may last for years.

When a young replacement queen has been bred and the old queen is still alive, dominance will determine whether the old queen will continue to reign or the new one will inherit the hive and colony. The winner stays in the nest, retaining the honeycombs and the largest part of the colony, while the loser flies from the nest with a large retinue of worker bees to found a new colony. In this way new swarms split off from existing and established swarms when these become too large.

A migrating swarm first assembles outside but near the nest of the parent colony. Considerable lobbying can be observed as 'movers' try to pull bees out of the hive to join them while 'stayers' try the opposite. Eventually equilibrium is achieved, and the migratory swarm flies off to find a new nesting site.

Fascinating fact

In very old bee colonies the bees are smaller. This is because the breeding cells become progressively smaller, due to accumulating cocoon residues. As a result, the workers that develop in these cells become smaller and smaller.

Large old colonies also become very aggressive, giving rise to the false claim that a different species of small, aggressive bees occurs in South Africa.

The migrating swarm now parks itself somewhere in a tree while scouts go hunting for suitable cavities. On their return, the scouts will perform a dance to convey the directions to these prospective nesting sites; some bees will watch them and go out to investigate. Returning investigators will either repeat the dance or, if they are not impressed, try the locality indicated by another scout. In this way, a highly democratic majority opinion about where to start a new hive is reached, and the whole swarm moves into the chosen shelter and builds wax combs.

Worker bee larvae are switched from a diet of royal jelly to one of pollen and honey after their first three days. Adult workers live off honey alone. During spring, when hive activity is high, workers may work themselves to death within three weeks. During winter months, when there is little activity, they may live for six months. Queens live for four to six years, and may make additional nuptial flights in this time to replenish their sperm supply. As new queens can be bred indefinitely, a new, well-protected nest may become centuries old.

Castes

A hive of honeybees comprises one queen and up to 80,000 worker bees. In spring males or drones are bred. In summer, up to about 10 per cent of the hive may consist of drones that don't work at all and are fed by the workers. The drones spend their days at the leks (mating swarms) and their nights in the hive. When autumn arrives, they are unceremoniously evicted, and pathetic, starving drone swarms may be seen outside the entrances of hives.

The drone or male honeybee (left) is the product of an unfertilised egg.

Although all worker bees look the same, they do a variety of specialised jobs, depending on their age. (This system is called progressive polyethism.) These jobs are as follows.

- A worker bee spends the first days of her life cleaning the combs and feeding the larvae. The glands that produce royal jelly are now fully developed in the worker.
- On day 11, her duty shifts to storing pollen and honey brought in by fieldworkers, concentrating nectar to honey and building combs.
- On day 15, her wax glands are fully developed for building combs and her royal jelly glands start degenerating.
- On day 18, she may be promoted to guard duty at the nest entrance; her aggression also peaks.
- On about day 20, she will make her first forays into the outside world, starting with carrying water and eventually she will undertake the specialised gathering of nectar and pollen.

Feeding

Honeybees live exclusively off nectar (or honey, its concentrated form) and pollen. Both of these can be stored almost indefinitely. The only other nutrient in the hive is the royal jelly that workers produce from their glands.

One of the functions of worker bees is to store nectar in the comb and ripen it to honey.

Fascinating fact

Interestingly, if the nest requires it, worker bees can revert to earlier specialisations. For example, they can redevelop their royal jelly or wax glands if brood care or comb building is urgently required – even after the glands have already atrophied!

Worker bee gathering nectar

Natural enemies

Bees have a great variety of enemies, both outside and inside their hives. Workers are exposed to predation by spiders, birds, including several specialist bee-eaters, and many other predators such as robber flies, dragonflies and mantids. Some predators, for example bee pirate wasps (*Palarus* sp.), are specialist predators of honeybees.

Within their nest, bees are exploited by wax moths (*Galleria* sp.) that can digest the combs and ruin the whole hive. Fruit chafers, small hive beetles (*Aethina tumida*) and death's-head moths (*Acherontia atropos*) steal honey out of the combs.

Some mammals rob bee colonies as part of their regular diet. Humans (sometimes with the collusion of honeyguide birds) are certainly the worst of these honey thieves, with honey badgers a close second.

Bees also have to contend with body parasites such as bee lice, *Varroa* mites, which cause a disease called varoosis, and internally parasitic Strepsiptera and Conopidae flies.

Honeybees comprise a large part of the diet of several species of bee-eater.

Ant workers tend to the queen's brood – here they carry pupae containing their siblings.

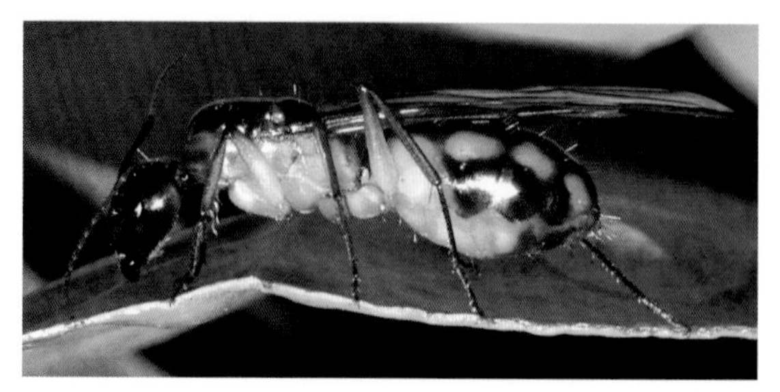

Winged queen ant

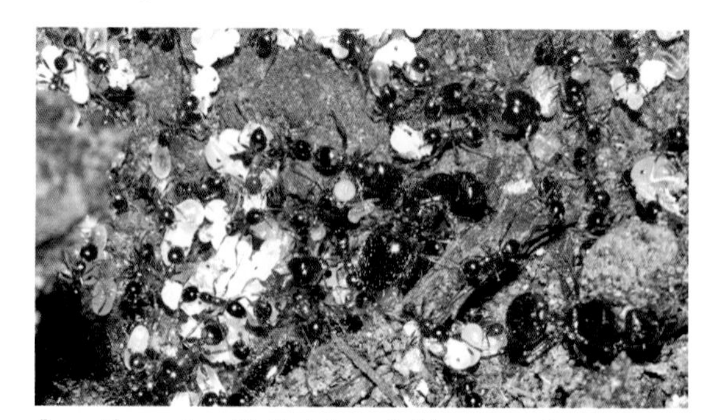

Argentine ants with their brood of larvae and pupae

ANTS

While many bees and wasps are solitary, all ants are social, like termites, and no solitary species are known. However, in ants, sociality and specialisation have developed to such extremes that it is difficult to discuss their biology as a group.

Colony life cycle

In many species, normally winged males and females swarm out to found their own colonies – similar to termites. After mating, the female chews off her own wings before starting the colony on her own. The male dies soon after breeding.

However, there are variations. In some species the female does not start a new colony, but acts dead and allows herself to be hauled into an ant colony of a different species. She may then hijack a section of the nest with her minute offspring, who simply narrow the tunnels – a strategy employed by thief ants (*Carebara* sp.). In other cases, the queen may kill the legitimate queen of the nest, and then gradually hijack the whole nest with the help of her own offspring.

There are also ants that, like honeybees, may leave the nest, taking a queen with them to form a new colony. As they move off, workers can be seen carrying 'undecided' workers in two different directions: back to the nest or towards the group leaving the nest. In some cases, these new colonies do not sever their ties with the parent colonies, and huge, interconnected supercolonies with many 'queen nodes' result. These supercolonies can span tens of kilometres. One such example is the imported Argentine ant (*Linepithema humile*).

The spermatheca of an ant queen must preserve millions of spermatozoa for years, as the queen has lost her wings and cannot repeat her mating flight. Queens are known to reach 30 years of age and workers may attain 10 years. Queens can be replaced, as in the case of bees, and some species keep several queens simultaneously as a matter of course.

Castes

An enormous variety of castes can be found in ant nests, with some species including 18 different forms. Apart from the queen, the colony nearly always contains both soldier and worker castes. In addition, various specialist castes are found. 'Entrance plugs' are soldiers with conical heads that can block the entrance to the nest (see Chapter 8). 'Millers' are soldiers with huge heads and flat mandibles that are used for breaking and grinding seeds. Some specialised worker ants, known as 'honey pots', store liquids in their bodies, eventually becoming immobile. Portable miniature workers are produced by some ants to serve as bodyguards; they ride on the backs of foraging worker ants, protecting them from parasites.

All of these castes comprise sterile females. Males are only bred for the seasonal nuptial flights, and do not participate in any of the nest activities.

Feeding

Most ants prey on other insects and their eggs. They are partial to sugar and they will harvest nectar from accessible flowers. Since they do not have any means of storing nectar, 'honey pot' ants are used to store this commodity.

Ants, such as cocktail ants (top) and pugnacious ants (above), can overpower and transport prey many times their own size through co-operative behaviour.

An ant feeds on 'honeydew' excretions of aphids.

Ants are particularly keen on the sweet honeydew excretions of sap-sucking insects such as aphids, leafhoppers and scale insects. They will often carry these insects into their nests for protection during their winter hibernation.

Harvester ants specialise in the collection of seeds and store these in granary cavities in their nests. These ants play an important role in seed propagation, since they do not necessarily consume all the seeds they harvest (see Chapter 11).

Natural enemies

Ants' worst enemies are probably other ants. Apart from the 'thieving' and 'hijacking' ants referred to, there are ants that depend entirely on the workers of other ant species to maintain their nests and rear their brood. These slave-driver colonies consist of a queen and soldiers only. They waylay other worker ants, carry them to their nest and force them into 'slave labour'.

Ants are also territorial insects, and when food supplies decrease in autumn, territorial wars often break out between colonies of the same species. Soldiers will then try to dismember or eventually decapitate each other, while workers carry off the corpses as legitimate spoils of war. The nest of the losing colony is subsequently plundered and completely devastated.

DRUG ABUSE

Adult ant beetles have large swollen antennae with glands that secrete a drug-like substance that visibly intoxicates ants, and to which they seem to become addicted. Ants will, in fact, drag these ant beetles into their nests and feed them their own brood in order to obtain their fix!

Large feelers of an ant beetle

ANT NESTS

Ants employ a great variety of designs and materials to build their nests.

- Most ants tunnel in soil.
- Some construct cardboard nests in trees.
- Other species live in cavities in wood or thorns.
- Weaver ants (*Oecophylla* sp.) spin leaves together using silk to form their arboreal nests.
- Army ants form their 'nests' entirely out of living workers. These nomadic predaceous ants have to stop over in their massive raids to allow the queen an egg-laying cycle of approximately two weeks. During these stopovers, the ants form a nest, complete with tunnels and chambers, from interlinked and immobile ant workers.

Army ants 'nesting'

An array of arthropod predators feed on ants, including spiders that camouflage themselves by mimicking ants. Among the larger animals, ants have relatively few enemies. This can be attributed to their possession of unpalatable formic acid and their ability to give nasty bites or even stings. Ants do, however, have hundreds of parasites in their nests, including fish moths, caterpillars of various blues, many species of ant chafers, and ant beetles. Most parasite larvae manage to pass themselves off as ant larvae, so that the worker ants then feed and groom them.

However, many of the hundreds of mites, millipedes, centipedes and other arthropods living in ant nests probably do not seriously exploit the ants. They merely use the well-protected and well air-conditioned dwelling place the ants provide.

11

The role of insects

Insects play a vital role in all terrestrial ecosystems. Unfortunately, the impact of their activities is often overlooked because of their small size. There is also a common misconception that all insects are pests, causing untold damage to plants, crops and even animals. A closer look at their ecological role will reveal how important they are in the healthy functioning of ecosystems.

Ant on a carnivorous honeydew

ROLE IN GLOBAL ECOLOGY

The easiest way to demonstrate the importance of insect activities in terrestrial ecology is by means of an 'experiment'. Let us suppose a completely safe, broad-spectrum insecticide is discovered that would not poison or harm any other living beings, and governments in southern Africa agree to eradicate all pests by blanket-spraying the subcontinent with the new insecticide. Now, let us assess the impact of this decision.

The first wave of extinction: animals

Within days, insect-eating vertebrates and other 'non-insect' arthropods will start to die. A few weeks later, the following terrestrial species will have become extinct (figures rounded off):

- birds: about 550 out of 960 species;
- amphibians: all 160 species in southern Africa;
- reptiles: approximately 380 out of 600 species;
- freshwater fish: about 160 out of 370 species;
- mammals: an estimated 200 out of 350 species.

Within a few short weeks, 1,450 out of 2,460 species – well over half of all vertebrates – will have died out due to starvation. After a short interval, about 30 per cent of the surviving species will disappear. They are the predators that usually feed on the insectivorous birds, reptiles, amphibians, mammals and fish that had died earlier on.

In one season, more than 1,750 of the 2,460 vertebrate species in southern Africa will have vanished, as more than three-quarters of all

A great number of vertebrate and arthropod species are wholly dependent on insects as a food source, including (left to right) the African hoopoe, Cape dwarf chameleon and the golden orb-web spider.

vertebrate animals directly or indirectly depend on insects for food.

In the meanwhile, about half of the estimated 10,000 'non-insect' arthropods will die of starvation, and predators, particularly spiders and scorpions, will disappear.

In the 1950s, Zululand, a region in KwaZulu-Natal, was blanket-sprayed with the pesticide DDT to eliminate the tsetse fly. Although the insect escaped eradication, it is likely that many other species were exterminated, including some that would remain forever unknown to science.

The second wave of extinction: plants

The absence of insects causes a ripple effect in the plant kingdom. At first, a small number of insect-eating plants such as honeydews and Venus flytraps die. Then the flowering plants start disappearing because more than 85 per cent of them depend on insects for pollination and successful seed production and dispersal.

Annuals will be wiped out within a year. Perennials will persist until they reach the end of their life span, but in the absence of insects to pollinate them they will be unable to reproduce, eventually becoming extinct.

Along with the flowering plants, more animals die out, especially birds, bats and other species that live off dicotyledonous plants pollinated by insects. Of all the animals, only the grass feeders and decomposers remain, and the parasites and predators that survive on them.

The last wave of extinction: soil

The most gradual, and the most fatal, consequence of the extinction of insects is the degradation of topsoil. Dead plant litter and animal remains no longer get buried and decomposed by insects, but dry out on the surface before being burnt or washed away. The soil becomes hard and compacted because of a lack of the millions of tunnels dug by termites, ants and larvae to aerate it and facilitate water penetration. At the same time, dead soil deep down is not brought to the surface, so no new soil is formed, leading to further degradation. In only a few decades, topsoil is eroded away and the underlying dead clay or bedrock is exposed. The last vegetation disappears, and with it all remaining animal life.

Dicotyledonous plants are flowering plants whose seeds have two lobes. There are more than 200,000 species in this group.

CO-EVOLUTION WITH PLANTS

Apart from their key ecological functions, insects are also responsible for thousands of sophisticated interactions that help to maintain a balance of numbers in ecosystems. The most fascinating examples of co-evolution are found in the close association between insects and plants. These species have cohabited on the planet for hundreds of millions of years.

Peculiar pollinators

Flowers use colours, shapes and smells to attract specific insect pollinators (see Chapters 6 and 8). The 'reward' flowers offer for pollination by insects is usually nectar, but carrion flowers (*Stapelia* sp.) use the scent of rotten meat to trick blowflies into spreading their pollen (see Chapter 8).

The toad plant (*Huernia hystrix*) mimics the appearance and smell of rotting meat to lure blowflies for pollination.

The forelegs of the *Rediviva* species of bee (inset) are specifically adapted to collect oil from the long lateral tubes of the flowers of various *Diascia* species.

Other flowers attract and reward insect pollinators with nothing but heat. This is a substantial benefit for insects that otherwise would have to generate the required temperature to activate their flight muscles themselves. Flowers that perform this function include those of the huge delicious monster and the arum lily.

Rediviva bees rely on oil found in special tubes under the flowers of *Diascia* spp. to feed their offspring. As they collect the oil with their specially adapted long front legs, pollen is being deposited on their bodies. Bees and flowering plants have co-evolved matching morphological characteristics – such as long front legs adapted to the oil tubes of a particular plant species – to limit competition between bees and to maintain species-specific pollen transfer between flowers.

Except for pollen and honey, bees need resin to produce propolis, which they use to line their nests, whereas solitary bees harvest resin to seal off their tunnels. Some flowers, for example *Dalechampia* spp., secrete resin instead of nectar to lure and reward pollinators.

Probably the most complex pollination interaction is between figs and fig wasps. These minute wasps breed in small fruit ('pips') inside figs. The fig has special florets with short styles for the use of the wasps. It also has normal florets with longer styles, thereby keeping the seed out of reach of the wasp's ovipositor and preserving it for

'EXPLODING' POLLEN PACKS

Wild solanums, and some other flowers, have pollen packs that explode in response to the vibration created by the wings of buzzing bees. Normally, solitary bees specialise in this form of pollination. In the photograph below, the vibration of the insect's wings is replicated by using a tuning fork, thereby triggering the release of pollen.

Pollen released from a wild solanum flower, with the aid of a tuning fork

its own reproduction. The male wasps that have developed inside the fig are wingless, whereas the females are winged. The females pick up pollen, as well as the small males, and then escape through an opening under the fig to pollinate and infest other figs. The shape of the opening and the shape of the wasp match like lock and key, preventing cross-infestation.

Due to their small size and relatively short life cycle, the wasps could not survive a winter between the reproductive cycles of the fig. Fig trees therefore also produce a special (infertile) harvest of winter figs, solely to keep the wasp population going!

Fly bushes and assassin bugs

Two species of fly bush in the Western Cape have evolved a curious roundabout interaction with insects. These plants entrap insects in a sticky secretion, but cannot digest them. A particular assassin bug that lives on these bushes has evolved special footpads that do not adhere to the sticky sap. The bug sucks out the entrapped prey; in return, the plant absorbs the assassin bug's faeces, which is a crucial source of nitrogen.

Some plants have nectar glands on the outside of their flowers to attract ants.

Ants and plants

Ants are a great asset to many plants, as they prey on leaf-eating insects and their eggs. These include caterpillars of moths and butterflies, beetles, crickets and locusts.

The branches and leaves of many plants, such as hibiscus and acacia, have extra-floral nectaries. These are nectar glands situated outside the flower for the express purpose of attracting ants. The patrolling ants automatically then rid the plant of its pest insects.

Enlarged acacia thorns, filled with sweet tissue, are often occupied by ant colonies (see Chapter 5). It would seem that the main purpose of these enlarged thorns is to attract ants, as they provide the same sanitation service that those attracted by nectaries do.

Some species of ant farm sap-sucking insects such as plant lice and leafhoppers. Despite conventional wisdom these insects do not damage plants to the extent we think they do. The honeydew they excrete falls on the ground, directly below the plant, where it stimulates the growth of nitrogen-binding microbes and the formation of soluble nitrogen. For the plant, the additional nitrogen is a good exchange for the removal of sap and sugars by the sapsuckers.

The most productive co-evolution between ants and plants, however, involves the elaiosomes ('ant bread') attached to the seeds of fynbos plants such as the pincushion protea. This 'ant food' is rich and flavoured, and easily accessible to the ants, while the actual seed is hard and unpalatable. Ants that

> The spread of plant and animal diseases by sap- and blood-sucking insects is one of several mechanisms that keep the number of animals and plants at a sustainable threshold level, necessary for the survival of these species.

Bean weevils feed exclusively on legume seeds.

carry these seeds to their nest will eat the 'ant bread' and in springtime throw out the seeds with the nest refuse. In this way, the ants are rewarded with nutritious morsels during winter in return for dispersing the seeds in the spring.

Insects prevent overpopulation

Insects play a major role in regulating plant and animal numbers in terrestrial ecosystems. Not only do they regulate the numbers of most other insects through parasitism and predation, they also keep the populations of vertebrate species and plants within bounds.

Many plant seeds are destroyed by seed bugs or seed borers. In acacias, seed borers may destroy 98 per cent of seeds. This probably limits the unsustainable proliferation of these trees more effectively than any other environmental factor.

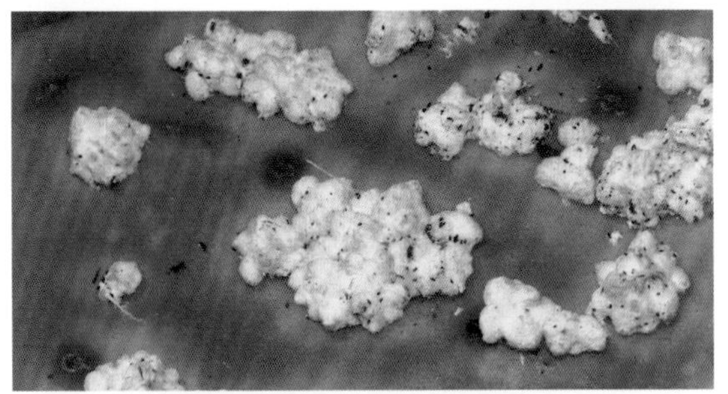

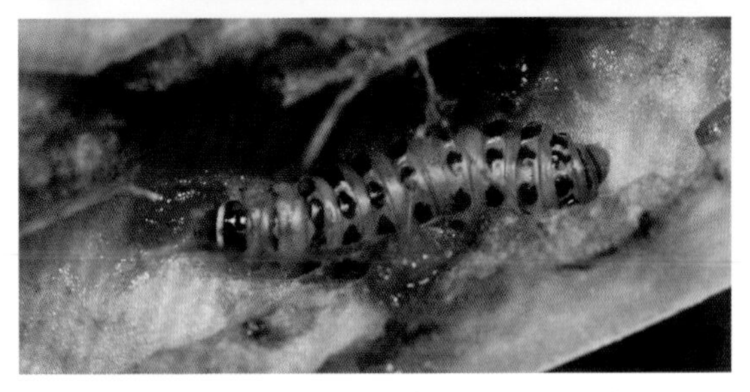

Cochineal bugs (top and centre) and the caterpillar of the cactus moth (above) have been introduced to stop the spread of prickly pears in the Eastern Cape.

INSECTS AND HUMANS

A few insects yield products valuable to humans, but the key functions they perform in maintaining natural ecosystems are the main benefit they bestow on us. Increasingly, these functions are being integrated into artificially managed systems.

Controlling pests and invaders

The use of predatory or parasitic insects to control insect pests and weeds is termed 'biological control'. Most pests and weeds proliferate because they were introduced to new continents without their natural enemies, which normally controlled their numbers. These natural enemies can be introduced (preferably without *their* enemies!) to suppress pests and weed species. In this process, it is crucial to ensure that the newly introduced natural enemies are host-specific, and will not migrate to indigenous species. Host switches do occur, and could create worse problems than the original one.

Classic examples of successful biological control against weeds are the importation of cochineal bugs and the caterpillars of the cactus moth (*Cactoblastis cactorum*) to control the proliferation of prickly pears in the Eastern Cape and gall-forming wasps to suppress the spread of the *Acacia longifolia* bush in the Western Cape.

Ladybeetles, and their larvae, can be effective in controlling aphids and some scale insects.

Parasites, predators and pathogens of insect pests are bred in rearing factories, or insectaries, for release by farmers to control their insect pests.

The advantages of this approach to pest control are obvious: the environment and consumers are protected from harm caused by insect poisons and pests' natural enemies are preserved. Once established, natural enemies control pests progressively more effectively, thus eliminating the need for additional pest control costs. The most important insects now bred as natural enemies in insectaries are parasitic wasps (Braconidae and Chalcidoidea families), ladybeetles and lacewings.

Pollinators of crops and orchards

Fruit farmers are particularly dependent on bees and other insects for pollination of orchards, since most fruit will not set without it. The honeybee (*Apis mellifera*) is used extensively for this purpose, and some bee farmers specialise in providing pollination services. Successful commercial pollination depends on orchards being densely populated with bees, making it impossible for swarms to gather nectar in significant quantities. This effectively makes honey production and commercial pollination mutually exclusive.

Honey and beeswax

Southern Africa is not self-sufficient in apiary products. The local climate and vegetation are subject to large year-on-year fluctuations, resulting in unpredictable honey yields from one season to the next.

Fascinating fact

In other parts of the world there have been experiments using different pollinators, such as the European bumblebee, but in Africa no pollinators other than honeybees have been employed commercially.

Commercial pollination services are used on fruit farms across South Africa.

The local honeybee industry has also suffered severe setbacks in the past few decades. First came the introduction of the incompatible Cape honeybee (*Apis mellifera capensis*) into other parts of the country. This was followed by the accidental importation of several bee pests and diseases. The result was a reduction in honey production from over 30kg per hive to only 18kg in one decade.

SILK MOTHS

Silk production has been tried several times in South Africa, but no real success has ever been achieved. Although the climate is suitable, it seems that we cannot compete with the East when it comes to the cheap, skilled and diligent labour needed to make a success of this industry.

Silkworm farm

Bee farmers also have to cope with the incredibly ingenious honey badger and, worse, an endemic human criminal element. Nevertheless, the honey industry is not negligible. Apart from the provision of pollination services, about 3,500 tonnes of honey are produced annually. Beeswax, though largely replaced by synthetic products, is still an expensive and sought-after product for candles and precision moulding.

Traditional and medicinal use

Using the larvae of the Bushman arrow-poison beetle (*Polyclada* spp.) to make a deadly poison, enlisting ant and termite soldiers to stitch wounds, and exploiting blister beetles ('Spanish fly') for their putative aphrodisiac qualities are some examples of how humans have employed insects for traditional and medicinal purposes. While many of these practices have fallen out of favour, this is not the case with the maggots of blowflies, which are still commercially available for cleaning septic wounds. These maggots very selectively feed on dead tissue only. They also secrete antibiotics to combat bacteria that compete with them for food.

The Bushman arrow-poison beetle and its larvae and pupae contain a powerful toxin.

Insects are useful laboratory animals. Their fast reproduction and the lack of public sentiment towards them make them ideal for use in experiments.

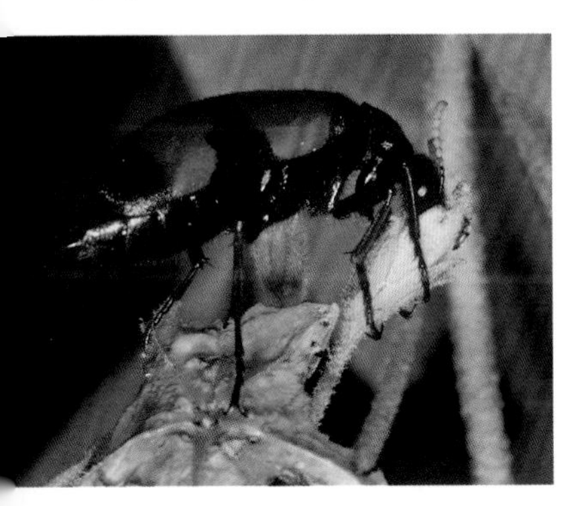

Despite its toxicity, cantharidin produced by blister beetles has been used in low doses as a putative aphrodisiac for centuries.

Fascinating fact

French physician Ambroise Paré (*c.* 1510–1590) was the first doctor to employ maggots to help heal wounds in the 16th century. Later, during the First and Second world wars, the application of live maggots prevented many a wounded soldier from dying from gangrene – as these larvae dissolve dead tissue and kill bacteria, thereby disinfecting the wound.

Blowfly maggots

Insects as food

On average, insects are 1.5 times as nutritious as red meat. The inhabitants of Africa (and other tropical regions) have traditionally harvested and consumed insects wherever economical quantities of non-poisonous species could be found.

Termites are harvested when they swarm through special traps and are marketed in a dried form throughout Africa. Families often traditionally own and inherit large termite colonies for harvesting.

Caterpillars of mopane moths (left) and cabbage tree emperor moths (centre) as well as locusts (right) are widely consumed by humans in southern Africa.

Mopane worms (*Imbrasia belina*) and other emperor moth caterpillars are also favourite foods. They are eaten fresh, dried or even preserved and canned. Thousands of tonnes of these caterpillars are consumed annually.

In all regions where locusts are found, particularly the swarming species, humans have harvested them. Some large bugs are considered a delicacy, and traditional communities harvest them diligently.

Giant stink bugs of the Tessaratomidae family are a delicacy for the Venda people of Limpopo.

Insects as ecological indicators

It has become increasingly common for insects to be used as ecological indicators to help detect changes in the natural environment. Most insects are extremely specialised and thus highly sensitive to particular environmental conditions.

A decomposing carcass produces a fixed sequence of chemicals and smells that change even within hours. The many fly and beetle species utilising such a carcass are highly specialised and are attracted at very specific stages of decomposition. A branch of forensic entomology, pioneered in South Africa in the 1970s, uses the presence or absence of these various decomposer species to determine time of death of animals, including humans.

The pollution of rivers and streams can be gauged by the presence or absence of different species of mayfly.

The degree and forms of pollution in rivers and streams can also be monitored by the presence or absence of specialised water insects, for example mayflies. Such surveys can often be conducted more cheaply and faster than chemical analyses.

The use of insects as indicators has certainly not been fully exploited. Potential areas for application include weather prediction, assessing air pollution, degradation of terrestrial ecosystems, soil quality and climate change.

Modern cultural uses

A specimen of a rare beetle, collected locally and illegally, has fetched $20,000 on the international collectors' market!

Due to growing awareness of the biological environment, people have come to know insects better and to appreciate their diversity. Millions of people worldwide collect insects for their beauty and for biological interest. Since insects are usually fast and prolific breeders, they can mostly be collected without endangering wild populations and ecosystems. As collectors are

Entomology research depends on professionally curated reference collections.

prepared to spend money on their hobby, insects can generate revenue in terms of ecotourism and direct sales to this market. This revenue is hardly being exploited in Africa.

INSECTS AND DISEASES

The propensity of insects to carry and transmit diseases makes them the most dangerous creatures by far.

Killer insects

Killer diseases, such as malaria, yellow fever, typhus fever and plague, are transmitted by insects. Malaria and yellow fever are passed on by mosquitoes, typhus fever by lice and plague by fleas. Although all these diseases can now be treated, historically they have resulted in more human deaths than all other causes put together. For example, more people have died from malaria than have been killed in all known wars in history.

Malaria is caused by parasites transmitted to humans by infected female *Anopheles* mosquitoes. Because the malaria parasite can camouflage itself chemically, vaccination has proved impracticable, and malaria remains the prime killer disease in Africa, particularly among children.

Plague wiped out at least 25 per cent of the human population of 15th-century Europe. In the history of Europe, more wars were won or lost due to plague and typhus fever than through military action. In eastern Europe, over five million people died of typhus fever during the First World War, and typhus victims of the Napoleonic Wars are estimated at 20 million.

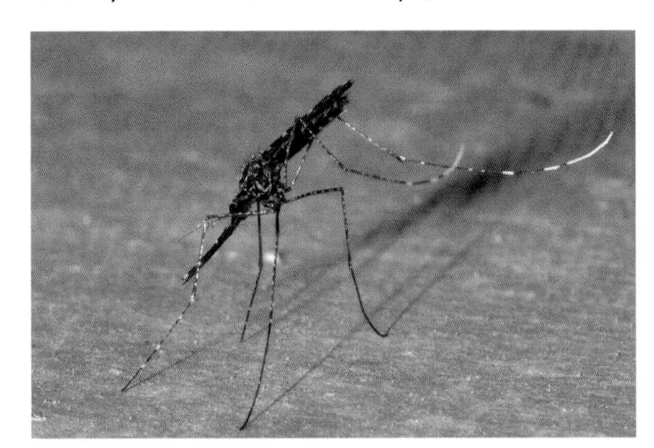

Malaria, Africa's most deadly disease, is transmitted by female *Anopheles* mosquitoes.

Nowadays, yellow fever, typhus and plague are no longer considered serious threats, as they can be successfully treated or prevented using modern medicine.

Threats to domestic animals

While ticks are undoubtedly the most important disease vectors among livestock, insects also have a hazardous, and sometimes catastrophic, effect on domestic animals. Horse sickness, which still periodically decimates the South African horse population, is transmitted by biting midges (*Culicoides* spp.). Nagana in cattle (and sleeping sickness in humans) is transmitted by tsetse flies. Unless treated, the disease can be fatal.

Flies are also responsible for much direct damage to livestock. Apart from the irritation and loss of condition, cattle suffer from attacks by various families of blood-sucking flies, which may carry disease-causing organisms. Damage caused by blowflies, bot flies and nasal flies can lead to serious livestock losses.

Venomous insects and humans

Many insects are highly poisonous. As humans are unlikely to ingest them, they hardly pose a threat to us, but domestic animals may be seriously at risk, and even killed, if they ingest, for example, blister beetles or flower beetles while grazing.

Venomous insects, on the other hand, pose a more serious threat to humans. In Africa, honeybee stings kill more people than all other wild animals put together do, including lions, crocodiles, elephants and snakes. These high fatalities can be ascribed to a fairly widespread prevalence of bee sting allergy, as well as the extremely aggressive nature of the African honeybee.

Other insects whose stings can be very painful are paper wasps and even solitary wasps, such as velvet ants.

Giant water bugs and assassin bugs can inflict extremely painful bites owing to proteolytic enzymes in their saliva. These enzymes aid the digestion process by breaking down protein.

Caterpillars of pear slugs (left) and tussock moths (right) have 'hairs' that can penetrate human skin, causing a variety of reactions, from itchiness to severe dermatitis.

There are insects whose venomous secretions can result in great discomfort for humans. When the setae or 'hair' of caterpillars of pear slugs and some moths and butterflies become embedded in the skin, they release a toxin that can cause hours of excruciating pain, welts and itching. In some humans, these hairs may even cause dermatitis.

Lastly, there are insects with poisonous and venomous secretions that can have debilitating and harmful effects on humans. Ground beetles, stink bugs and blister beetles secrete extremely irritating and foul-smelling defensive fluids from their abdomens. These can cause blisters on sensitive skin and may also severely harm the mucous membranes of organs such as the eyes.

AGRICULTURAL PESTS

Insects are regarded as formidable pests in agriculture, so much so that an overwhelming number of research programmes, textbooks and scientific journals have been dedicated to understanding the role of insect pests in agriculture and exploring mechanisms to control them.

In fact, insects generally cost farmers an average of about 20 per cent of all harvests – either in damage, or in the form of costly pest control. No other living creatures on earth have a comparable impact on the economy.

In spite of their devastating effect, the number of harmful insect species is surprisingly low. Pests justifying control measures in South Africa number

The defensive secretions of stink bugs (left), blister beetles (centre) and ground beetles (right) can inflict intense pain.

only about 100 species out of a total of perhaps 100,000. Even with some marginal and sporadic pests added, all our insect pests comprise only about 500 species, or 0.5 per cent of the total number of insect species.

About 90 per cent of agricultural insect pests fall in three orders: bugs (Hemiptera), beetles (Coleoptera) and moths (Lepidoptera).

Damage caused by sapsuckers

Bugs cause three kinds of damage to plants. Firstly, some species of scale insect, for example pernicious scale (*Quadraspidiotus perniciosus*), have extremely toxic saliva, which can kill off their host.

Secondly, leafhoppers, aphids, jumping plant lice and whiteflies spread plant diseases from infected plants to healthy ones. These viruses are often lethal and can wipe out whole orchards or crops.

Sap-sucking insects, such as leafhoppers (top), may transmit dread diseases. Others, like aphids (above), damage plants outright.

Waxy scales are well protected against insecticides and are therefore hard to control.

Mealy bug numbers may reach pest proportions because ants protect them against their natural enemies.

Lastly, waxy scales and mealy bugs can cause physical harm by killing growth points and badly hampering photosynthesis through honeydew secretions and concomitant fungal growth. Aphids and other heteropteran families may also contribute to this type of damage.

Damage caused by beetles

Considering that they constitute two-thirds of all insect species, only a small percentage of beetles are regarded as agricultural pests, and none of them poses a serious threat.

Chafers are known to damage flowers and foliage.

Fruit chafers may despoil fruit and flowers.

Some species of ladybeetle and their larvae (right) can seriously damage foliage.

Longhorn beetles are one of several beetle families whose larvae bore in timber.

Fascinating fact

The larvae of hide beetles will feed on dried animal matter such as furs, skins, biltong and museum specimens of animals.

Hide beetle larva feeding on uncured sheep skin

Chafers may do some leaf damage, and their larvae may feed on roots of lawn grasses and cereals. Some beetles will damage flowers, fruit chafers and blister beetles being the main culprits. Others are voracious leaf-eaters, for example citrus weevils (*Sciobius* spp.), leaf-eating ladybeetles on vegetables, and false cut worms (toktokkie larvae), which attack seedlings at ground level.

Probably the most serious damage beetles can cause is to wood and timber. Except for termites, all consumers of wood are beetles, particularly longhorn beetles, shot-hole borers, bark borers and powderpost beetles.

Beetles will also attack stored goods. Grain stores are often demolished by grain beetles (*Oryzaephilus* spp.), maize weevils (*Sitophilus* spp.) and bean weevils, in the case of legume seeds.

Damage caused by caterpillars

Moth caterpillars constitute the most serious threat to agriculture. Mealies are attacked by maize stem borers (*Busseola* spp.) and boll worms (*Helicoverpa* spp.), with the latter also surviving on dozens of other crops. False codling moths (*Cryptophlebia* spp.) attack virtually all fruit, and several other caterpillars feed on a wide range of hosts, from grain to trees in forestry plantations. Caterpillars also attack certain dead organic products. Clothes moths (*Tineola* spp.) will destroy untreated clothing, whereas meal moths (*Ephestia* spp.) and grain moths (*Sitotroga* spp.) are major pests of stored cereals.

Occasionally, dramatic outbreaks of army caterpillars (*Spodoptera* spp.) can wreak havoc as these 'army worms' march across pastures and grain fields, leaving only stubble behind.

Pests in minor insect orders

There are also several serious crop pests in some of the minor insect orders. These include thrips, which feed on citrus, tomatoes and a variety of other crops; fruit flies, which attack virtually all fruit and the fruit of vegetables; and leaf-mining flies, which can cause considerable damage to tomatoes and other crops.

Finally, let us not forget the locusts. Growing carelessness in the control of hopper swarms is likely to lead to the reappearance of large swarms in Africa. In 1591, hopper swarms invaded Italy from Africa, and more than a million people died as result of the famine that followed the invasion. In Africa, they could certainly cause worse damage, even today.

False codling moth larvae attack a large variety of fruit and seeds.

Found in several insect orders, leaf miners are very hard to control.

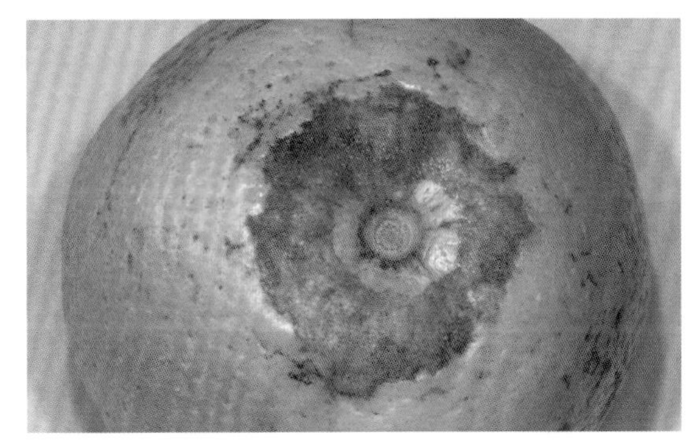

Citrus thrips cause damage to the peel around the calyx of oranges, but without any effect on the fruit.

12

Identification

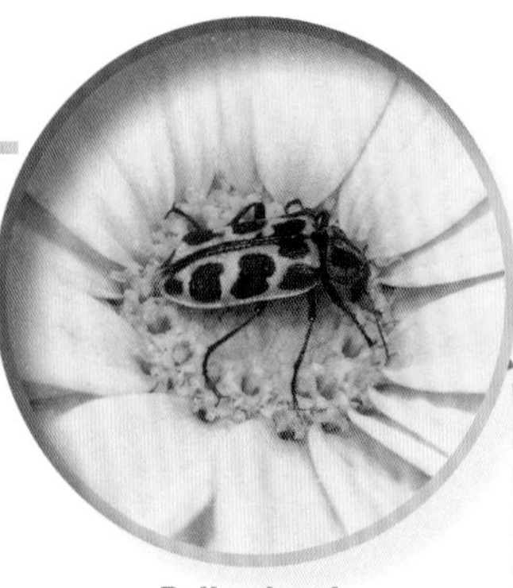
Pollen beetle

An estimated 80,000 insect species have been described in southern Africa to date. Undoubtedly, there are still many new species that await discovery, description and naming. In fact, the discovery of new families is not unheard of and even new orders and suborders may well be found and added to our already vast insect kingdom.

This chapter presents an overview of the insects most likely to be encountered in southern Africa. Given the great number of species, the chapter is organised according to **groups** – orders, suborders and families. Of the more than 660 family groups occurring in the region, 70 of the best known, most visible and species-rich families were selected for identification purposes, representing 80 per cent of the most common insects.

- Entries are arranged in a logical sequence, starting with descriptions of orders and suborders (where applicable), followed by families. Easily noticeable features, along with biology and habitat, are described and, with a few exceptions, photographs or illustrations are provided.
- Insect sizes given indicate body length – from head to tail without any appendages (antennae, legs, wings, mouthparts or abdominal appendages).
- The number of species listed under each entry is based on records of species described and named in southern Africa. Generally, species names have been avoided, as even specialists would be unable to distinguish one species from another using only a brief description and a photograph.
- Barring a few adjustments, the classification of insects in this chapter is based on the definitive work on local insect families in southern Africa, *Insects of southern Africa* by Clarke H. Scholtz and Erik Holm (Protea Book House, 2008).

Adult antlion

WHAT INSECT IS THAT?

Identifying insects can be rather daunting. The steps outlined below will help you determine the family group of the insect you wish to identify. Based on careful observation of the specimen in question:

1. Select the most likely insect order to which the insect could belong.
2. Compare the specimen at hand with photographs and illustrations in the relevant order and family sections to find the closest match.
3. Read the family description to see whether it corresponds with the characteristics, behaviour and location of the insect you want to identify.
4. Review related family entries to check that you have not confused the insect with one in a different family or order.

THE HEMIMETABOLOUS ORDERS

These are the more primitive insects. They undergo a simpler metamorphosis, and lack a pupal stage in their life cycle. Most of the southern African orders (21) and their suborders fall into this category.

SILVERFISH, FISH MOTHS

ORDER: ZYGENTOMA (ALSO CALLED THYSANURA)

Small to medium-sized (3–15mm). Wingless insects. Mostly small, with spool-shaped, scaled bodies and three long tails (cerci). Live in humus, under bark and inside ant and termite nests. Sand dunes are home to some species, of which the three tails have been reduced to nodules. In ant and termite nests, small, stubby types with short tails are found. A number are household pests.

- 2 families; 48 species.
- Can be confused with bristletails (Archaeognatha).

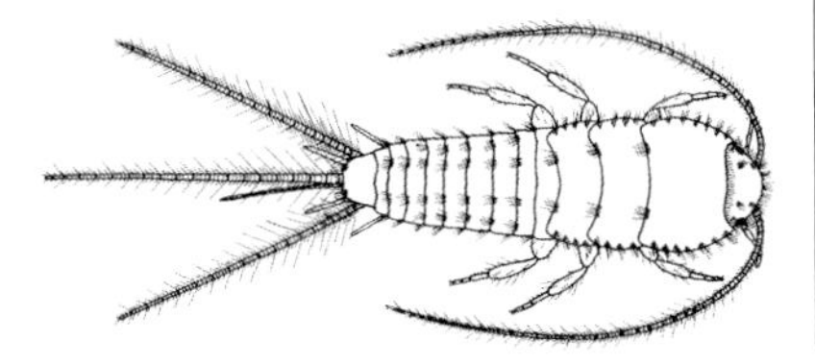

BRISTLETAILS

ORDER: ARCHAEOGNATHA

Medium-sized (10–15mm). Wingless. Similar to silverfish; also with three tails, but with a hunchback. Jump by jerking tail downward and towards the head. Found mostly in humid forests and along rocky coasts. Feed on decomposing plant matter, algae and lichen.

- 1 family; 18 species.
- Can be confused with silverfish (Zygentoma), but the hunchback is distinctive.

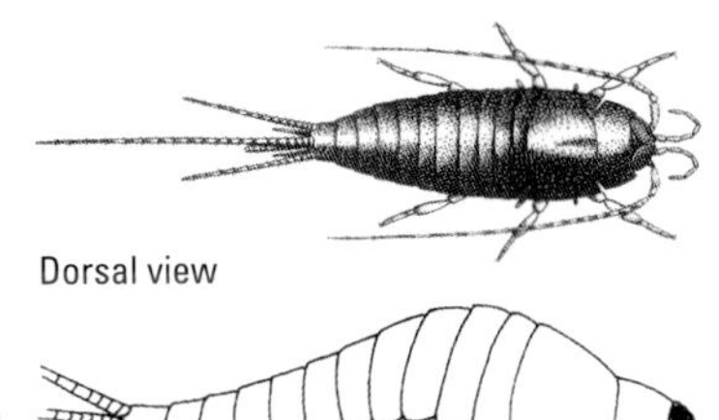

Dorsal view

Lateral view

MAYFLIES

ORDER: EPHEMEROPTERA

Medium-sized (mostly under 10mm). Winged. Uniquely for winged insects, adults have long front legs, two or three very long tails (cerci), and exceptionally small hind wings (front wings are 'normal'). Adults' lifespan is short, sometimes only one day. Adults always close to water; nymphs live in water. Nymphs have three tails and leaf-shaped gills on the sides of the abdomen. Moult into 'duns' and then into adults.

- 11 families; 180 species.
- No other flying insects have such long 'tails'.

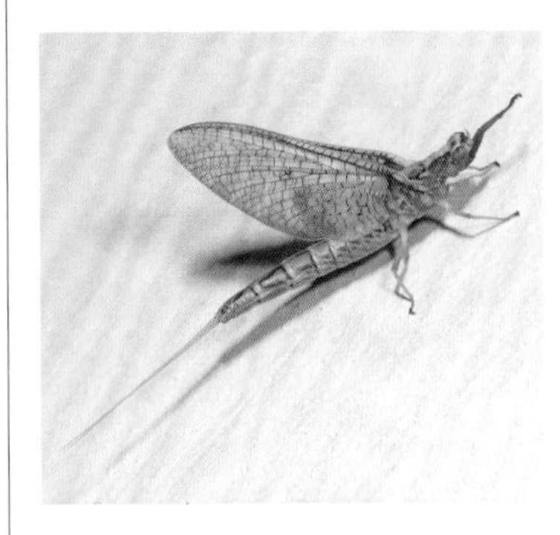

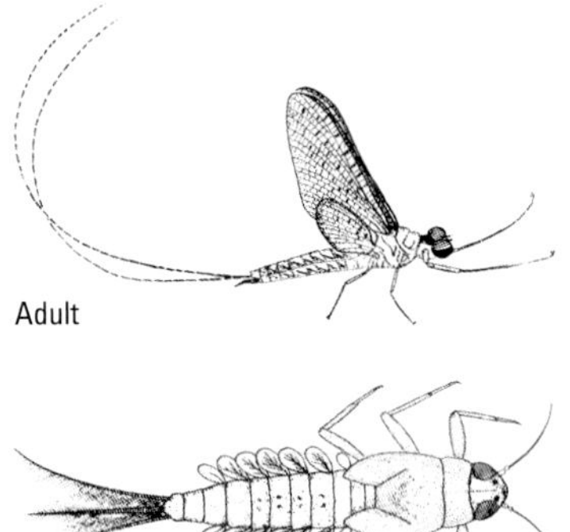

Adult

Nymph

DRAGONFLIES AND DAMSELFLIES

ORDER: ODONATA

Medium-sized to very large (20–120mm). Insects in this order have long, straight abdomens, large eyes, forward-directed legs, four similar wings with notches in the middle of the front margin and short, hair-like feelers. There are two easily identifiable suborders: damselflies (Zygoptera) and dragonflies (Anisoptera).

DAMSELFLIES

Suborder: Zygoptera

Medium-sized to very large (15–70mm). Distinguished from dragonflies (Anisoptera) by more delicate build, wings that mostly taper towards the base and that can be folded backwards when resting, and eyes on the sides of the head with more than an eye's width space between them. Nymphs live in water and have leaf-shaped gills at the end of the abdomen.

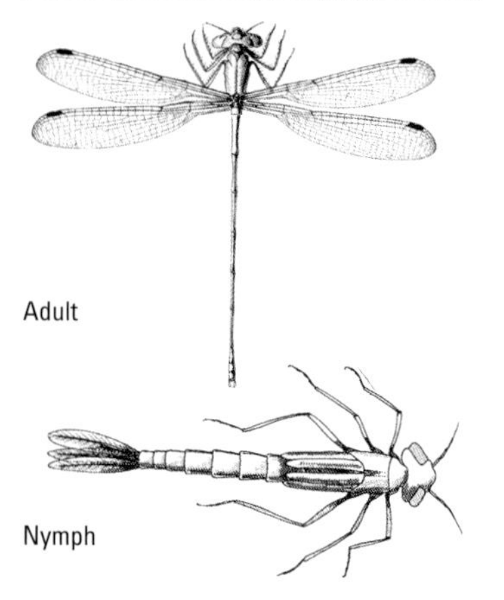

Adult

Nymph

- 7 families; 95 species.
- Can be confused with dragonflies (Anisoptera) and antlions (Myrmeleontidae), but the latter have well-developed antennae, no indentations on the front margins of the wings and the orientation of the legs is not forward.

DRAGONFLIES

Suborder: Anisoptera

Large to very large (30–120mm). Differ from damselflies (Zygoptera) in that they have a more sturdy build, their wings do not taper towards the base but extend sideways during rest, and the eyes occupy almost the entire head, often touching in the middle. Nymphs live in water. Gills are located inside the rectum, through which water is sucked in and squirted out to propel the nymph forward.

- 4 families; 127 species.
- Can be confused with damselflies (Zygoptera) and antlions (Myrmeleontidae).

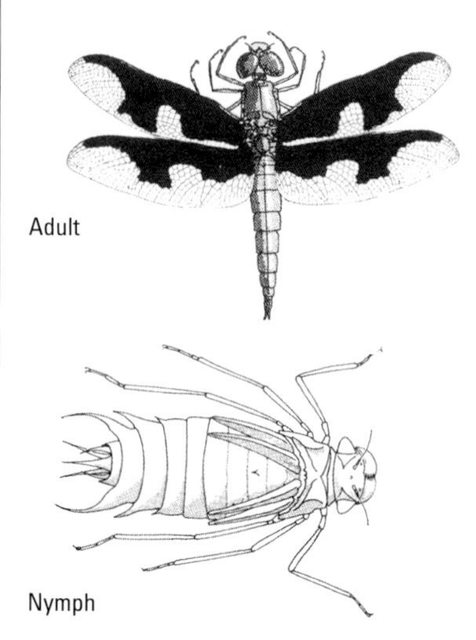

Adult

Nymph

ROACHES, COCKROACHES

ORDER: BLATTARIA (ALSO CALLED BLATTODEA)

Small to large (5–50mm). Flat insects, with soft, leathery shell and long, thin antennae. Two short tail appendages are present. The breastplate (pronotum) covers the head, which is oriented downward. Most species have four functional wings, but a number of species are permanently wingless, either only in the female sex or in both sexes. Omnivorous; found anywhere in or near organic waste. A number of species are cosmopolitan household pests.

- 4 families; 180 species.
- Can be confused with some katydids (*Oecanthus* spp.) and stoneflies (Plecoptera), but they do not have the distinctive breastplate and hidden head of cockroaches. Stoneflies have four equally translucent wings; forewings of cockroaches are more hardened and opaque than the hind wings.

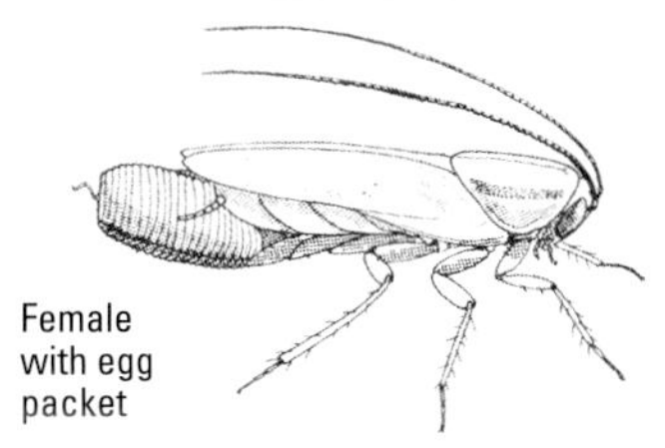

Female with egg packet

TERMITES

ORDER: ISOPTERA

Small to medium-sized (workers and soldiers: 2–12mm). Live in subterranean colonies as true social insects. Workers and soldiers have soft, poorly pigmented bodies, hardened head capsules, and are always wingless and blind. Only large harvester termites have eyes. Reproductive males and females look similar to workers but are larger, and have wings and eyes. The four wings look identical and are much longer than the body. Wings are shed after mating flights. Queens become extremely enlarged.

- 5 families; 135 species.
- Can be confused with cockroaches (Blattaria). Winged termites resemble cockroaches, but differ in that their wings are identical and much longer than the body and the breastplate is not flattened and does not cover the head. Workers and soldiers differ significantly from ants (Formicidae), as they lack the hard carapace and thin stem between abdomen and breast and the characteristic angled antennae found in ants.

Northern and southern harvester termites

Family: Hodotermitidae

Medium-sized (8–13mm). Workers and soldiers have eyes. Live in subterranean nests with small openings; wander about outside their nests on cool days. Mainly snip off grass (*Hodotermes* spp.) or small twigs (*Microhodotermes* spp.) in sections and carry these to their nests. Serious pests on grass and grazing land when combined with drought and overgrazing.

- 2 species.

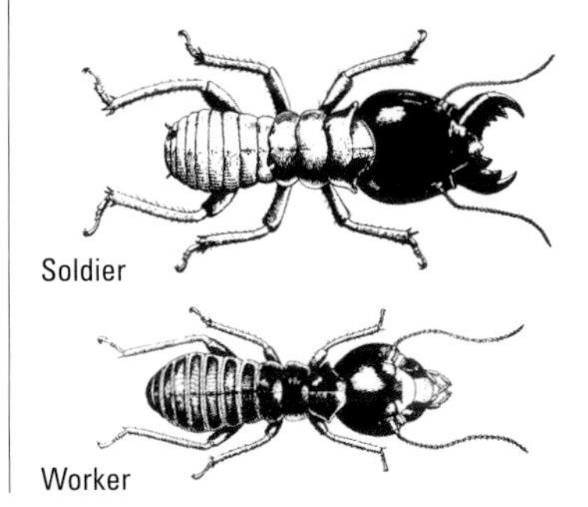

Soldier

Worker

Black-mound termites

Family: Termitidae

Subfamily: Termitinae

Small (workers: 3–6mm). Found in small colonies under rocks, decaying wood or dung pads, often living in the nests of other termites. Nest mostly without a visible structure above the ground, but sometimes typical black 'anthills' can be seen. Most feed on humus or dead wood. Only a few species are pests.

- 190 species.

Termite queen

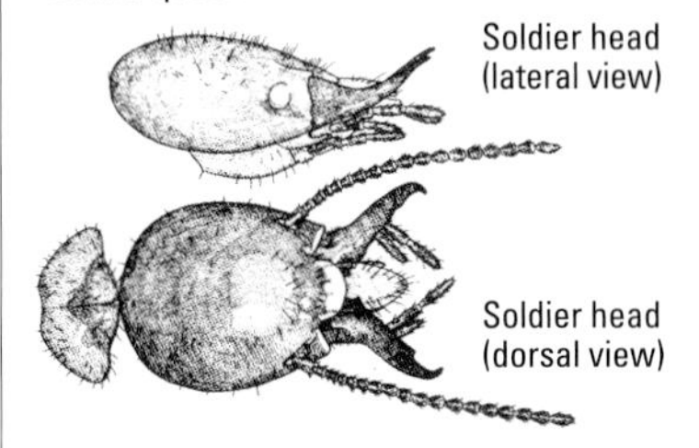

Soldier head (lateral view)

Soldier head (dorsal view)

Fungus-growing termites

Family: Termitidae

Subfamily: Macrotermitinae

Medium-sized (workers: 8–13mm; soldiers: up to 25mm). These insects are large in comparison with other termites. Build enormous colonies. Carry bits of wood to their nests and make fungus gardens. Termites feed on the fungi. Nests have either large 'chimneys', closed at the top, or short, open chimneys surrounded by clay floors. Both species are serious pests of timber.

- 2 species.

Termite queen

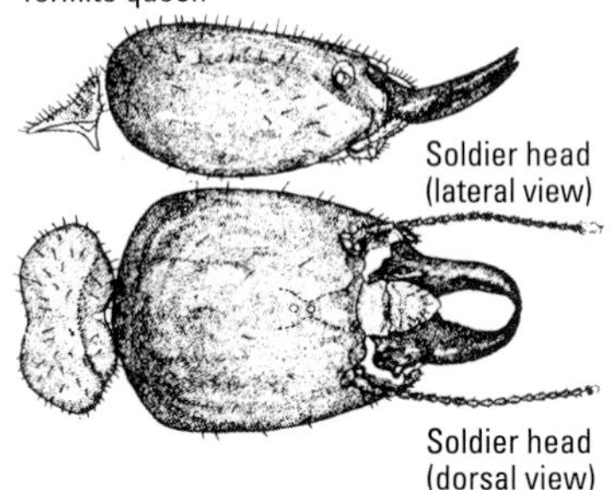

Snouted harvester termites

Family: Termitidae
Subfamily: Nasutitermitinae

Small (workers: ±5mm). Soldiers have snout-shaped heads with which they are able to squirt a sticky acid as defensive fluid. Nests mostly dome-shaped, but other designs are also found. At night workers carry grass

and other plant material to their nests. *Trinervitermes* spp. can denude grassland pastures.

- 12 species.

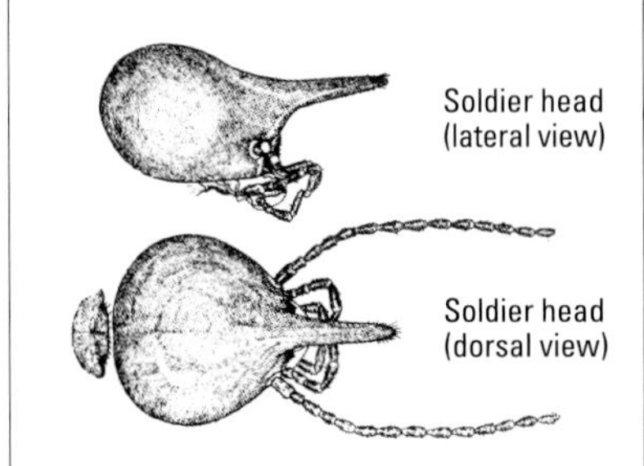

HEEL-WALKERS, GLADIATORS

ORDER: MANTOPHASMATODEA

Medium-sized (10–20mm). Insects of this recently discovered order look like wingless mantid nymphs, but forelegs are not modified for grasping, as in mantids. Antennae long, eyes prominent. Predators of small insects, with a distinct way of walking on their 'heels', hence the name 'heel-walkers'.

- 3 families; ±20 species (This order was discovered only in 2002 and is still being studied and analysed.)
- Can be confused with mantids (Mantodea) and small stick insects (Phasmatodea), but are more sturdy in build and have prominent eyes.

MANTIDS

ORDER: MANTODEA

Medium-sized to very large (20–150mm). Large eyes, flexible triangular head with long antennae, and forelegs modified for grasping prey. In winged species, the forewings are narrower and slightly hardened, but hind wings are wide and membranous. All are camouflaged ambush predators of other insects.

- 7 families; 186 species.
- Can be confused with mantidflies or mantispids (Mantispidae); however, the hind wings of the latter fold roof-like over the abdomen and are not flat as in mantids. Several families of stink bugs (Heteroptera) also include species with grasping front legs, but these can easily be distinguished from mantids by their sucking mouthparts.

Flower mantids

Family: Hymenopodidae

Large (25–45mm). Often brightly coloured with striking patterns or well camouflaged against a floral background. Usually with lateral lobes on the thorax and/ or spines on the head. Females are sometimes wingless.

- 27 species.

Gargoyle mantids, cone-headed mantids

Family: Empusidae

Very large (70–85mm). Slender with leaf-like lobes on the four hind legs and (split) conical projections from the top of the head. Antennae of males long and combed.

- 4 species.

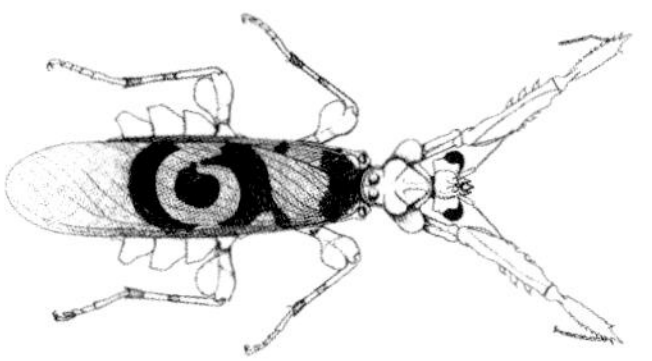

Bark mantids

Family: Amorphoscelididae

Large to very large (30–60mm). Sturdily built, body fairly flat. Grey bark patterns for camouflage. Lies flat against bark.

- ±20 species.

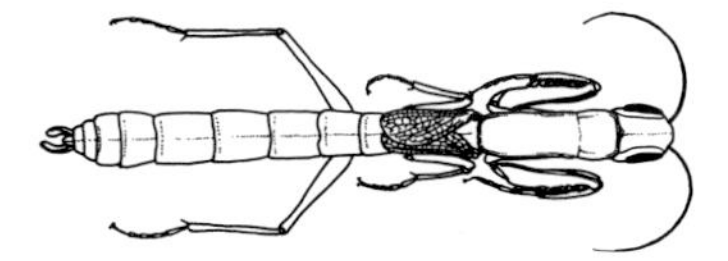

Common mantids

Family: Mantidae

Medium-sized to very large (11–80mm). Foliage or grass mimics. Family includes the majority of mantid species.

- 130 species.

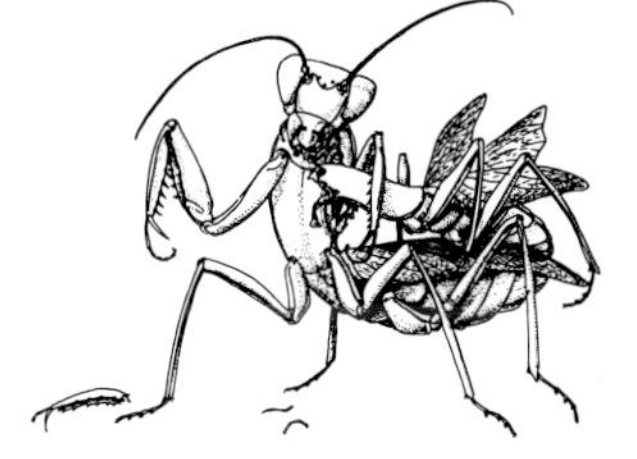

EARWIGS

ORDER: DERMAPTERA

Medium-sized to large (8–50mm). In winged species, short, square forewings cover membranous hind wings. Dorsal segments of the abdomen are exposed; abdomen has a pair of noticeable forceps (modified cerci) at the rear end. Many species wingless. Live in tunnels and crevices. Mostly plant feeders, but some species are predatory. Nocturnal.

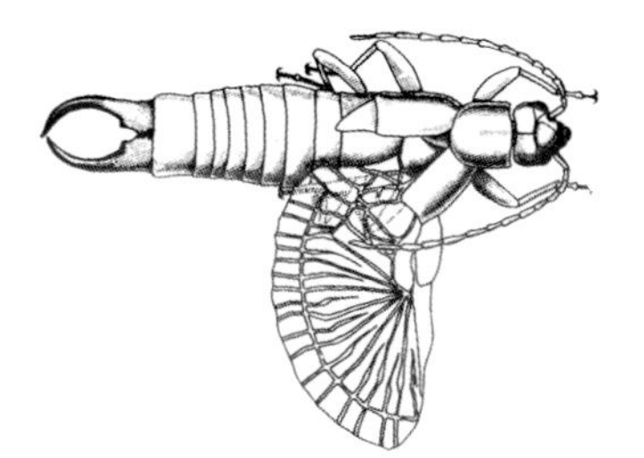

- 5 families; 36 species.
- Can be confused with rove beetles (Staphylinidae), which have similar antennae and mandibles. Earwigs are easily identified by abdominal forceps; rove beetles have only two small, thin jointed 'tails'.

Cane rat earwigs

Family: Hemimeridae

Medium-sized (±10mm). Previously considered a separate order, known as Hemimerina. An external parasite found on cane rats. Unusual among earwigs; flattened, with a soft body and special hair clamps on the legs, blind and wingless. Abdominal forceps are reduced to two segmented tails, a condition otherwise found only in certain earwig nymphs.

- 2 species.

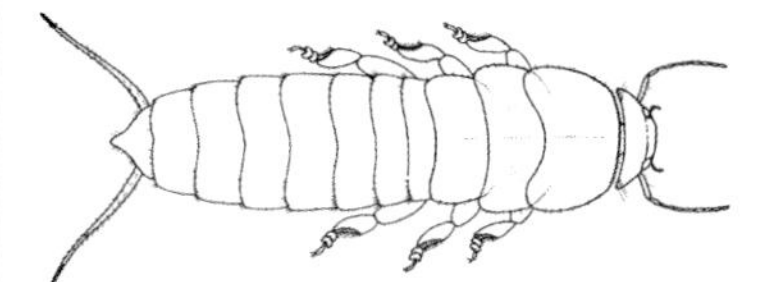

WEB-SPINNERS OR EMBIIDITS

ORDER: EMBIODEA (ALSO CALLED EMBIOPTERA OR EMBIIDINA)

Medium-sized (5–25mm). Live communally in silk tunnels, usually under stones or loose bark. Characteristically, first segment of front foot is swollen; femur of hind legs is enlarged. Swollen feet segments contain silk glands, enabling all stages (from nymphs to adults of both sexes) to spin silk for their tunnels. The enlarged hind legs enable web-spinners to run backwards inside their tunnels. Certain species have winged males. Feed on lichen, moss and dead organic matter.

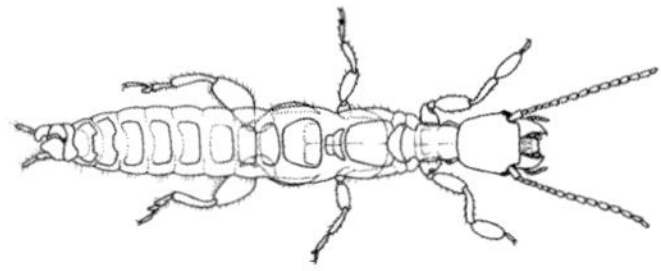

- 3 families; 37 species.
- Can be confused with stoneflies (Plecoptera), winged termites (Isoptera) and wingless earwigs (Dermaptera), but in all cases the swollen segments of the front legs are diagnostic. The wings of web-spinners are shorter than those of termites and the abdominal forceps seen in earwigs are absent. They also bear some resemblance to thrips (Thysanoptera), but the feet (tarsi) of thrips are enlarged on the last segment, the head is slimmer than the abdomen, and the wings have a border of long bristles.

STONEFLIES

ORDER: PLECOPTERA

Medium-sized (5–25mm). Antennae and two abdominal appendages rather long and thin. Four membranous wings folded flat on or laterally around the abdomen. Head forward-pointing, eyes prominent. Adults always near river banks; nymphs live in water. Adults are agile runners (they also run on water) and do not fly readily. Nymphs resemble those of mayflies (Ephemeroptera), but have gills on the thorax. Empty skin cases shed during the final nymph stages are often found stuck to rocks along river banks.

- 2 families; ±35 species.

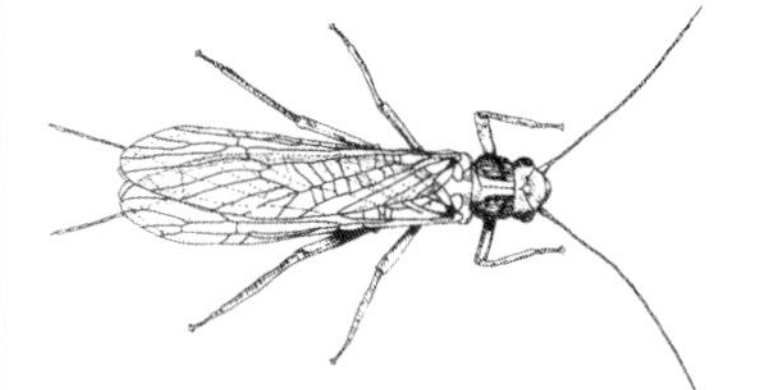

- Can be confused with cockroaches (Blattaria) and some crickets (Gryllidae), but the hind legs of the stonefly are not modified for jumping (as in most crickets). Also similar to web-spinners (Embiodea).

STICK INSECTS

ORDER: PHASMATODEA (ALSO KNOWN AS PHASMIDA)

Very large (60–250mm). Thin, stick-like insects with elongated thoracic segments. Thorax and abdomen approximately the same length. Head directed forward, eyes small. Some are wingless; winged types have slim leathery forewings. Sit still or in rocking motion on host plant; very well camouflaged.

Winged species are attracted to lights at night.

- 2 families; 32 species.
- Can be confused with heel-walkers (Mantophasmatodea) and mantids (Mantodea), but front legs are not modified for grasping.

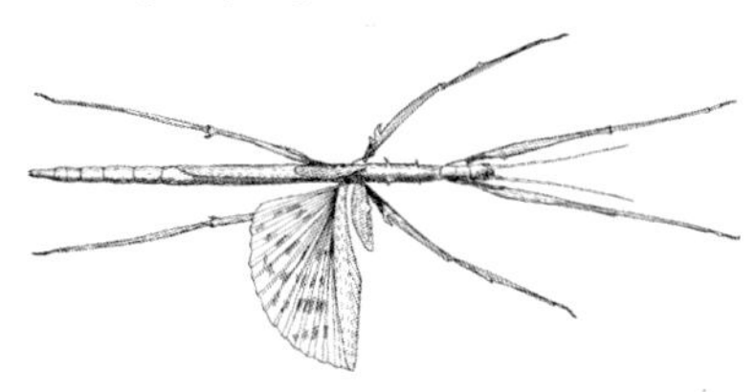

PSOCIDS OR BOOKLICE
ORDER: PSOCOPTERA (=PSOCODEA)

Small to medium-sized (1–10mm). Soft insects with unusually large, mobile heads, long antennae, and four identical wings that fold 'roof-like' over the abdomen when at rest. Wingless species occur. Feed on algae, fungi, lichen on bark, and dead plant matter. Some infest old books and cereals.

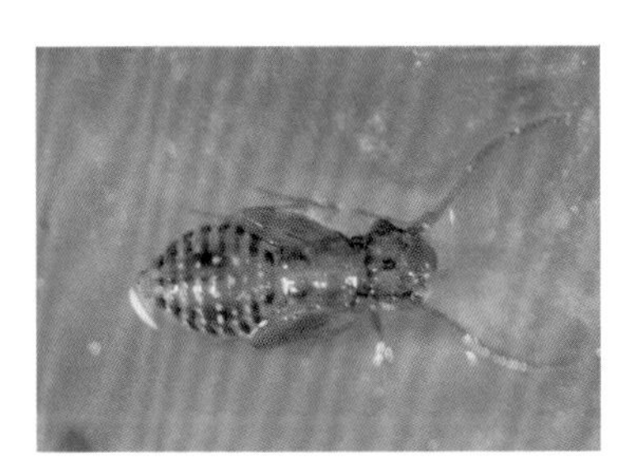

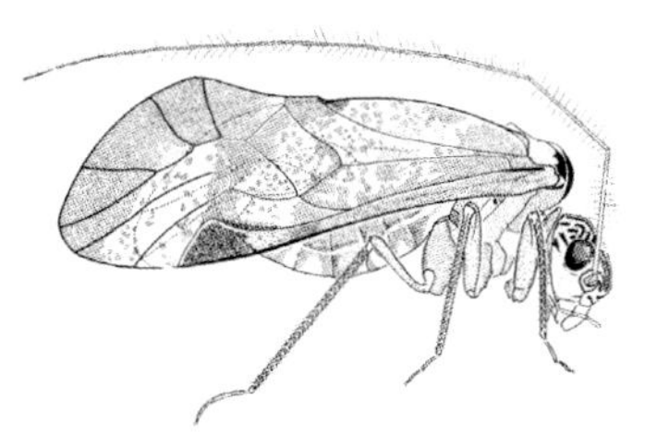

- 18 families; 80 species.
- Can be confused with some small bugs (Hemiptera), for example jumping plant lice (Psyllidae) and leafhoppers (Cicadellidae), but these have short antennae, hind legs that are adapted for jumping, and sucking mouthparts. Wingless Psocoptera species may be confused with certain lice (Phthiraptera), but the latter have short antennae and claws on the feet.

LICE
ORDER: PHTHIRAPTERA

Mostly small with some medium-sized species (1.5–11mm). Parasites of birds and mammals. Always flattened, with claws on their feet (tarsi) that enable them to cling to the hair or feathers of their host. Possess biting or piercing-sucking mouthparts, which are directed forward. Cement eggs or 'nits' to the hair or feathers of the host.

- Can be confused with bedbugs (Cimicidae), but these do not have tarsal claws and their sucking mouthparts are underneath the head. Bee lice (Braulidae) are similar, but they are found only on bees and their mouthparts are directed downward.

BIRD LICE
Suborder: Amblycera

Small to medium-sized (2–8mm). Very host-specific; almost all live on birds. Also found inside throat pouches of pelicans.

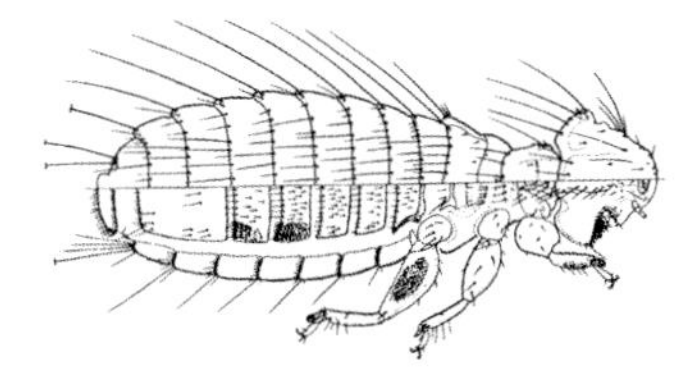

- 4 families; 318 species.

BITING BIRD LICE
Suborder: Ischnocera

Small to medium-sized (2–12mm). Biting mouthparts without long proboscis. Extremely host-specific; almost all are found on birds. Eggs (nits) glued to feathers of host (see photograph below).

- 2 families; ±630 species.

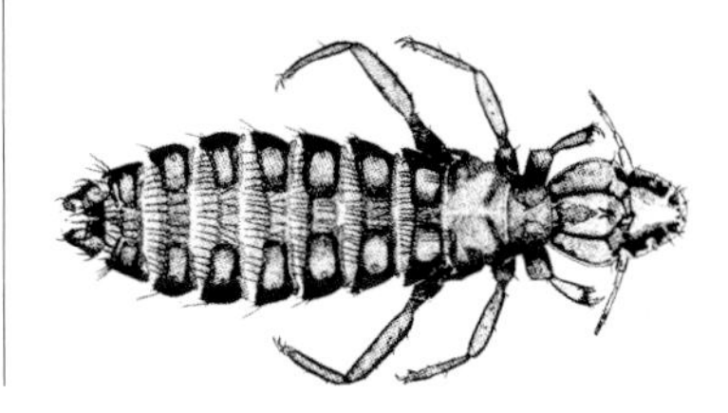

ELEPHANT LICE

Suborder: Rhynchophthirina

Small (4mm). Characterised by an elongated proboscis. Found on elephants and warthogs.

- 1 family; 2 species.

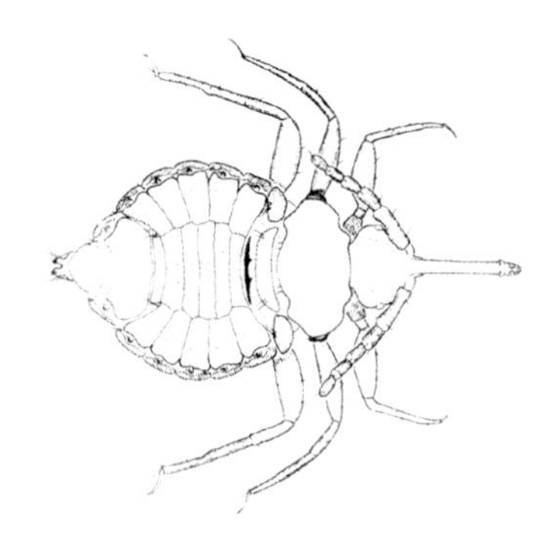

MAMMAL LICE

Suborder: Anoplura

Small (1–3mm). All have sucking mouthparts. Live on mammals. The well-known head and body louse (*Pediculus humanus*) and pubic louse (*Phthirus pubis*) found on humans belong to this suborder.

- 12 families; ±130 species.

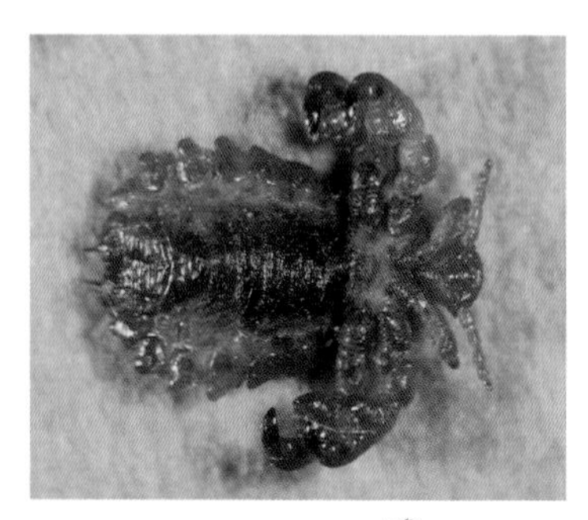

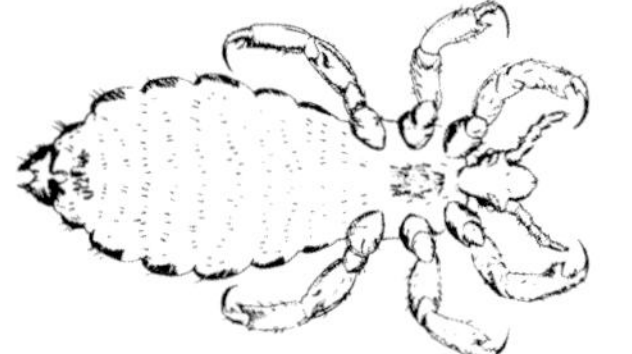

THRIPS

ORDER: THYSANOPTERA

Small (1–2mm). Slender thorax. Head narrower than abdomen. Mouthparts are skewed and asymmetrical. Last tarsal segments are enlarged and bulbous. Winged species have fringed wings. Found on flowers, but also elsewhere on plants. Most species grate plants and then drink the plant juice. Some are predators of small insects and mites; others feed on fungus. A number of species are serious agricultural pests on a variety of crops.

- 6 families; 282 species.
- Can be confused with web-spinners (Embiodea).

Hair-fringed wings

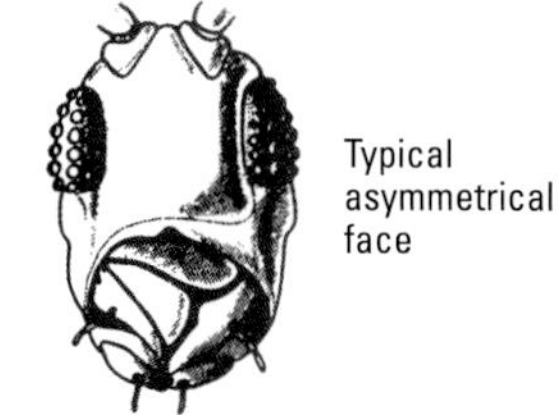

Typical asymmetrical face

CRICKETS, KATYDIDS, GRASSHOPPERS, LOCUSTS

ORDER: ORTHOPTERA

This order contains two relatively distinct suborders: long-horned crickets and katydids (suborder Ensifera) and short-horned grasshoppers and locusts (suborder Caelifera). Winged and wingless species occur in both suborders. Front wings are sturdier and tougher than hind wings. Hind legs are enlarged, with a stout femur, and are adapted for jumping in most families.

- 20 families.
- Cannot be confused with any other insects, as the modified hind legs are very distinctive. Families that do not have enlarged hind legs for jumping – mole crickets (Gryllotalpidae) and bladder grasshoppers (Pneumoridae) – can be identified by their unique appearance.

CRICKETS, CRICKET-LIKE FAMILIES

Suborder: Ensifera

Long antennae that exceed body length. Hearing organs are located on the fore-tibiae, and sounds are produced by rubbing together the edges of the forewings. Females have long ovipositors. Mostly nocturnal.

- 10 families.
- Can be confused with grasshopper-like families (Caelifera), but long antennae are diagnostic.

Katydids, bush crickets, long-horned grasshoppers

Family: Tettigoniidae

Medium-sized to very large (20–103mm). Mostly green, sometimes dull brown, with very long, thin antennae. Forewings mostly broad and leaf-shaped; used to imitate leaves as camouflage. Females have a large sickle-shaped ovipositor. A few very large but slender predatory species have spiny protrusions on the tarsi. Most are plant eaters; others are aggressive predators whose bite will draw blood. Nocturnal.

- ±160 species.
- Can be confused with grasshoppers (Caelifera), but long antennae and ovipositor of female are distinguishing characteristics.

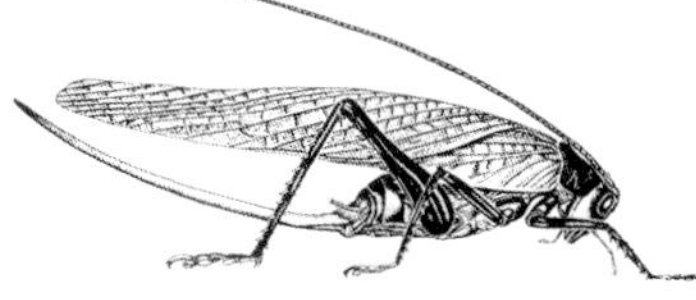

Female with long ovipositor

Mole crickets

Family: Gryllotalpidae

Medium-sized to large (20–30mm). Forelegs extremely modified for burrowing. Forewings are reduced and do not cover the longitudinally folded hind wings. Nymphs take up to two years to reach adulthood. Dig tunnels in moist soil. Feed on roots, and are sometimes a pest in lawns.

- Only 4 species (all in the genus *Gryllotalpa*).

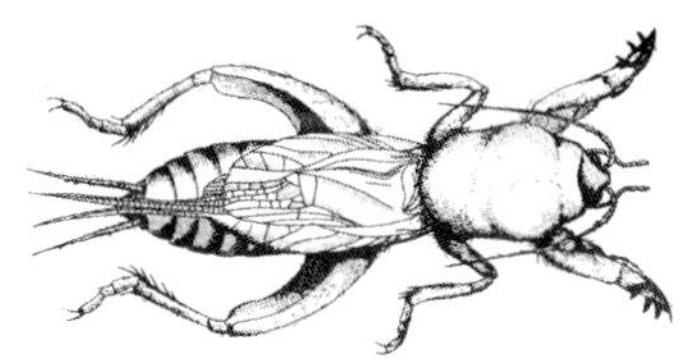

King crickets, Parktown prawns

Family: Anostostomatidae

Medium-sized to very large (20–70mm). Clumsy and wingless. Males often sport grotesquely enlarged mandibles. The Parktown prawn (*Libanasidus vittatus*) is a well-known member of this family. Most species are omnivorous and nocturnal, and have a variety of habitats, both moist and dry.

- 14 species.

Armoured ground crickets, corn crickets

Family: Bradyporidae

Mostly large (21–50mm). Wingless crickets with distinctive spiky protrusions on the large hardened pronotum and dorsally on the abdomen. Hind femur only slightly enlarged. They walk rather than jump. Short wing stumps under rear end of the thoracic shield are used for stridulation. In arid areas (the Karoo, Namibia and the Kalahari), their numbers may greatly increase during autumn, when they become cannibalistic and

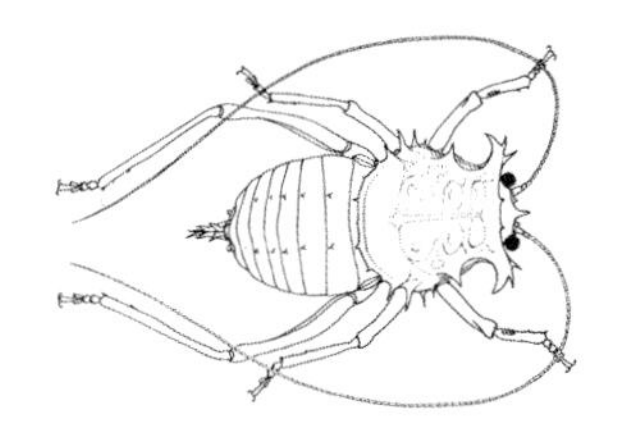

devour each other. Some species are, from time to time, regarded as agricultural pests.

- 14 species.

Dune crickets

Family: Schizodactylidae

Medium-sized (10–25mm). Pale, wingless crickets, with characteristic swollen fore- and middle tibiae and broad, branched 'sand shoes' on tarsi. Strong hind legs make for long-distance jumps. Found in sand dunes of Northern Cape, Namibia and the Kalahari.

- 8 species (all in the genus *Comicus*).

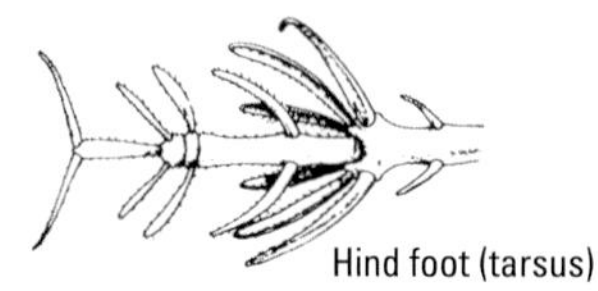

Hind foot (tarsus)

Crickets

Family: Gryllidae

Medium-sized to large (10–40mm). Winged or wingless crickets with relatively long abdominal appendages (cerci). Winged males stridulate using their forewings. Males are territorial and will attack each other. True crickets are omnivorous or plant feeders. Family includes well-known common household species, such as the house cricket (*Gryllus bimaculatus*), the thermometer cricket (*Acanthogryllus fortipes*) and tree crickets (*Oecanthus* spp.).

- More than 70 species.

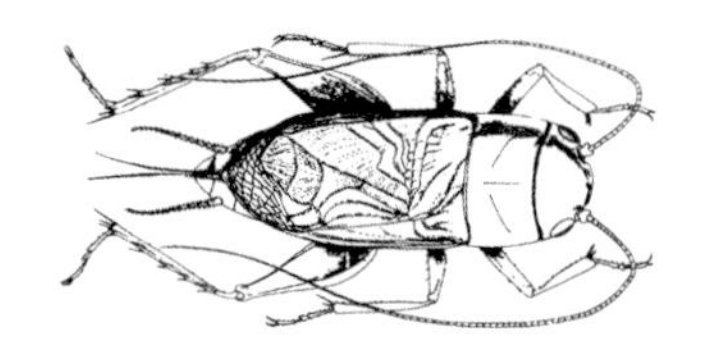

GRASSHOPPERS, GRASSHOPPER-LIKE FAMILIES

Suborder: Caelifera

Grasshoppers and their relatives have short antennae (less than half their body length), short ovipositors and markedly short cerci. Hearing organs are located on the sides between the thorax and abdomen. Stridulation happens by rubbing the hind legs against the forewings or abdomen. Mostly diurnal.

- 10 families.

Water grasshoppers

Family: Tetrigidae

Medium-sized (5–15mm). Thoracic shield extended in such a way that it covers the wings to the rear. Found along freshwater shores; can swim well by kicking with hind legs. Diurnal; sometimes attracted to lights at night.

- 23 species.

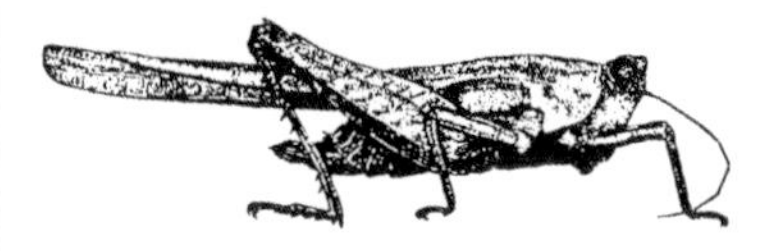

Bladder grasshoppers

Family: Pneumoridae

Large to very large (40–90mm). Males green, with balloon-like inflated abdomens. Females have a more 'normal' build and are wingless. Hind legs are not adapted for jumping. Males produce a loud hoarse sound with their abdomen as amplifier. Stridulate by rubbing hind legs against abdominal ridges. Found in coastal dune fields around South Africa.

- 17 species (almost entirely endemic to South Africa).

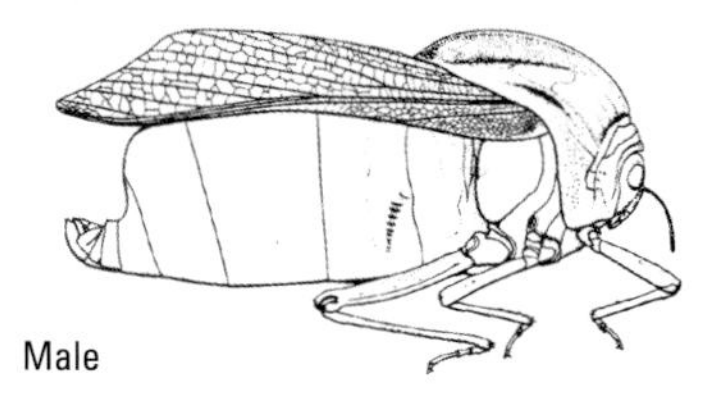

Male

Rain locusts, saw-backed locusts

Family: Pamphagidae

Very large (50–75mm). Prominent keel-like crest on pronotum. Blade-shaped antennae often broad. Well camouflaged on bark. Males of *Lamarckiana* spp. produce an incessant noise on summer nights.

- More than 71 species (often very localised).

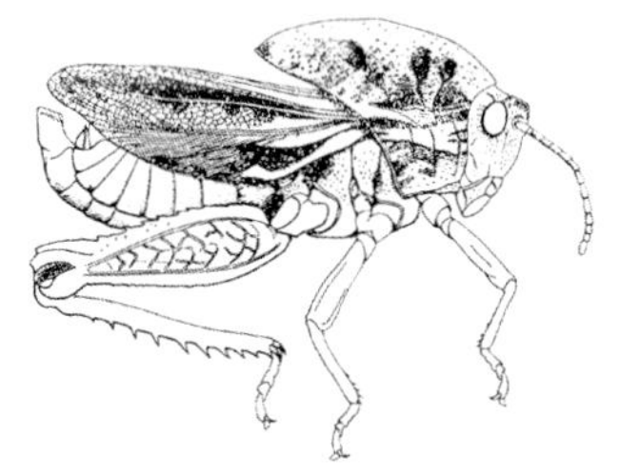

Foam grasshoppers, stink locusts, lubber grasshoppers

Family: Pyrgomorphidae

Large (25–75mm). Either wingless (see photograph below) or with winged and wingless individuals in the same species. All secrete poisonous haemolymph through reflex bleeding and are unpalatable or inedible. Their bright coloration warns predators of their inedibility. Nymphs (and sometimes adults) often form swarms.

- 40 species.

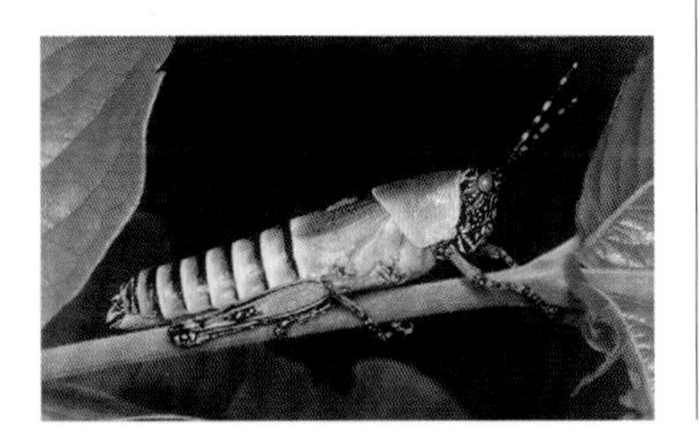

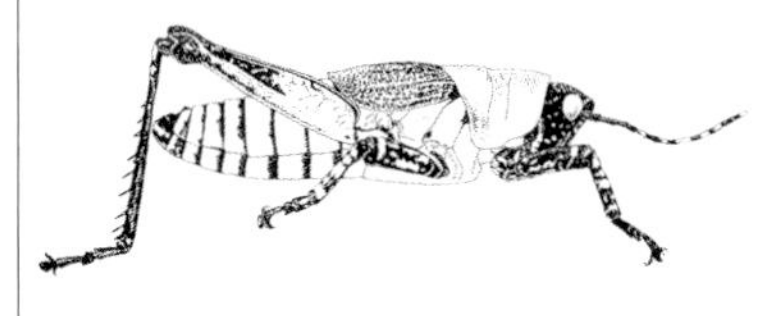

Bush grasshoppers

Family: Lentulidae

Medium-sized to large (15–36mm). Mostly wingless.

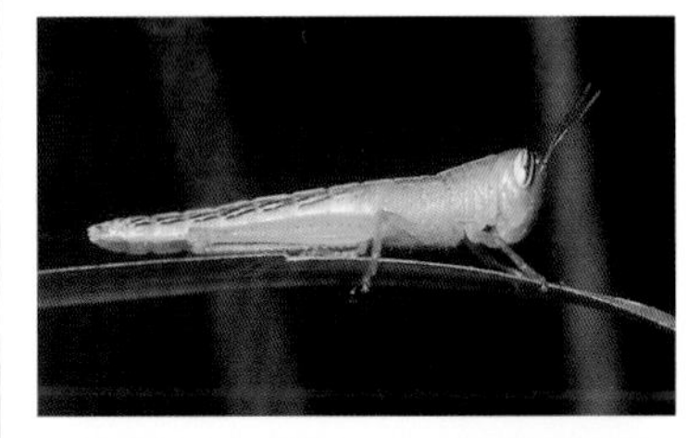

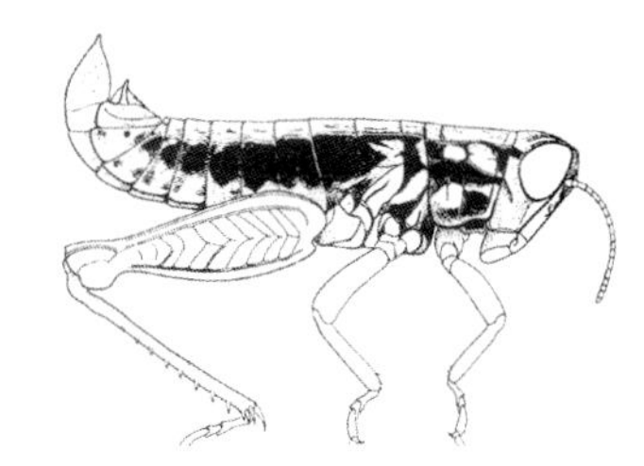

Prefer leaves to grass for feeding. Easily confused with the nymphs of other grasshopper families.

- 50 species (mostly localised, with the largest diversity of species in the world found in South Africa).

Stone grasshoppers

Family: Lathiceridae

Medium-sized to large (16–40mm). Always with broad, squat build. Antennae are short and can be withdrawn into special grooves, possibly to protect against the sandblasting effect of the desert wind. Coloration matches the sand or gravel of their desert habitat. Found only in the Namib Desert.

- 5 species.

Locusts, short-horned grasshoppers

Family: Acrididae

Medium-sized to very large (20–72mm). Includes locusts in both migratory and solitary forms. Almost all true locusts are winged and have hearing organs located laterally on the abdomen. Some species have brightly coloured hind wings that are only displayed during flight. Several short-horned grasshoppers have an elongated head with eyes placed near the top of the head, and are grass mimics. Most species are well camouflaged, blending with the vegetation on which they feed or the ground where they rest.

- ±360 species.

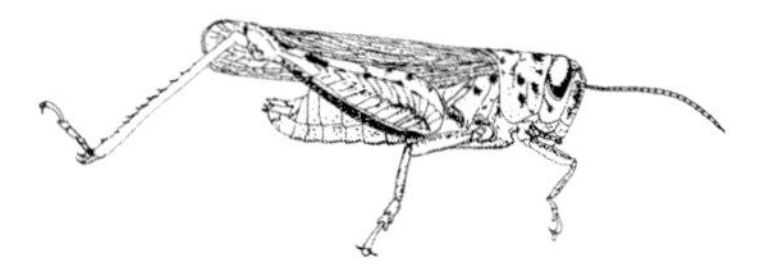

BUGS

ORDER: HEMIPTERA

This is the largest order of hemimetabolous insects in which the young develop into adults without going through a pupal stage. This highly diverse order comprises three suborders: Heteroptera (stink bugs and water bugs), Auchenorrhyncha and Sternorrhyncha.

Heteroptera includes unusual families such as Cimicidae (bedbugs) and the aquatic bugs (18 families in South Africa). The families of Sternorrhyncha include aphids (Aphididae) and their relatives, and the scale insects in the superfamily Coccoidea, some of which are barely recognisable as insects. Auchenorrhyncha contains those insects that look more or less like cicadas (Cicadidae).

- 92 families.
- Not likely to be confused with any other order, although two winged flies, mosquitoes and gnats (Diptera) have piercing-sucking mouthparts that are directed downward, a feature they share with hemipterans.

STINK BUGS AND WATER BUGS

Suborder: Heteroptera

The front ventral half of the forewing is hardened. In winged forms, wings lie at rest next to a large triangular central shield (scutellum), forming a distinctive X pattern on top of the abdomen. Stink glands are common in most families.

- 19 families.

Bedbugs

Family: Cimicidae

Small to medium-sized (4–7mm). Flattened, wingless, with oval abdomen. All are nest parasites of birds and mammals.

- 10 species.
- Can be confused with lice (Phthiraptera), but the sucking mouthparts of bedbugs are positioned downward, not forward. The claws typical of lice are absent in bedbugs.

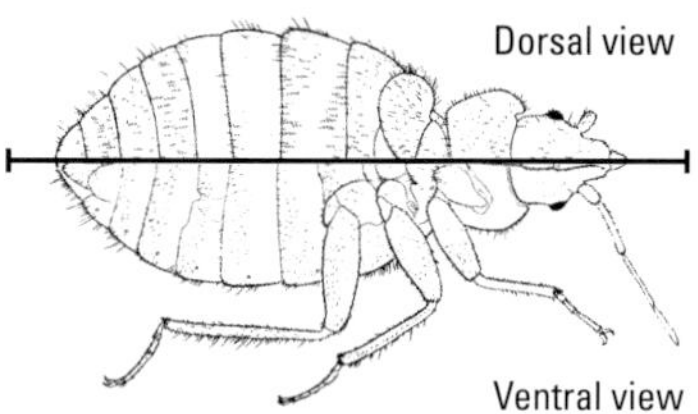

Leaf bugs, capsids

Family: Miridae

Small to medium-sized (2–12mm). Delicate bugs with thin antennae and legs. Wings are angled sharply downwards in rear half. Most live by sucking plant juices, but some prey on other insects.

- 250 species (probably still hundreds undescribed).

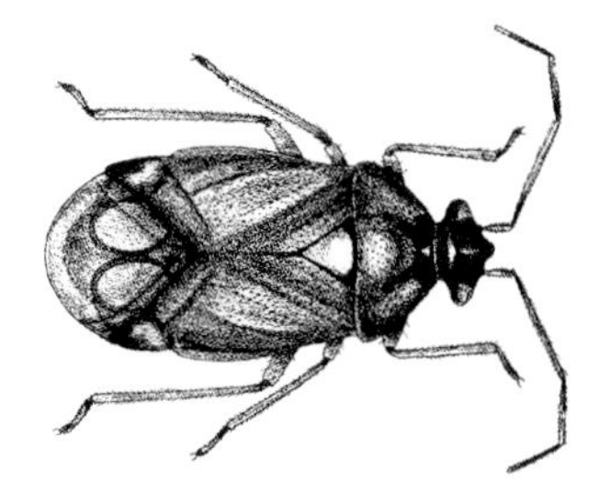

Lace bugs

Family: Tingidae

Small to medium-sized (2–7mm). Easily recognisable by species-specific lace-like patterns on wings and thorax. Live on and suck plant juice under leaves, causing white spots on vegetation. Some species cause galls.

- 200 species.

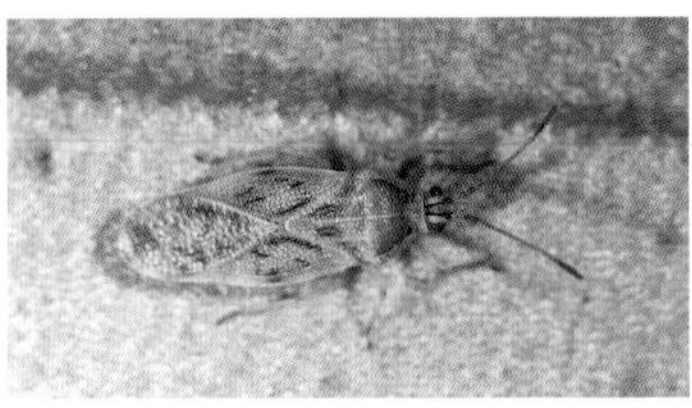

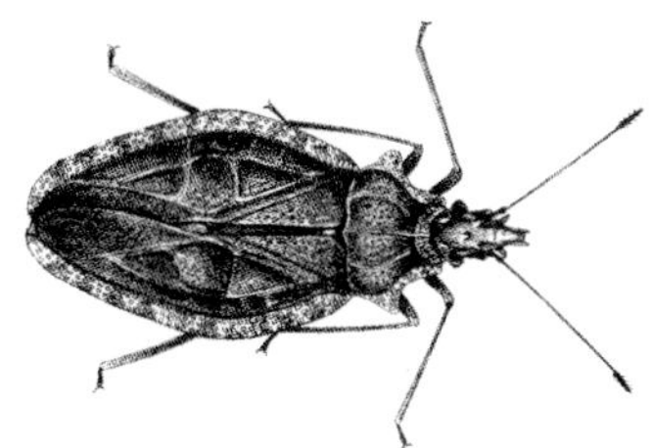

Assassin bugs

Family: Reduviidae

Medium-sized to large (5–40mm). Body shapes vary, from long and slender to robust and clumsy. Distinctive features are the long 'neck' at the back of the head and strong piercing-sucking mouthparts that, when viewed laterally, appear as a hardened snout (rostrum) curving in a sabre-like fashion from the front of the head. Stink glands and bright warning colours are often present; some slender species are well camouflaged in grasses. One subfamily has modified forelegs for grasping, similar to mantids (Mantodea). Assassin bugs are predators of other arthropods and are sometimes specific about their prey (usually other insects, but millipedes in some). Inflict a painful bite to humans in self-defence.

- ±500 species.

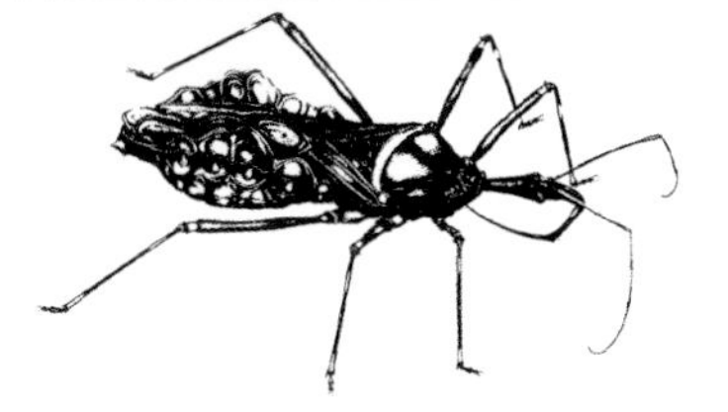

Twig wilters, squash bugs, leaf-footed bugs

Family: Coreidae

Medium-sized to large (5–40mm). Flattened dorsally, characteristic lateral protrusions on thorax and abdomen, and conspicuously coloured tips on antennae. Legs are leaf-like, often enlarged; spines may be present. Some species squirt a foul-smelling substance from their stink glands at the coxa over quite a distance. Suck plant juices from shoots, causing them to wilt.

- 150 species.

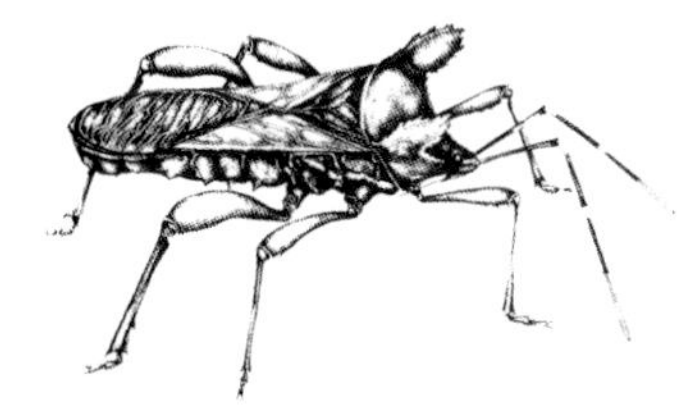

Cotton stainers, red bugs, fire bugs

Family: Pyrrhocoridae

Medium-sized (5–20mm). Oval-shaped, flattened dorsally, with bright (red or yellow with black) colour markings. Mate for days on end, attached tail-to-tail; males and females equally adept at walking backwards and forwards. Suck plant juices, mostly from seeds, but also shoots. The African cotton stainer (*Dysdercus nigrofasciatus*) is a serious pest on cotton.

- 35 species.
- Can be confused with seed bugs (Lygaeidae), but have more veins on their wings (more than seven), and lack simple eyes (ocelli).

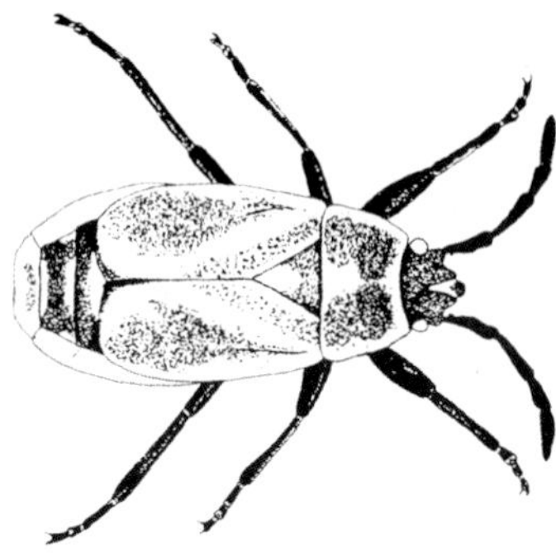

Seed bugs, ground bugs

Family: Lygaeidae

Small to medium-sized (2–20mm). Appear similar to red bugs (Pyrrhocoridae), but have fewer veins on their wings (fewer than six), and ocelli normally present. Some species are brightly coloured, but most are a dull grey. Often found congregating in large groups. Suck plant juices, mostly from seeds. The family has half a dozen subfamilies, which some regard as full families.

- 420 species.

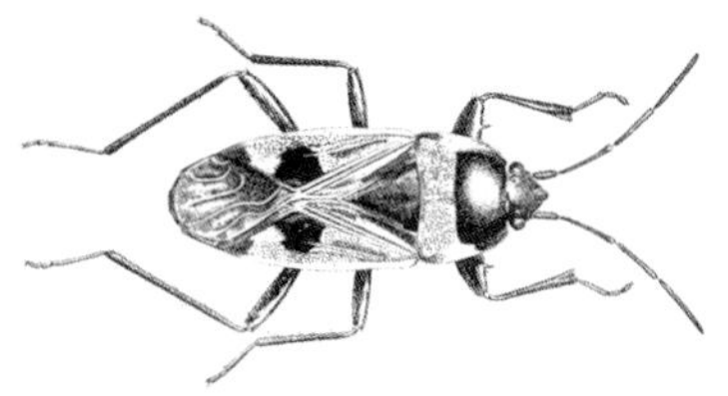

Burrowing bugs

Family: Cydnidae

Medium-sized (5–10mm). Glossy black or brown with smooth oval shape and large scutellum (shield). Glands in the thorax secrete a pungent odour. Normally found under the ground, where they live. Suck sap from roots. In sandy regions, attracted to lights at night after rain, often in very large numbers.

- 30 species.

- Can be confused with giant water bugs (Belostomatidae), but burrowing bugs have spiky protrusions on the legs and are not adapted for swimming. Can be distinguished from shield bugs (Pentatomidae) by their well-rounded thoracic edge and strong spines on the legs.

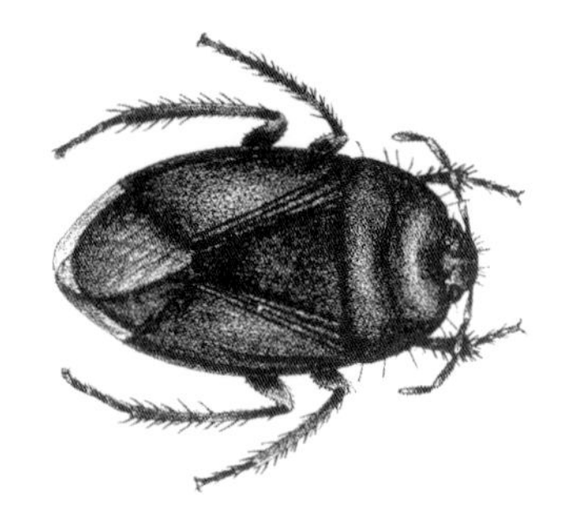

Pill bugs

Family: Plataspidae

Medium-sized (5–20mm). Oval and convex. The strongly enlarged scutellum covers the entire abdomen. Found in tropical parts of South Africa.

- 25 species.

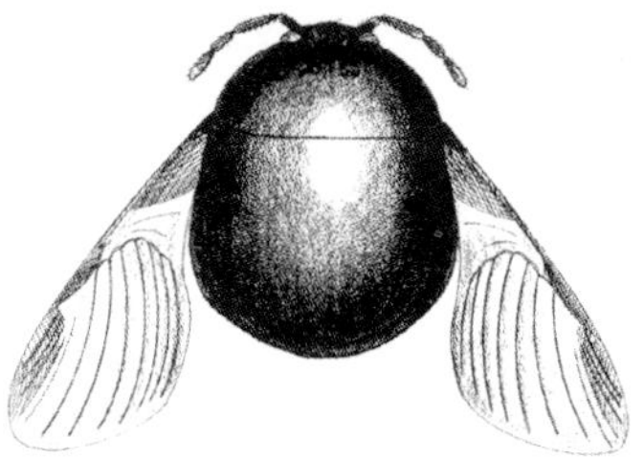

- Can be confused with beetles (Coleoptera), but mouthparts adapted for sucking. Shield over the wings does not have a seam down the middle. Differ from shield-backed bugs (Scutelleridae) (see below) in having an oval and extremely convex shape.

Shield-backed bugs

Family: Scutelleridae

Medium-sized (6–20mm). Scutellum enlarged and extended over the entire abdomen. Certain species are brightly coloured. All species suck plant sap.

- 30 species.

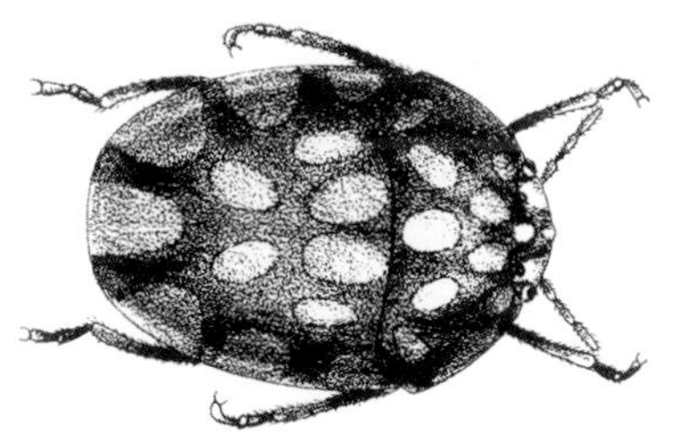

- Can be confused with beetles (Coleoptera). Some resemble weevils (Curculionidae) or jewel beetles (Buprestidae), but are distinguished by their sucking mouthparts and the absence of a seam down the middle of the back of the abdomen, which is characteristic of all beetles.

Inflated bugs

Family: Tessaratomidae

Medium-sized to large (15–30mm). Distinctive shape, green to yellow coloration. Sapsuckers on shrubs and trees. Some species become very abundant and are used as food by local people.

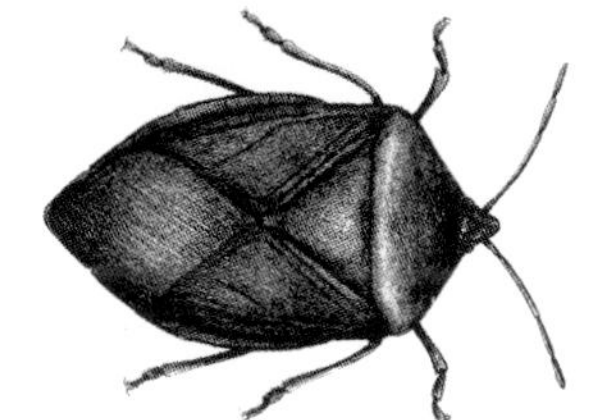

- 10 species.
- Can be confused with shield bugs, which they resemble, but in inflated bugs the dilated abdomen is wider than the pronotum.

Stink bugs, shield bugs

Family: Pentatomidae

Medium-sized (15–20mm). Distinctive shield-shaped body with a large triangular scutellum (shield). Thorax of most species has spiny protrusions on the sides. All species have stink glands, and most feed on plant sap. A few species are agricultural pests, but some are predators on other insects.

- 300 species.
- Can be confused with inflated bugs and burrowing bugs (Cydnidae).

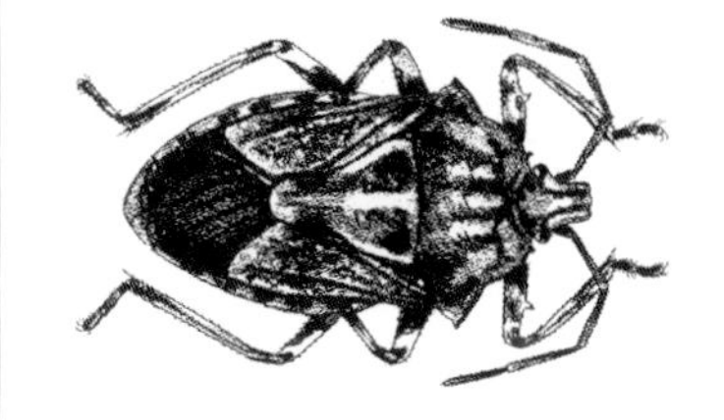

Water striders

Family: Hydrometridae

Medium-sized (±10mm). Very thin and elongated, dull bugs. Predominantly wingless. Eyes positioned in the middle of an extremely elongated head. Occur at or on fresh water. Feed mostly by sucking dead insects.

- 5 species.
- Can be confused with small stick insects (Phasmatodea), but have sucking mouthparts. The mouthparts of water striders look similar to those of several species of assassin bug (Reduviidae), but the legs of water striders are set more widely apart.

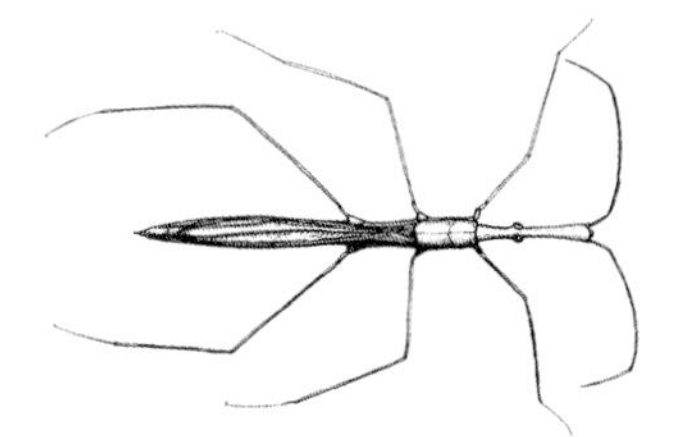

Pond skaters

Family: Gerridae

Medium-sized (5–20mm). The four hind legs are extremely long and thin; forelegs are folded, and modified for grasping. Utilise surface tension of water and long legs to walk on top of water. Hunt insects that have fallen into the water.

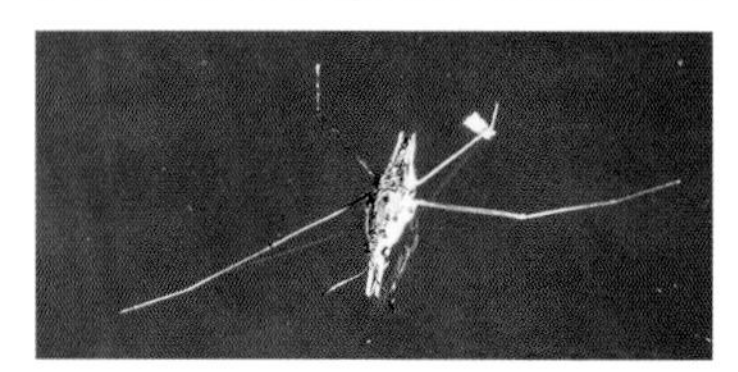

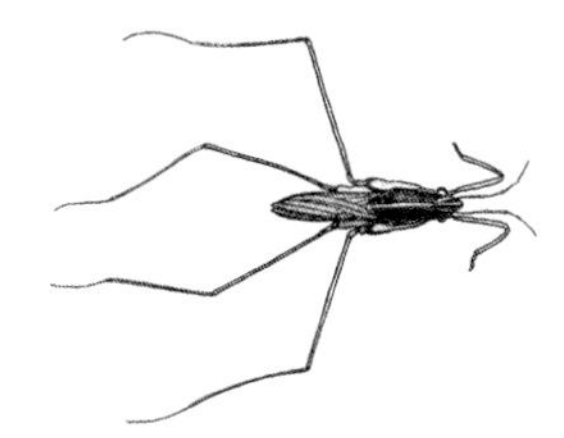

- 16 species.

Water boatmen

Family: Corixidae

Small to medium-sized (1–8mm). Flat, elliptical aquatic bugs. Hind legs are modified into large 'oars' for underwater swimming. Feed predominantly on plant matter (which is unusual for water bugs), but some species feed on plankton or gnat maggots. Fly at night.

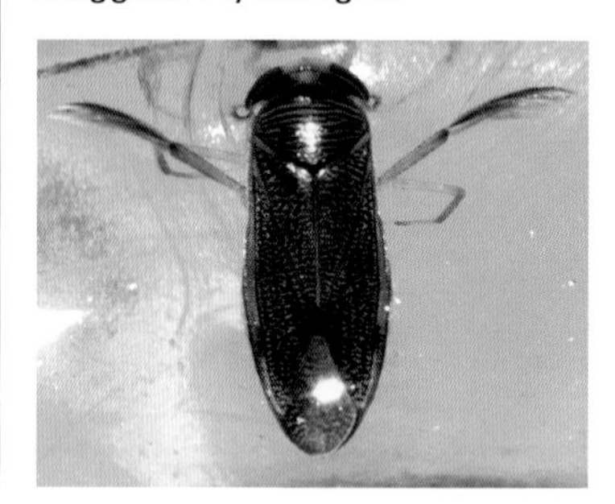

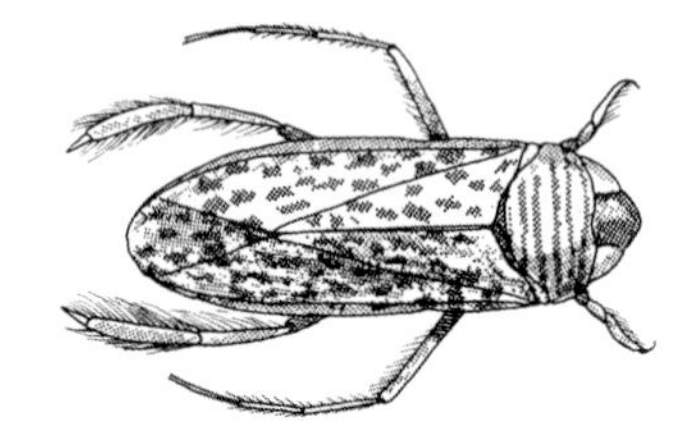

- 26 species.
- Can be confused with backswimmers (Notonectidae), but the keel-shaped back is absent and they do not swim upside down. Look similar to saucer bugs (Naucoridae), but differ in having broader heads and oar-shaped hind legs.

Backswimmers

Family: Notonectidae

Small to medium-sized (4–11mm). Characteristic keel-shaped back. Hind legs resemble long oars; front legs modified for grasping. Swim upside down under the water surface. Predators of small aquatic insects. Can fly at night.

- 28 species.
- Can be confused with water boatmen (Corixidae).

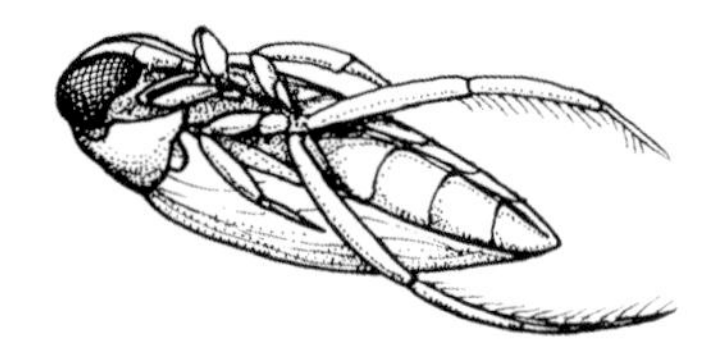

Water scorpions

Family: Nepidae

Medium-sized to large (without 'tail', 20–45mm). Flat, long to oval, with raptorial forelegs, thin middle and hind legs, and an abdominal breathing tube

that exceeds their body length. Swim or walk under water among vegetation, with 'snorkel' protruding above the surface of the water for breathing. They are predators, feeding on aquatic insects and tadpoles. Can fly at night.

- 13 species.

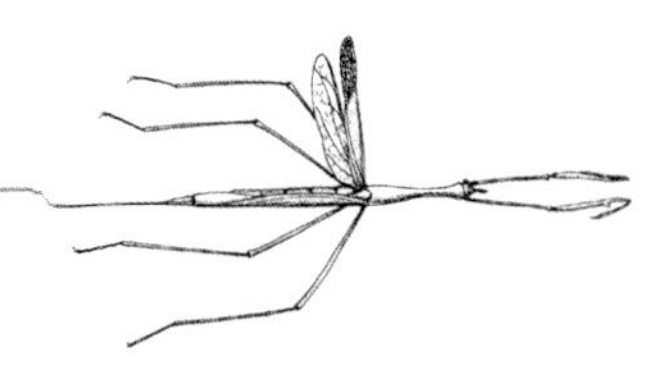

Saucer bugs

Family: Naucoridae

Medium-sized (9–14mm). Live under water but do not have significantly modified legs for swimming. Nocturnal fliers.

- 11 species.
- Can be confused with water boatmen (Corixidae), but the body is broader and oval.

Giant water bugs

Family: Belostomatidae

Medium-sized to very large (12–80mm). Raptorial forelegs; four hind legs adapted for swimming. Forward-projecting piercing-sucking mouthparts. All species are predators. Nocturnal fliers.

- 10 species.

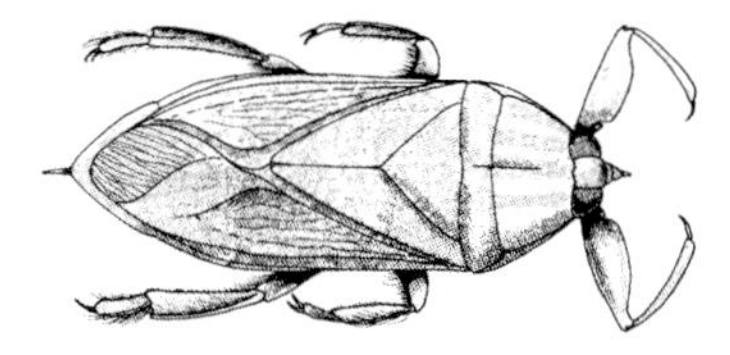

Suborder: Auchenorrhyncha

Forewings uniform in appearance from front to back, slightly more hardened than hind wings. Wings folded roof-like over body when resting. No stink glands. Antennae reduced to spiky hairs.

- 21 families.

Lantern bug group

Superfamily: Fulgoroidea

This superfamily, also known as the grouping Fulgoromorpha, is extremely diverse, and the easiest way of identifying its members is by elimination: small bugs without stink glands (Auchenorrhyncha) that are not cicadas, spittle bugs, leafhoppers, treehoppers or mealy bugs, and that do not belong to any of the aphid or scale insect groups (Sternorrhyncha), belong to this superfamily.

- 15 families; 260 species.

Long-winged snout bugs

Family: Derbidae

Medium-sized (10–15mm). Wings are held upright.

- 14 species.

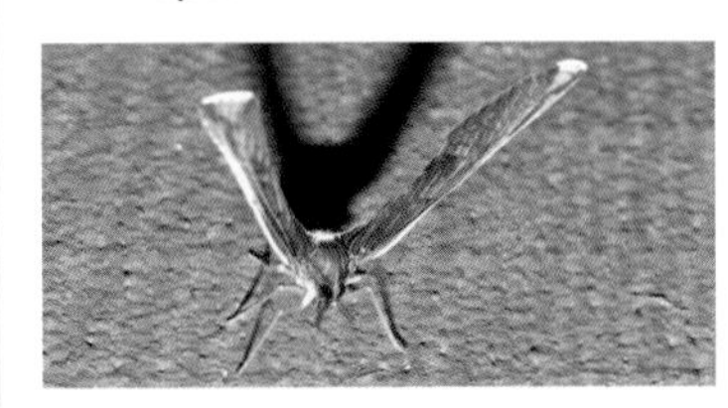

Lantern bugs, snout bugs

Family: Fulgoridae

Medium-sized to large (10–40mm). Often with distinctive elongation of head into a horn-like protuberance.

- 22 species.

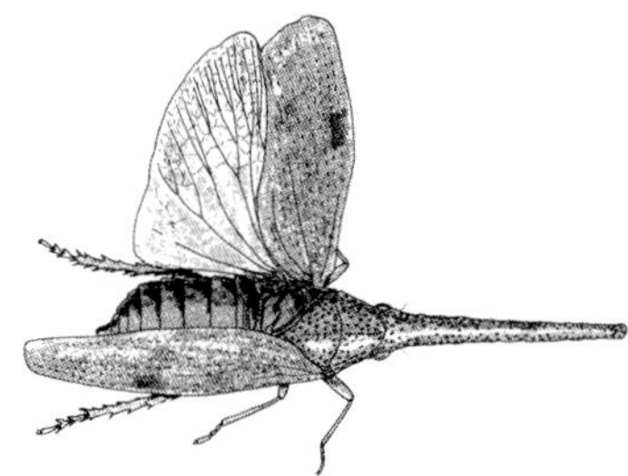

Dictyopharid planthoppers

Family: Dictyopharidae

Small to medium-sized (5–15mm). Broad wings and pointed heads.

- 41 species.

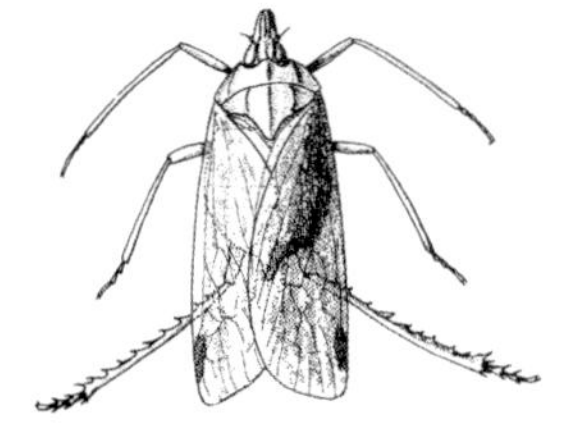

Moth bugs

Family: Flatidae

Medium-sized (8–12mm). Very broad wings that are folded roof-like, with a sharp peak, against the body when resting. Head with rounded ridge in front.

- 21 species.

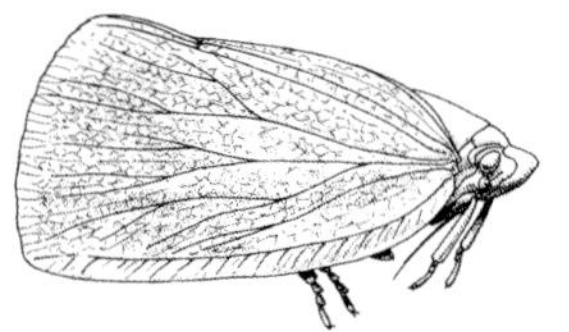

Fly bugs

Family: Ricaniidae

Small (±5mm). Moth-like plant-feeding bugs with flat, rounded wings that are not folded roof-like against the body when at rest.

- 10 species.
- Can be confused with moth flies (Psychodidae), but they do not have long, plumed antennae and are generally not hairy.

Lophopids

Family: Lophopidae

Medium-sized (±10mm). Wings noticeably broad and flattened. Forelegs enlarged and flattened.

- 7 species.

Cicadomorpha group

The following four families do not belong to the superfamily Fulgoroidea, but are representative of the informal group of plant-eating bugs known as Cicadomorpha, comprising several superfamilies.

Spittle bugs, froghoppers

Family: Cercopidae

Medium-sized (10–15mm). Opaque forewings, often brightly coloured. Nymphs bubble air through excreted plant sap, thereby protecting themselves in the 'bubble bath'.

- 33 species.
- Can be confused with small cicadas (Cicadidae), but the head is transversely blade-shaped in front, not a ridged bulge. Hind legs lack the spiny protrusions of leafhoppers (Cicadellidae) and are not adapted for jumping.

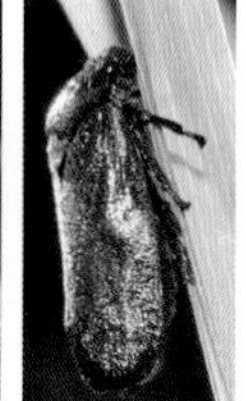

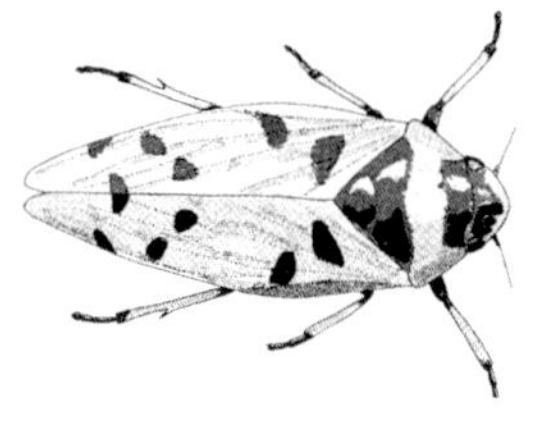

Cicadas, Christmas singers

Family: Cicadidae

Medium-sized to large (15–50mm). Some species with transparent wings, but more often with colour markings on wings. Thorax often with lateral extensions. Legs not adapted for jumping. Males have large membranes on the sides of the abdomen with which they produce their characteristic shrill sound. Nymphs live under the ground and have forelegs adapted for digging.

- At least 160 species.
- Can be confused with spittle bugs (Cercopidae).

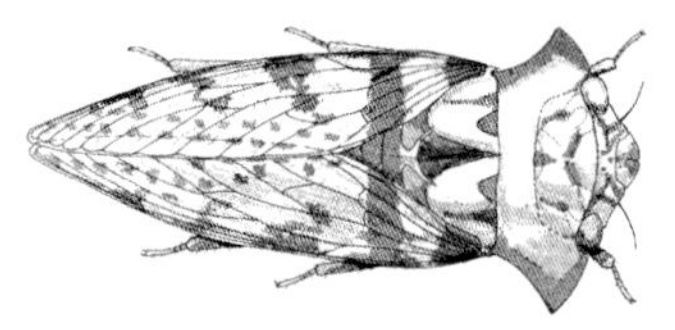

Leafhoppers

Family: Cicadellidae

Small to medium-sized (2–8mm). Mostly green or brown, with some brightly coloured. Body shape resembles that of cicadas (Cicadidae). Hind legs have spiky protrusions, similar to those of grasshoppers (Acrididae), and are adapted for jumping. Many species are agricultural pests; all are sapsuckers and some spread plant diseases.

- 350 species.
- Can be confused with several families of Fulgoroidea, but these all lack the spiked legs adapted for jumping.

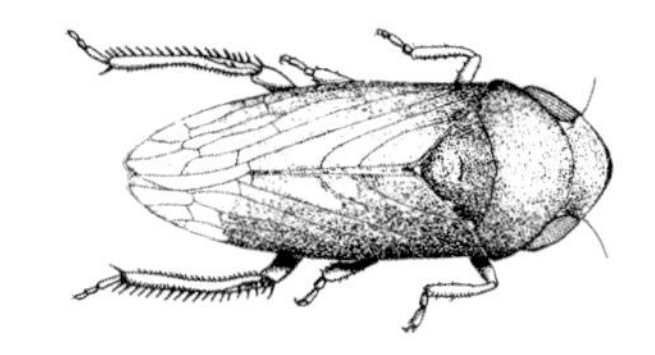

Treehoppers

Family: Membracidae

Small to medium-sized (4–8mm). Legs adapted for jumping. Wings are transparent. Distinct, prominent thorn-like growths on the pronotum, with one spanning the entire length of the abdomen and the others protruding laterally. Often mimic the thorns of their host plant.

- 120 species.

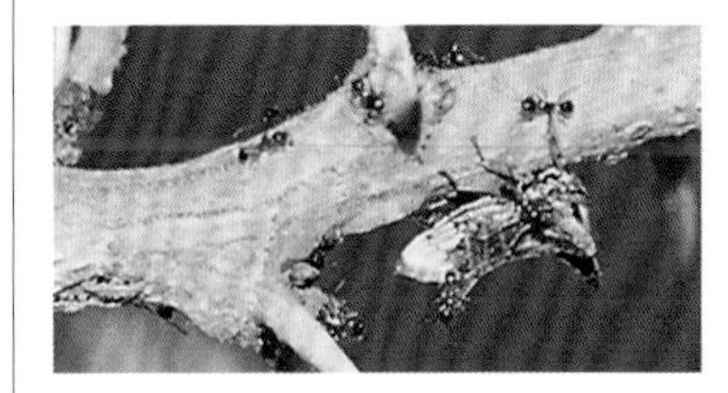

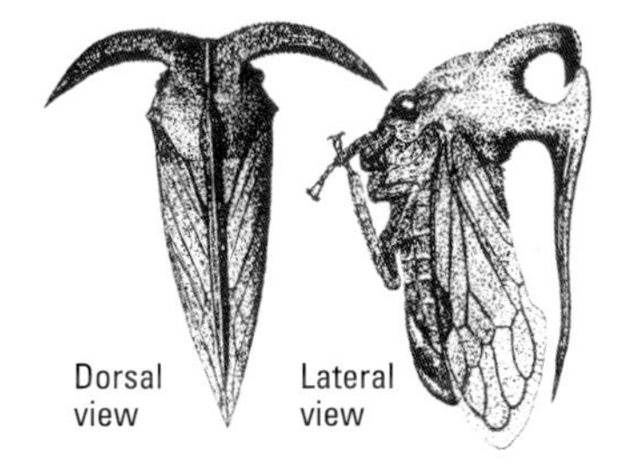

APHIDS, PLANT LICE, SCALE INSECTS AND THEIR KIN

Suborder: Sternorrhyncha

All winged species in this suborder have identical front and hind wings. Some species are wingless. This suborder includes all scale insects (Coccoidea), aphids and other scale-like insects.

- 19 families.

Jumping plant lice, psyllas

Family: Psyllidae (including Triozidae)

Small (1.5–5mm). Look like minute cicadas (Cicadidae), but with transparent wings, mostly with no colour markings. Hind legs lack spines and are adapted for jumping. Antennae well developed. The African citrus psylla (*Trioza erytreae*) transmits a virus to citrus trees that causes 'greening disease' and is an important agricultural pest.

- 61 species.

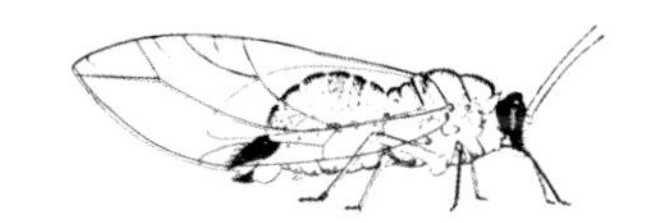

Whiteflies

Family: Aleyrodidae

Small (1–2mm). Wings shaped like those of moth flies (Psychodidae), but mostly covered in a white or grey powdery substance. Some transmit plant viruses and are serious pests.

- More than 20 species.
- Can be confused with moth flies (Psychodidae) and dusty-winged lacewings (Coniopterygidae), but are always much smaller.

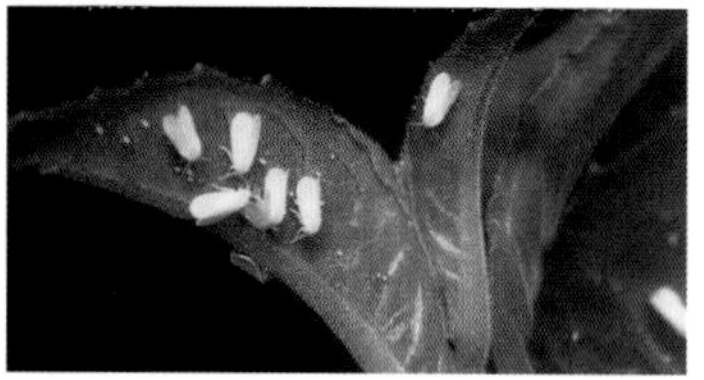

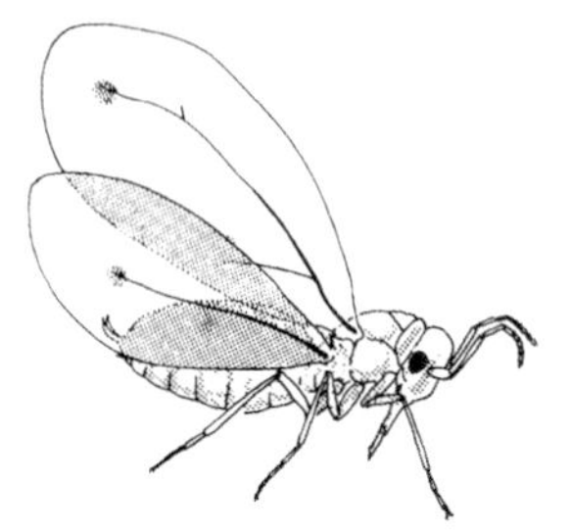

Aphids, plant lice, green flies

Family: Aphididae

Small (1–4mm). Mostly wingless; but winged individuals can be produced at times. Antennae are long and there are two protrusions (tubercles) on the tip of the round abdomen. Breed in large colonies on host plants and are tended by ants. Many species are agricultural pests.

- 165 species.

- Winged forms may be mistaken for jumping plant lice (Psyllidae), but, unlike Aphididae, they have longer abdomens and no tubercles on the abdomen. Males of soft-scale insects (Coccidae) differ from aphids in that they have only two wings.

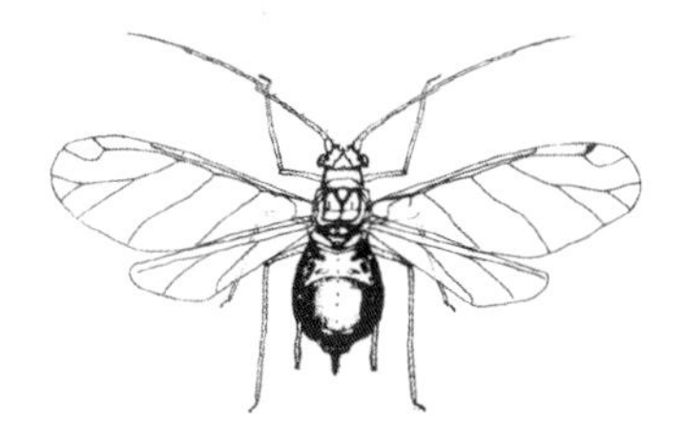

Scale insects and their kin

Superfamily: Coccoidea

All members of this superfamily are strictly plant sapsuckers but vary in host specificity. Females and larvae are always immobile, with reduced appendages, and are hidden underneath a wax-like or hard shell secreted by the insect. Males are small and winged, but do not feed. Many species reproduce parthenogenetically and therefore do not have males.

Young larvae are called 'crawlers' and either move actively or are carried on the wind until they reach a favourable place to settle and feed. They attach themselves and start developing their shells, which have a characteristic species-specific shape.

Most scale insects secrete honeydew that ants find irresistible. Ants are always found in the presence of such scale insects and they protect them against their natural enemies, parasitic wasps being the most common. Honeydew often causes the growth of fungus on the host plant.

Scale insects comprise some of the most serious agricultural, silvicultural and horticultural pests. They play a significant role in the international fruit trade, as infested fruit cannot be exported and marketed.

- 15 families.

Ground pearls, giant coccids

Family: Margarodidae

Small to large (ground pearls: 1–3mm; giant coccids: up to 40mm). Blob-like, with much reduced appendages. Readily recognisable by the shell they secrete. The females of ground pearls form cysts in distinctive glossy-gold shells underground, where all stadia suck root sap. Some giant coccids have bizarre growths, which are leathery and not hardened. A number of species are imported pests, for example Australian bug (*Icerya purchasi*), a worldwide

Ground pearl (encapsulated)

pest on citrus and other plants and one of the few known hermaphroditic insects.

- ±13 species (ground pearls); 4 species (giant coccids).

Soft-scale insects

Family: Coccidae

Small to medium-sized (1–25mm). Soft blob-like insects with a thin to very thick waxy shell. First-stage nymphs ('crawlers') actively seek out new host plants. Males have only two wings, are often red, and have long wax 'tails'. Intensively visited by ants for their honeydew. Several species are pests.

- 130 species.

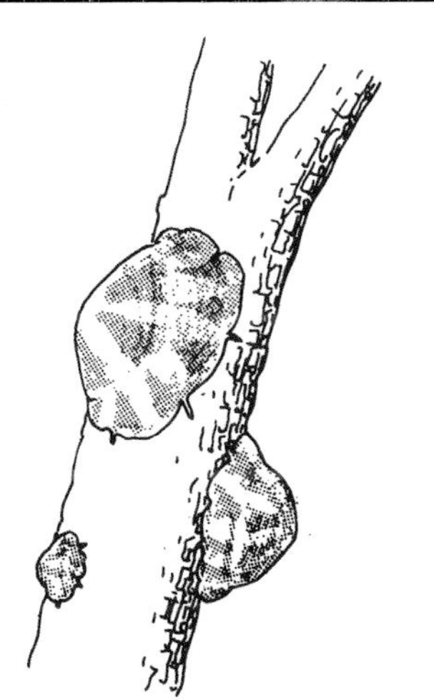

Armoured scale insects

Family: Diaspididae

Small (1–3mm). Blob-like, but with thin, hard shells. Do not secrete honeydew. Commonly found on leaves and branches of almost all indigenous plants. Several species are pests, for example, red scale (*Aonidiella aurantii*), which is found on citrus.

- 270 species.

Pupa

Mealy bugs

Family: Pseudococcidae

Small (2–5mm). Same as soft-scale insects (Coccidae), but with the secreted shell not attached to the host plant and covered with a powdery wax. Spiny protrusions along the sides and 'tails'. Ants are attracted by their copious secretions of honeydew. Serious pests on citrus and in vineyards; some can transmit plant viruses.

- 61 species (in South Africa).

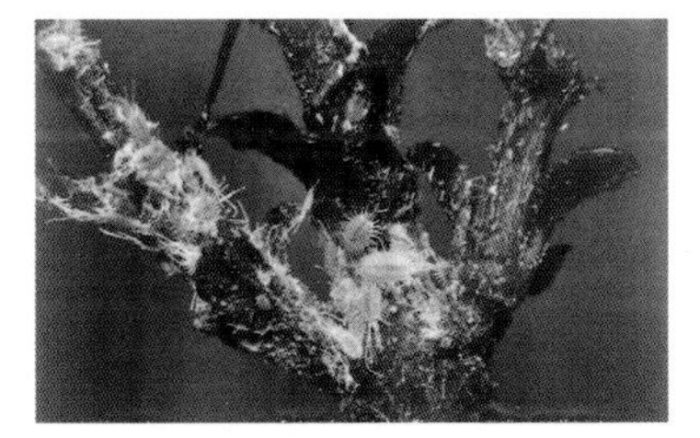

THE HOLOMETABOLOUS ORDERS

These are the more evolved orders with a pupal stage in their life cycle.

DOBSONFLIES, ALDERFLIES

ORDER: MEGALOPTERA

Medium-sized to very large (8–75mm). Primitive insects. Larvae are aquatic predators and have lateral abdominal gills. Adults resemble antlions (Myrmeleontidae). Pupae are present. Adults always close to water.

- 2 families; 7 species.
- Can be confused with antlions, but these insects lack the forward-pointing mouthparts and large fan-shaped hind wings of dobsonflies and alderflies. Also resemble stoneflies (Plecoptera), but stoneflies have abdominal appendages and downward-pointing mouthparts, unlike dobsonflies and alderflies.

LACEWINGS, ANTLIONS

ORDER: NEUROPTERA

Medium-sized to large (5–60mm). Predatory insects with prominent round eyes and long antennae. Abdomen is elongated, like that of damselflies and dragonflies (Odonata). Paired abdominal appendages are absent, and four similar wings, usually transparent, are folded roof-like over the abdomen. All adults are winged and are attracted to lights at night. Larvae have characteristically sickle-shaped jaws, which are hollow tubes with sharp points used to suck out the body fluids of their prey. Many species are beneficial to agriculture and gardening, as they prey on a variety of plant pests.

- 13 families; 350 species.

Dusty-winged lacewings

Family: Coniopterygidae

Medium-sized (5–8mm). Whole body and wings covered in white powdery exudates. Larvae live on plants, where they prey on small insects and mites.

- 14 species.
- Can be confused with small caddisflies (Trichoptera), but caddisflies are never white and have broader hind wings. Can also be confused with whiteflies (Aleyrodidae) and other hemipterans, but these families have sucking instead of biting mouthparts.

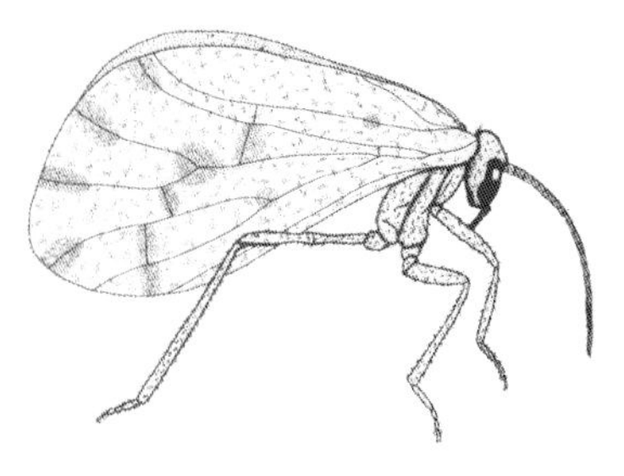

Mantidflies, mantispids

Family: Mantispidae

Medium-sized (6–25mm). Front legs modified for grasping, as in mantids (Mantodea). Constricted abdomen and typical colour patterns clearly mimic paper wasps (Vespidae). Eggs laid on short stalks; larvae are predators in egg pockets of spiders.

- 32 species.
- Can be confused with mantids (Mantodea), but wings of Mantispidae are similar and front wings are not leathery. No abdominal appendages. Similarity to paper wasps (Vespidae) is very superficial: raptorial front legs of Mantispidae are distinct.

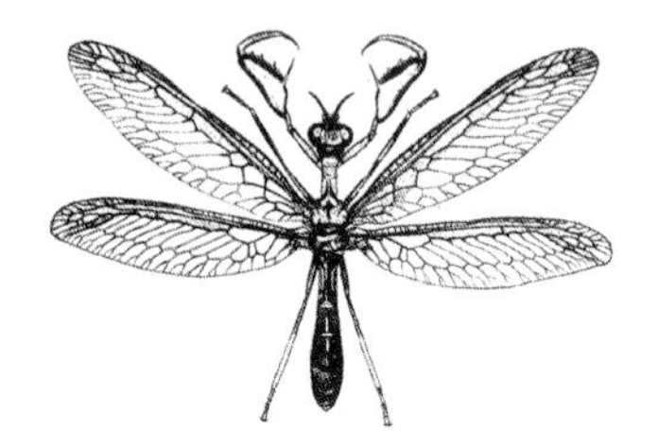

Brown lacewings, aphid wolves

Family: Hemerobiidae

Medium-sized (6–12mm). Brown with brightly coloured eyes. Wings are hairy and relatively broad. Larvae hunt aphids (Aphididae) and other small insects on plants.

- 22 species.
- Can be confused with caddisflies (Trichoptera), but brown lacewings and aphid wolves have functional biting mouthparts and lack the leg spikes and broad hind wings of caddisflies.

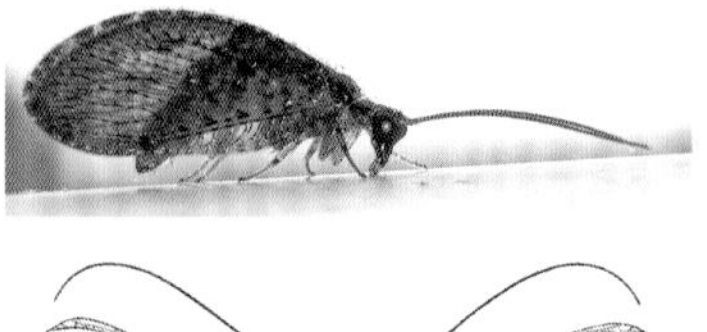

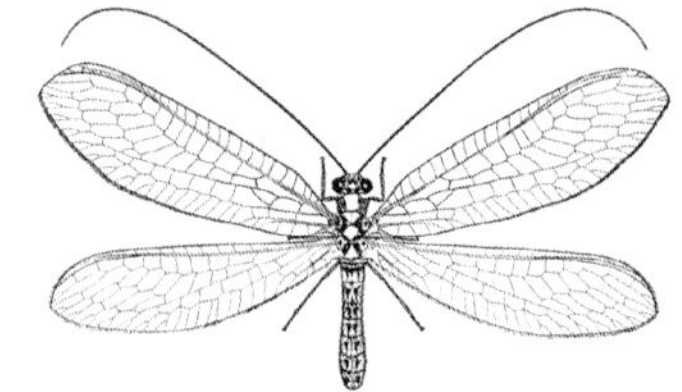

Green lacewings, golden eyes

Family: Chrysopidae

Medium-sized (7–20mm). Green, yellow or sometimes reddish, with bright metallic-coloured eyes. Generally built like brown lacewings (Hemerobiidae), but larger and slimmer. Eggs laid singly at the ends of long, slender silk

threads. Larvae hunt small arthropods, mostly aphids. Camouflage themselves by covering their bodies with waste, shed skin and shells of dead prey. Play an important role in biological pest control.
- 79 species.

Thread-wing lacewings, spoon-wing lacewings

Family: Nemopteridae

Medium-sized (10–20mm). Elongated hind wings, sometimes longer than 50mm. Forewings look the same as those of green lacewings (Chrysopidae), but hind wings are two to three times as long, extending into long threads or streamers, sometimes with a leaf-shaped dilation at the end. Larvae have long 'necks' (elongation of the first thoracic segment), and are free-living in loose sand, usually under rocks.

- 51 species (almost all known species are indigenous to the Karoo and Namaqualand).

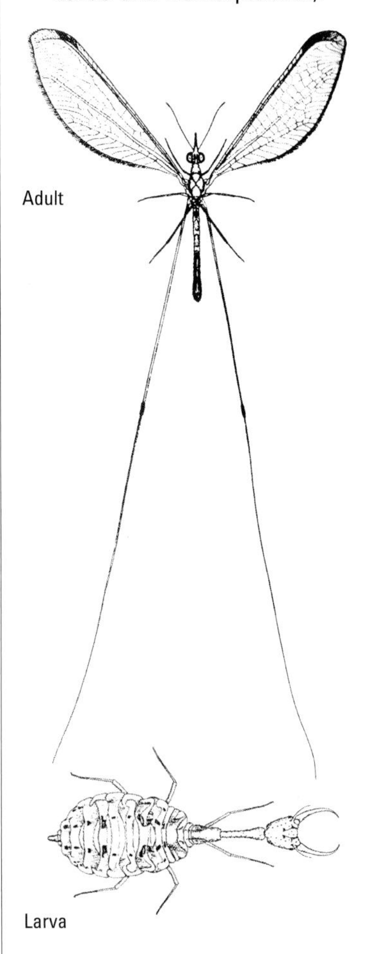

Owl flies

Family: Ascalaphidae

Medium-sized to large (20–40mm). Wings lace-like, very distinctive. Large ball-shaped eyes and long clubbed antennae. Both adults and larvae are hairy and well camouflaged on bark. Adults of a number of species have unusual sitting postures to lessen the chance of predators recognising them. Larvae are flattened and mostly hunt on bark; those of some species hunt on the ground.
- 79 species.

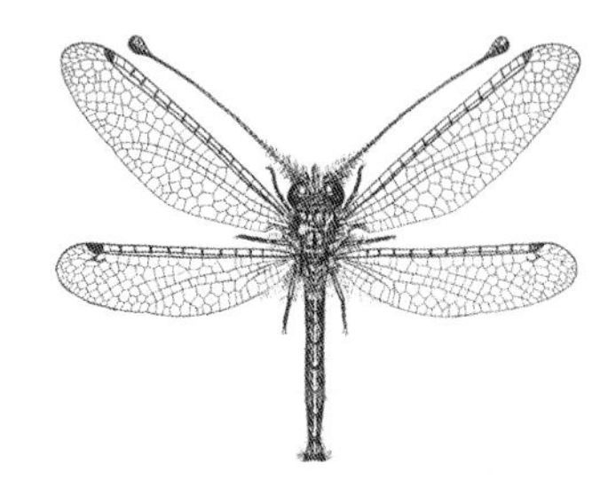

Antlions

Family: Myrmeleontidae

Medium-sized to very large (15–80mm). Resemble dragonflies in appearance, but with clearly visible antennae, mostly hooked at the ends. The four wings are similar and translucent. Adults predominantly nocturnal. Some of the larger species have yellow and black markings on their wings and are diurnal. The larvae of the smaller types (also known as 'moles' or 'joelies') make funnel-shaped pits in sand in order to capture their insect prey, mostly ants.

- 125 species.
- Can be confused with damselflies and dragonflies (Odonata) and dobsonflies and alderflies (Megaloptera). Diurnal species may look like moths (Lepidoptera), but have clearly visible biting mouthparts and lack a rolled-up proboscis. Wings are smooth and do not have the scale covering evident in moths.

HANGING FLIES
ORDER: MECOPTERA

Medium-sized (±20mm). Orange-brown, head extended into an elongated rostrum (snout-shaped), and with four similar, translucent wings. One Cape species is wingless. Hang by their forelegs and catch flying insect prey with any of their six legs – all modified for grasping. Larvae employ the same camouflage strategy as green lacewings (Chrysopidae). Locomotion like that of looper (geometrid moth) caterpillars (Geometridae).

- 1 family; 31 species.
- Can be confused with robber flies (Asilidae) and craneflies (Tipulidae), but species in both these families have only two wings and no specialised grasping tarsi. Certain ichneumon wasp species (Ichneumonidae) may look similar, but differ in not having grasping tarsi and a snout-shaped head.

FLEAS
ORDER: SIPHONAPTERA

Laterally flattened, with piercing-sucking mouthparts and hind legs adapted for impressive jumps. Almost all are parasites of mammals (mostly rodents); a few parasitise birds. Flea larvae look like maggots and live off organic waste in nests or dwellings.

- 8 families; 101 species.

Jigger or chigger fleas
Family: Tungidae

Small (1–3mm; engorged females up to 10mm). Females occur in sand and burrow into the skin of human feet. Embedded there, a female will grow subcutaneously to pea size while continuing to lay eggs in the sand via oozing pus. The eggs develop in the sand, and the cycle is repeated.

- 1 species (*Tunga penetrans*).

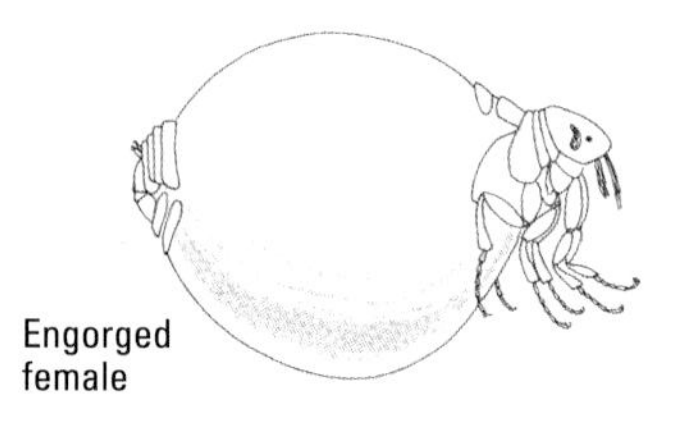

Common fleas
Family: Pulicidae

Small (1.2–3mm). This flea family contains species that are common

pests of humans and domestic animals. All have the normal appearance, structure and lifestyle of a flea, except for the stick-tight fleas (*Echidnophaga* spp.), which attach to their poultry hosts like ticks.

- 46 species.

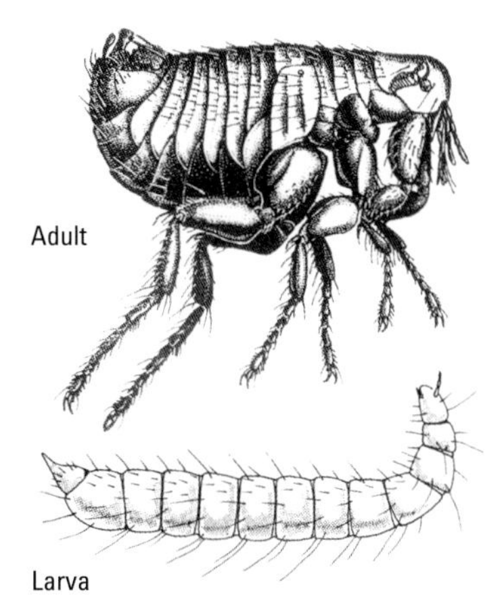

CADDISFLIES
ORDER: TRICHOPTERA

Small to medium-sized (2–25mm). Moth-like, with grey, hairy wings that fold roof-like over the abdomen when the insect is at rest. Antennae are long and thin, normally directed forward. Larvae are aquatic and spin longitudinal silk tubes or cases (covered with small stones and waste), often equipped with a sieve to filter out organic food particles from the water.

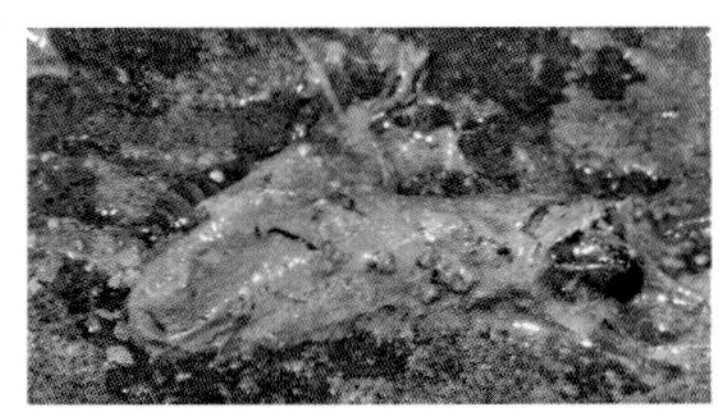

Aquatic larva

- 19 families; 262 species.
- Can be confused with brown lacewings (Hemerobiidae) and dusty-winged lacewings (Coniopterygidae). Most commonly mistaken for moths (Lepidoptera), but caddisflies lack the rolled tongue of moths and have hairs, not scales, on the body and wings.

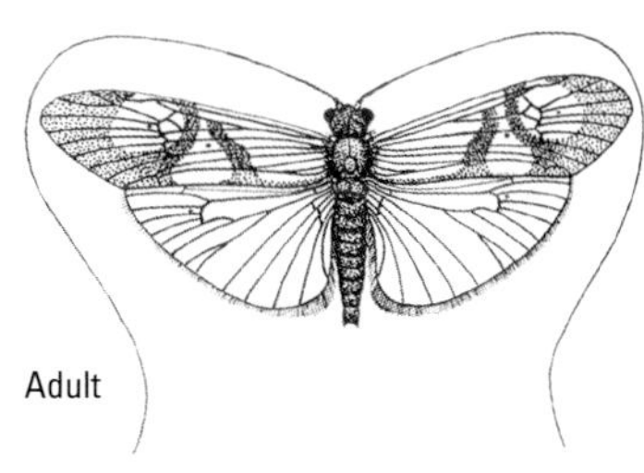

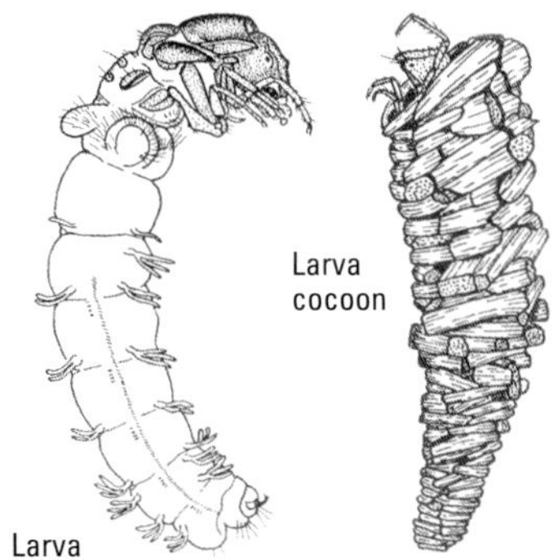

BEETLES
ORDER: COLEOPTERA

Beetles can be identified by a hardened shell that, in most species, covers the entire body. The hardened forewings (elytra) cover the abdomen and the hind wings; the latter are used only for flying. In flightless species the forewings are fused. All beetles have biting mouthparts (with jaws or mandibles). Simple eyes are absent. Antennae vary in shape, but are always developed and never reduced to hairy spikes.

- ±102 families (in South Africa; 174 worldwide).

Primitive beetles
Family: Cupedidae

Medium-sized (±20mm). Very primitive ('living fossils'). Forewings a network of veins and pits. Antennae long, thick and cylindrical. Larvae burrow into decaying wood. Only one species found in the region – in the coastal forests of KwaZulu-Natal and the Eastern and Western Cape.

- 1 species.

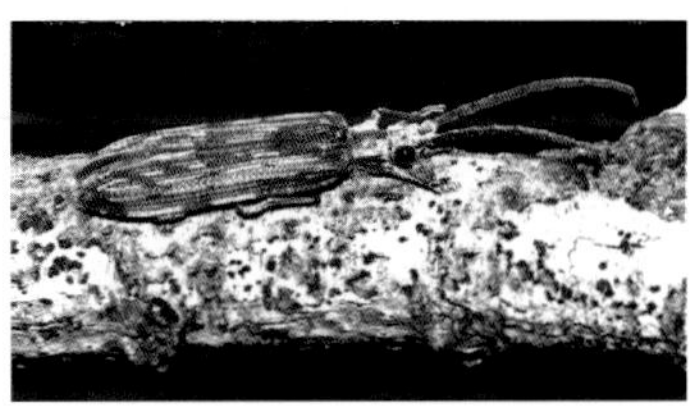

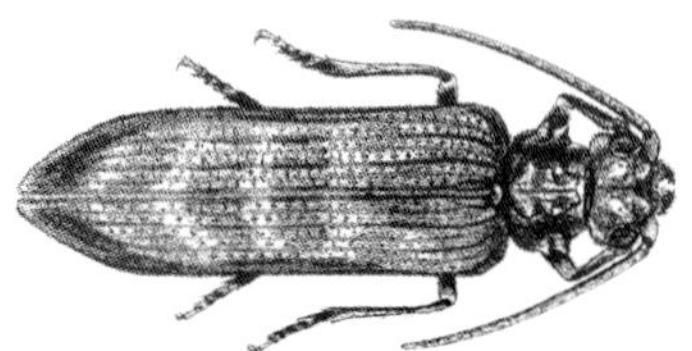

Ground beetles
Family: Carabidae

Diverse family of predatory beetles with a spike (on the trochanter) above the base of the hind legs. Subfamilies individually better recognisable than the family as a whole.

Ground beetles

Subfamily: Carabinae

Small to very large (3–60mm). Normally flattened beetles, with prominent eyes, sharp mandibles and long legs for running. Tapered 'waist' between thorax and oval abdomen. Some species equipped with abdominal glands that secrete or squirt a compound used in self-defence. Smaller species fly; larger species, for example *Anthia* spp., are wingless. All adults and larvae are predators. Attracted to and commonly found at lights.

- ±1,400 species.
- Can be confused with stag beetles (Lucanidae), especially those living in the ground, but ground beetles have slender antennae without an enlargement at the end.

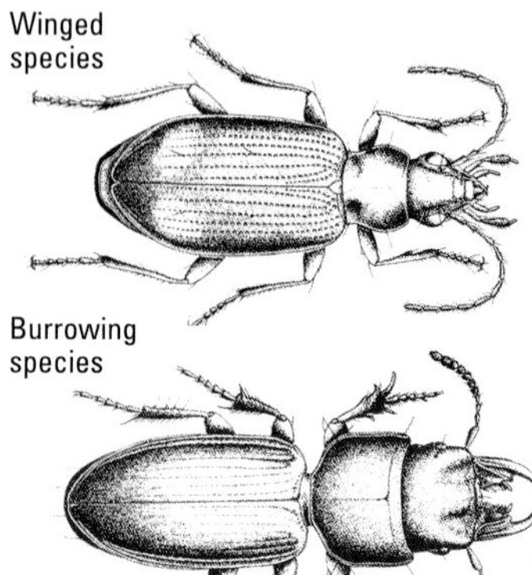

Tiger beetles

Subfamily: Cicindelinae

Medium-sized to very large (8–70mm). Prominent eyes and mandibles, long thin legs, and a narrow thorax. Smaller species often brightly coloured. Large species are wingless. Fast runners and fliers. Larvae hide in vertical ground tunnels and jump out to catch their prey. Adults are all predators.

- ±160 species.

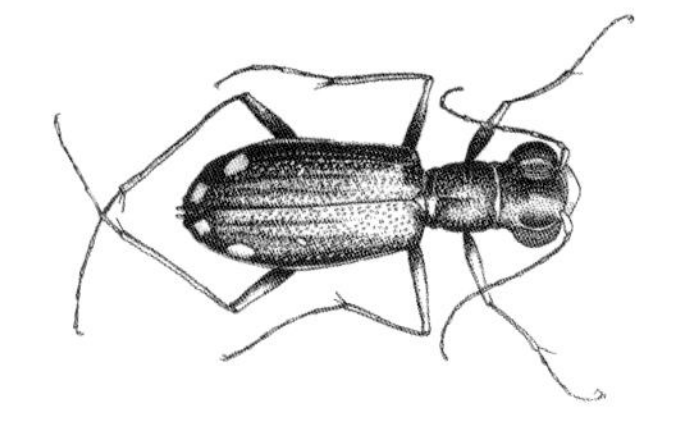

Ants' guest beetles, ants' nest beetles

Subfamily: Paussinae

Small to medium-sized (4–12mm). Always red-brown, winged, with characteristic cylindrical abdomen and broad, thick antennae. All species are parasites of ants (Formicidae). Nocturnal; attracted to lights at night.

- 85 species.

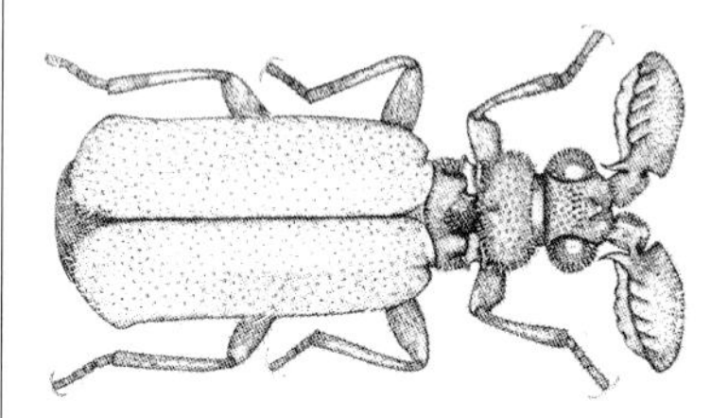

Predaceous water beetles

Family: Dytiscidae

Small to large (1–45mm). Flattened, oval and streamlined. Hind legs are large, oar-like and fringed with hairs. Both adults and larvae are underwater predators. Adults can stay under water for long periods by keeping a supply of air trapped beneath their wings, like an air bubble. Males have special adhesive suckers on front tarsi. Nocturnal fliers; attracted to lights at night.

- ±310 species.
- Can be confused with whirligig beetles (Gyrinidae) and water scavenger beetles (Hydrophilidae), but tarsi,

especially those of water scavenger beetles, which are flatter, are very different.

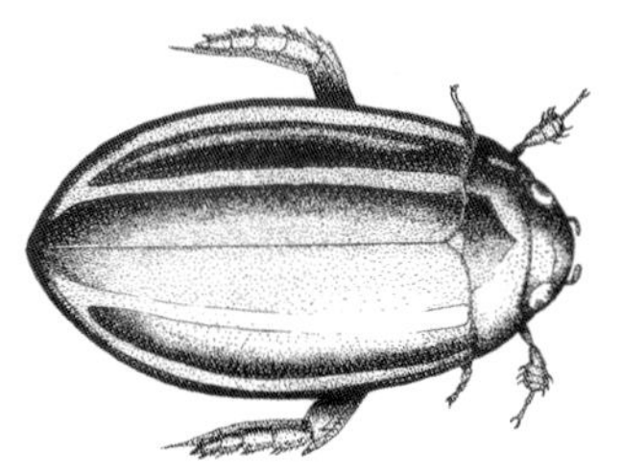

Whirligig beetles

Family: Gyrinidae

Small to medium-sized (4–17mm). Flattened, oval and streamlined. Grey to metallic coloration. Swim fast on water surface by using surface tension. Feed on insects that fall into the water. Often found in large groups. Nocturnal fliers; attracted to lights at night.

- 55 species.
- Can be confused with predaceous water beetles (Dytiscidae), but in whirligig beetles all four hind legs are short and oar-like and the eyes are divided into halves for seeing above and below the waterline at the same time.

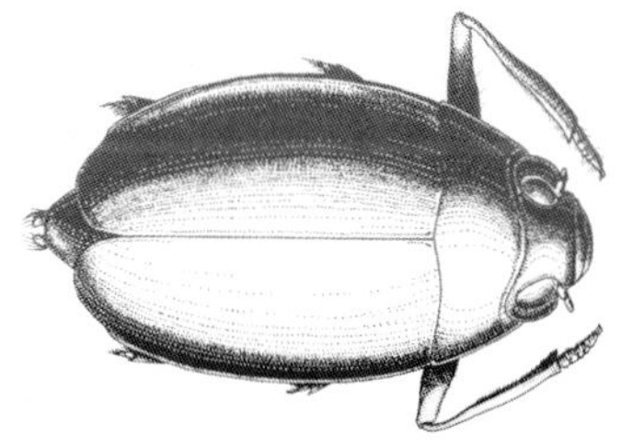

Water scavenger beetles

Family: Hydrophilidae

Small to large (1–50mm). Oval, convex and mostly shiny black. Very smooth and streamlined, but flat ventrally and with relatively normal legs. Live in moist environments, even under water. Scavenge dead and decomposing material. Adults are nocturnal fliers; attracted to lights at night.

- ±120 species.
- Can be confused with predaceous water beetles (Dytiscidae).

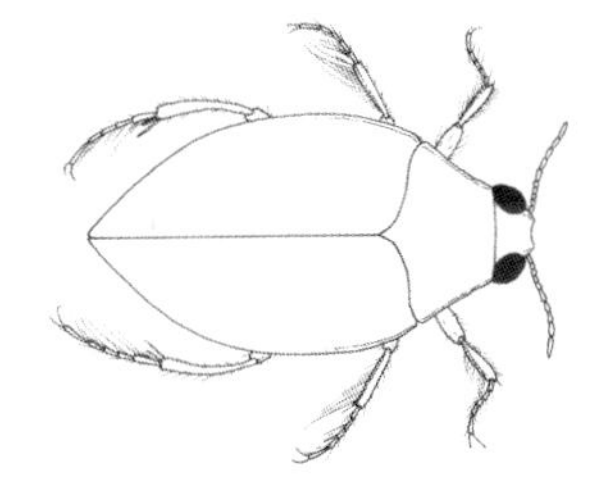

Steel beetles, hister beetles

Family: Histeridae

Small to medium-sized (1–20mm). Shiny black to green or metallic blue, sometimes with red spots. Perfectly oval with large heads and mandibles. The covering wings are slightly abbreviated so that the abdomen is exposed on top. Predators of fly maggots. Common under dung pads and in carcasses and other places where maggots breed. Nocturnal fliers; attracted to lights at night.

- ±300 species.

Carrion beetles

Family: Silphidae

Medium-sized (10–20mm). Metallic to grey. Flattened beetles with ridged wings. Abdomen protrudes far beyond the wings. Found under carcasses where larvae and adults feed on carrion.

- 3 species.

- Can be confused with rove beetles (Staphylinidae), but are much broader, with a prominent wing texture. In carrion beetles only two or three abdominal segments are exposed; in rove beetles more than five abdominal segments are visible.

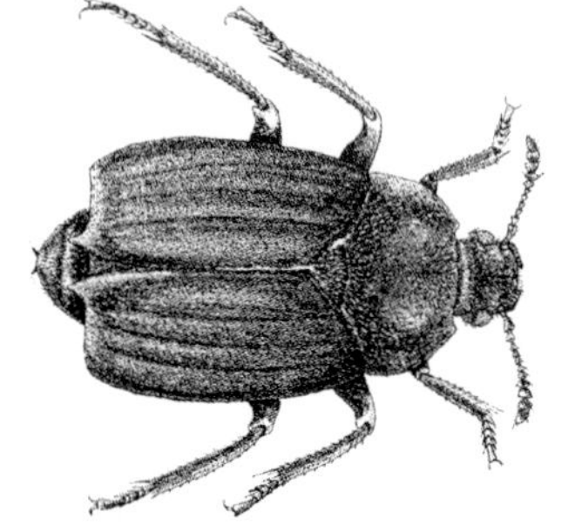

Rove beetles

Family: Staphylinidae

Very small to medium-sized (0.5–20mm). Bodies elongated, with reduced forewings under which the long hind wings are folded, leaving the long abdomen visible. Adults and larvae are mostly predators. Some species feed on fungi or plants; others parasitise nests of social insects. Attracted to lights at night.

- ±1,000 described species (a fraction of the estimated number of species).
- Can be confused with carrion beetles (Silphidae) and other short-winged beetles, for example ship timber beetles (Lymexylidae), but these beetles' hind wings do not fold up. Can also be mistaken for some short-winged longhorn beetles (Cerambycidae) and blister beetles (Meloidae), but the latter are large and bulky. Differ from earwigs by the lack of abdominal pincers.

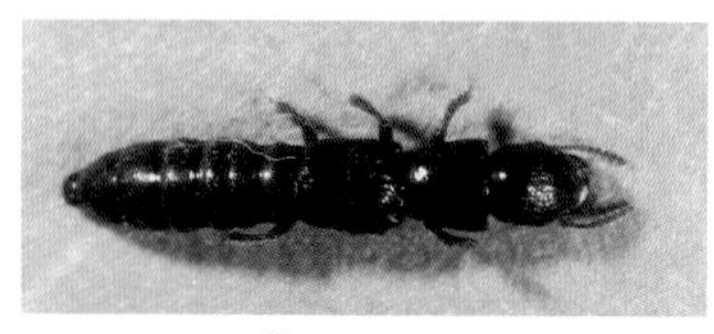

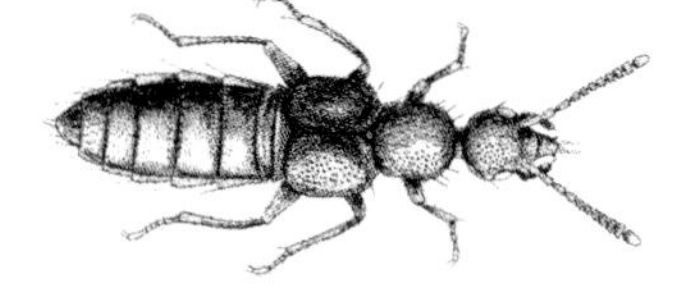

Dung beetle-related families

Superfamily: Scarabaeoidea

In southern African beetle families of this group, the last few segments of the antennae are prominently widened in a club-like fashion. All are relatively bulky, with a wide thorax, and have white, grub-type larvae with C-shaped bodies.

Stag beetles

Family: Lucanidae

Medium-sized to large (15–35mm). Slightly elongated beetles with toothed antennal tips and prominent, large heads and mandibles. The mandibles often have protrusions, especially in the males. The unusual wingless *Colophon* spp. (see photograph below), found only on mountains in the Western Cape, have a very large and prominent thorax. Larvae feed on decomposing wood or vegetable matter.

- 36 species.
- Can be confused with soil-dwelling ground beetles (Carabidae), but they have simple mandibles and their antennae are straighter and thinner than those of stag beetles.

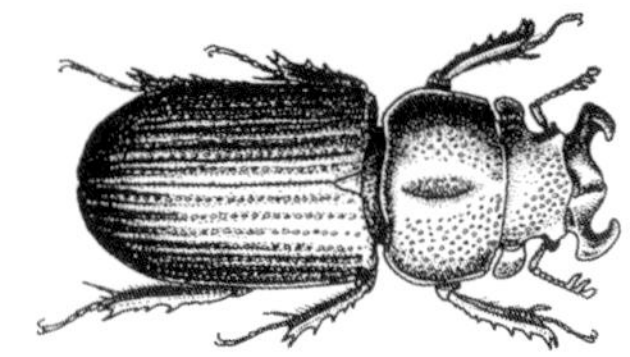

Winged stag beetle

Carcass beetles

Family: Trogidae

Medium-sized (5–20mm). Very convex, oval beetles, dull grey

to black with toothed antennal tips and distinctive knobbles on their backs. Live with their larvae under old dry carcasses. Apart from clothes moths (Tineidae), they are the only insects capable of digesting keratin. Some species are wingless. Winged adults are nocturnal fliers.

- 55 species.

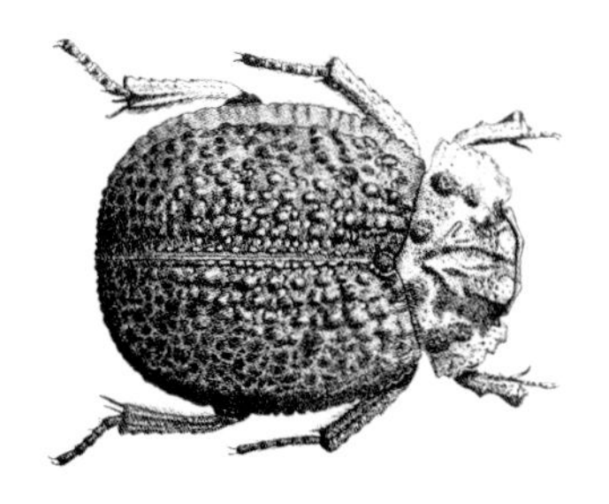

Truffle hunters

Family: Bolboceratidae (formerly Geotrupidae)

Medium-sized (10–25mm). Very convex, rounded beetles, with yellow to dark brown coloration. Males often have protrusions and a pitted texture on the thorax and head, with huge club-shaped tips on their antennae. Found in deep sand. Some species feed on underground fungi ('truffles'). Nocturnal fliers; attracted to lights at night.

- ±50 species.

Scarab beetles, dung beetles

Family: Scarabaeidae

Subfamilies are diverse, but all have typical C-shaped larvae that feed on dung. The antennae of all adults have ball-shaped tips that can fan open.

- ±3,000 species.

Dung chafers

Subfamily: Aphodiinae

Small to medium-sized (2–10mm). Slightly elongated, with a smooth body outline.

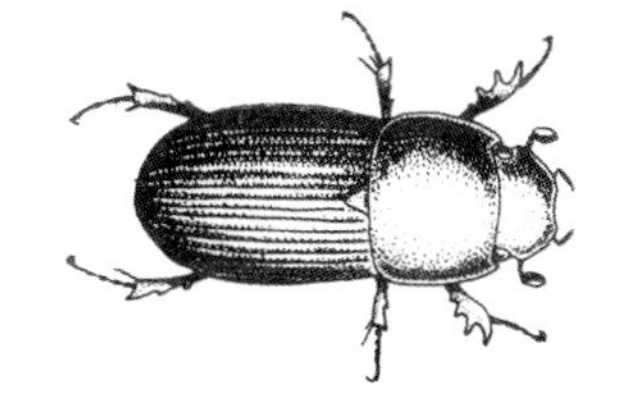

Yellow, brown or black. Live and breed inside dung pads. Often attracted to lights.

- At least 215 species.

Fruit chafers

Subfamily: Cetoniinae

Medium-sized to very large (10–65mm). Often beautifully coloured. Their flattened shield-shaped body differentiates them from other scarab beetles. Males often sport horns on their heads. A few females are wingless. Feed on sweet plant matter (flowers, fruit and sap from plant stems). Larvae are typically C-shaped; live in decomposing organic matter and crawl on their backs when unearthed. Adults diurnal. One subgroup is mostly nocturnal and its species live as parasites of ants or in bird nests.

- 255 species.

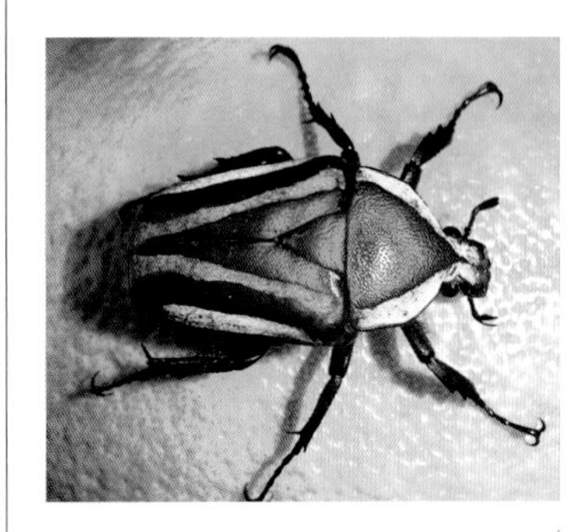

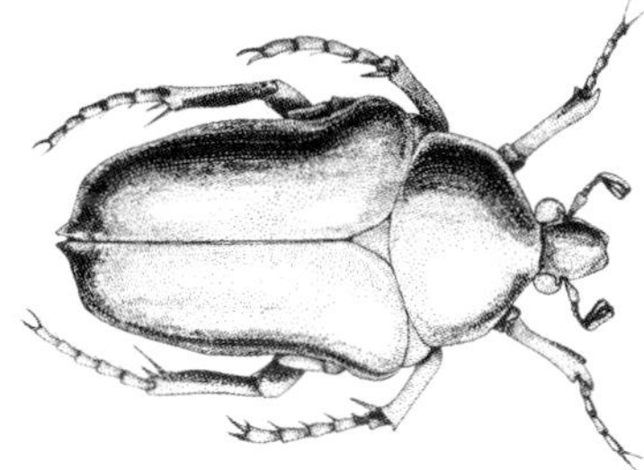

Rhino beetles

Subfamily: Dynastinae

Medium-sized to large (12–45mm). Elongated, rounded beetles. Adult males often have large horns. Larvae typically C-shaped; live on decomposing plant matter.

- 60–70 species.
- Can be confused with cockchafers (Melolonthinae), as smaller, hornless rhino beetles closely resemble these bugs. However, smaller rhino beetles can be distinguished by their harder and usually shiny black shell.

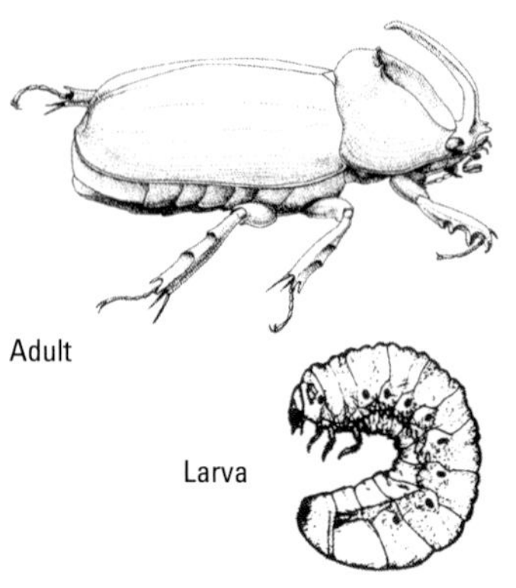

Cockchafers, spring beetles, chafers

Subfamilies: Melolonthinae; Rutelinae

Medium-sized (5–20mm). The two subfamilies are very similar and contain yellow to rust-brown beetles that are cylindrical in shape. Commonly found at lights at night. Rutelinae are distinguished by larger and uneven claws on the rear tarsi. Adults feed on leaves; larvae mostly feed on roots. A number are pests. Within Melolonthinae, monkey beetles (tribe Hopliini) constitute an unusual group (see second photograph below). These diurnal beetles, common in Namaqualand, feed on flowers. They have strongly developed and enlarged hind legs and claws, which they use to extract themselves from the flowers into which they bore.

- ±650 species, including ±300 Hopliini species (Melolonthinae); 450–500 species (Rutelinae).

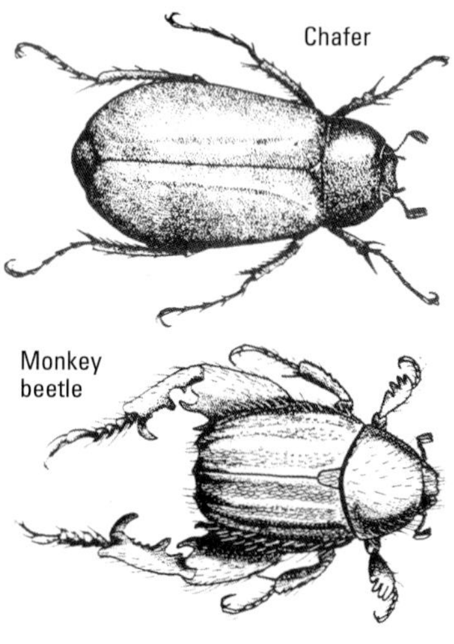

True dung beetles

Subfamily: Scarabaeinae

Small to large (3–50mm). A diverse group. Always stout and rounded, their length hardly exceeding their width. Coloration differs from black to bright metallic; colour mostly uniform over entire body with no markings or patterns. Forelegs are wide and toothed for digging and trowelling. Some species have males with large horns on their head and/or thorax. All larvae feed on carrion or dung. Adults often bury dung for their larvae – in the case of ball-rolling beetles (see second photograph below), dung balls are rolled away, often over significant distances. Most are nocturnal fliers, but diurnal species are common. Wingless species occur, such as the large Addo flightless dung beetle (*Circellium bacchus*) and Namib dung beetles (*Pachysoma* spp.).

- ±1,000 species.

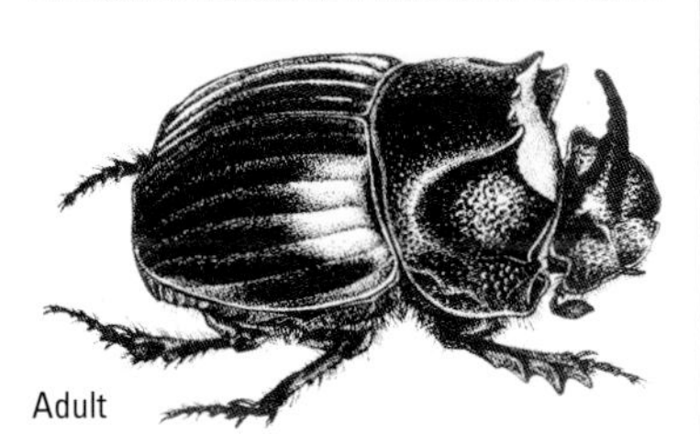

Adult

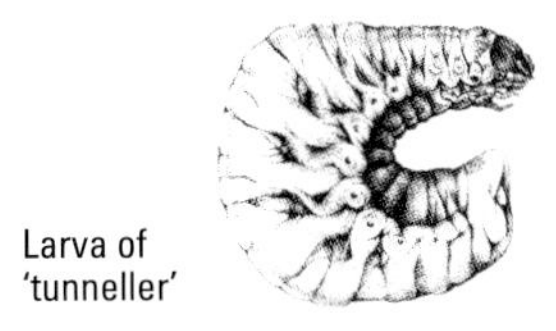

Larva of 'tunneller'

Jewel beetles, flat-headed borers

Family: Buprestidae

Very small to large (1.5–50mm). Bullet-shaped beetles, mostly slightly flattened; most species are very brightly coloured. Larvae have broad, flattened thoracic segments and are woodborers. Some smaller jewel beetles are leaf or grass miners, whereas others are free-living root feeders. Adults are diurnal fliers and sun-loving, and some visit flowers.

- ±1,000 species.

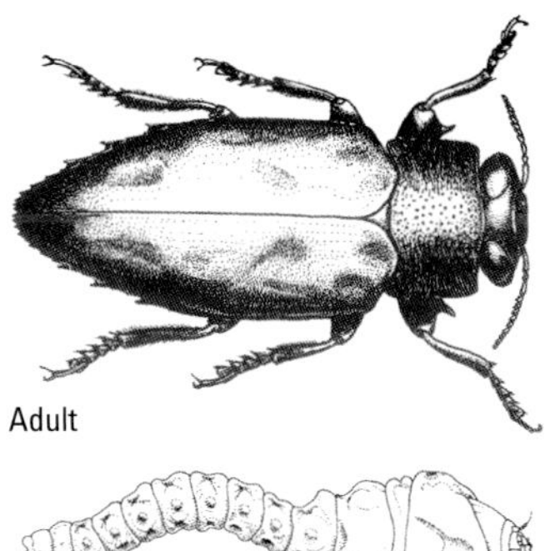

Adult

Larva of flat-headed borer

Click beetles

Family: Elateridae

Small to very large (5–80mm). Long elliptical shape is similar to that of jewel beetles (Buprestidae). Dull grey or brown, a few with coloured spots. Antennae sometimes plumed. Owing to a jackknife-type mechanism on the underside, between the pro- and meso-thorax, adults are able to leap into the air if they accidentally land on their backs or when grabbed by a predator. Larvae live in decomposing plant matter. Most are predators; others are plant feeders and even agricultural pests.

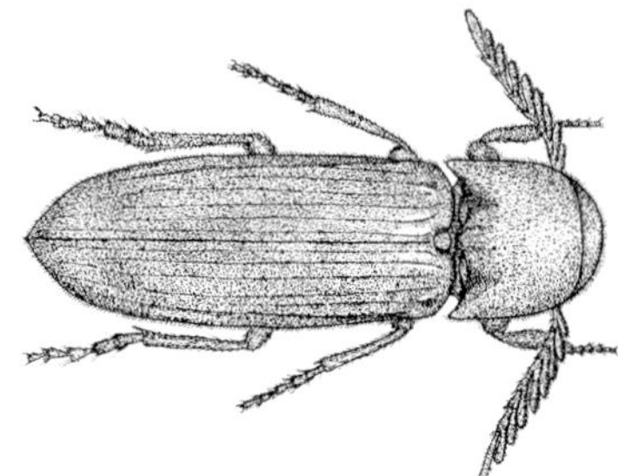

- ±700 species.
- Can be confused with jewel beetles (Buprestidae), but the hinged thorax and abdomen of click beetles are rounded where they meet across the front of the body, allowing the thorax to hinge by moving up and down.

Fireflies, glow worms

Family: Lampyridae

Medium-sized (6–22mm). Long, flattened beetles with leathery shells. Head covered by pronotum. The long abdomen is separately mobile from the wings. Males and females have light organs at the tip of the abdomen with which they signal a species-specific code to attract one another. Females are mostly wingless (glow worms). Poisonous.

- 30 species.

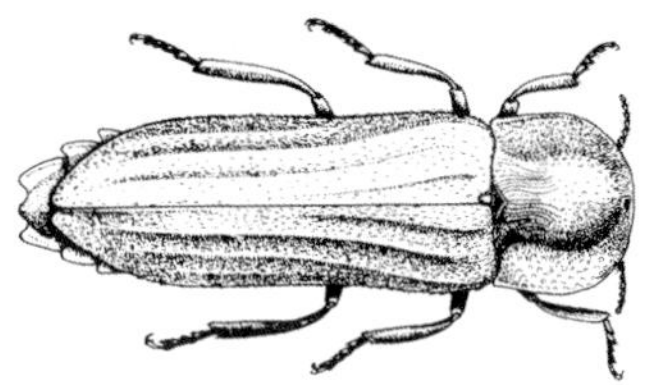

Net-winged beetles

Family: Lycidae

Medium-sized (6–22mm). Flat, wide, leathery-bodied insects with a distinctive colour pattern and a network of veins on the wings. The head is covered by the pronotum; antennae are serrated. The abdomen is separately mobile. All species mimic each other. Adults are also mimicked by stink bugs, moths, wasps and beetles in different families. Larvae hunt in compost; some also feed on fungi. Adults feed on flowers, often in large numbers of different species on one bush or shrub. Poisonous.

- 50 species.

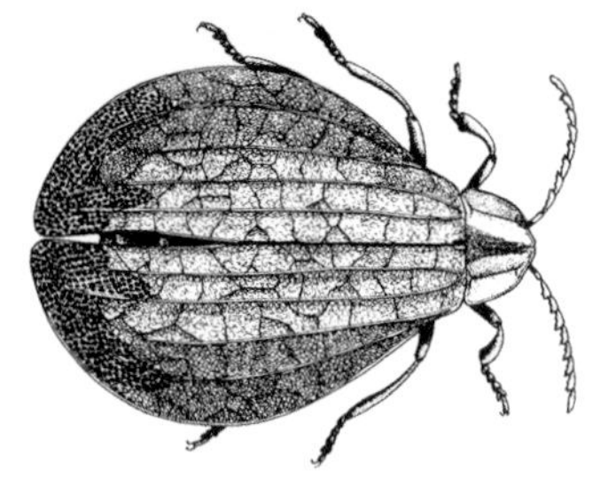

Hide beetles, museum beetles

Family: Dermestidae

Small to medium-sized (4–10mm). Oval to round, velvety texture on top, often with colour markings. Club-like antennae. Larvae and adults feed on dead animal matter; some are cosmopolitan pests, infesting stored goods and specimens in natural history museums. Adults of many species, however, are found only on flowers, and the species of one rarely seen group (subfamily Thorictinae) probably all live in ants' nests.

- 85 species.

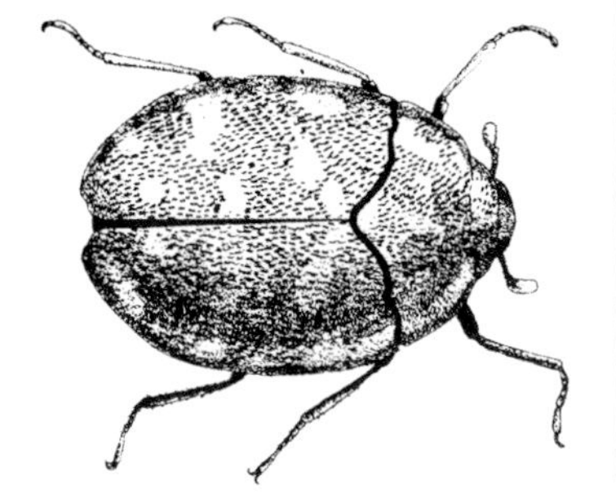

Shot-hole borers

Family: Bostrichidae

Small to large (2–30mm). Elongated and cylindrical (subfamily Bostrychinae) or elongated and flat (subfamily Lyctinae). The head of most species is downward-pointing and not visible from above. Pronotum laterally rounded; forewings terminated bluntly at the rear, sometimes with horn-like protrusions at the back or at the front and back. Bore perfectly round holes in wood, in which their larvae develop. Several species are important commercial timber pests. Small heaps of fine sawdust indicate infestation.

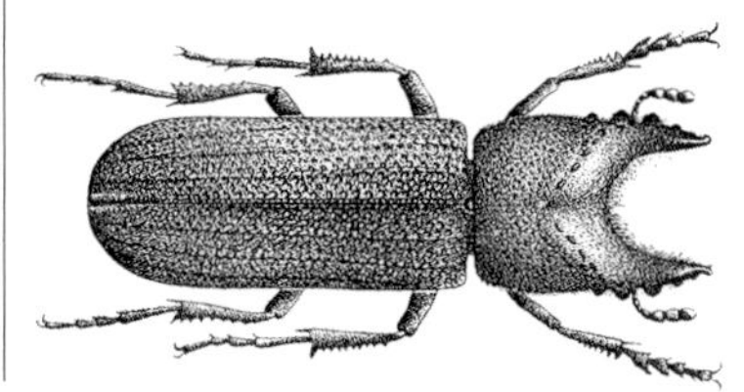

Others are serious pests of stored grain and worked bamboo. Attracted to lights at night.

- ±80 species.

Spider beetles

Family: Ptinidae

Small (2–5mm). Spider-like, with convex abdomen, reduced thorax, hidden head and long legs and feelers. Some have extremely long, thin appendages. All species are flightless. Larvae and adults feed on decomposing organic waste. Found only in arid environments in the western parts of southern Africa. Many species live under stones or rock overhangs or in caves.

- ±30 species.

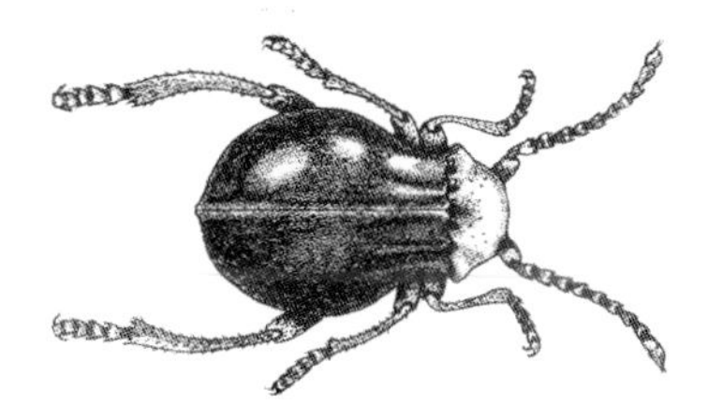

Furniture beetles, death-watch beetles

Family: Anobiidae

Small (2–5mm). Cylindrical shape; head downward-pointing. Adults not as blunted at the front and rear as shot-hole borers (Bostrichidae). Like shot-hole borers, they bore round, but smaller, holes in wood, particularly dry wood, untreated furniture and construction timber. Some species are pests in stored plant products, even tobacco. Death-watch beetles make a characteristic knocking sound.

- Anobiidae are very poorly researched and an accurate estimation of the number of species found in the region is not possible.

Adult beetle with larvae

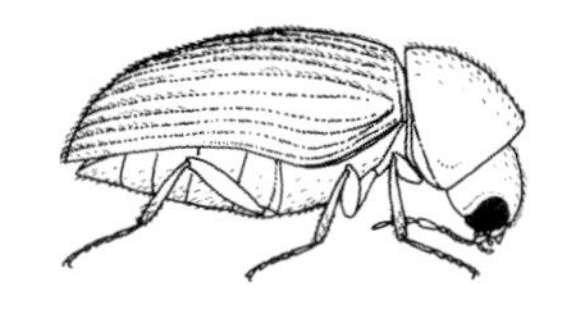

Chequered beetles

Family: Cleridae

Medium-sized (8–15mm). Cylindrical or elongated and flattened in shape, with large eyes and a narrow thorax. Often mimic the colour pattern of velvet ants (Mutillidae). Adults and larvae hunt other insects and larvae (primarily other beetles) on tree trunks and crawl into woodborer tunnels for this purpose. The adults of brightly coloured beetles are often found on flowers; less colourful ones seem to be nocturnal and are attracted to lights at night.

- Almost 200 species.

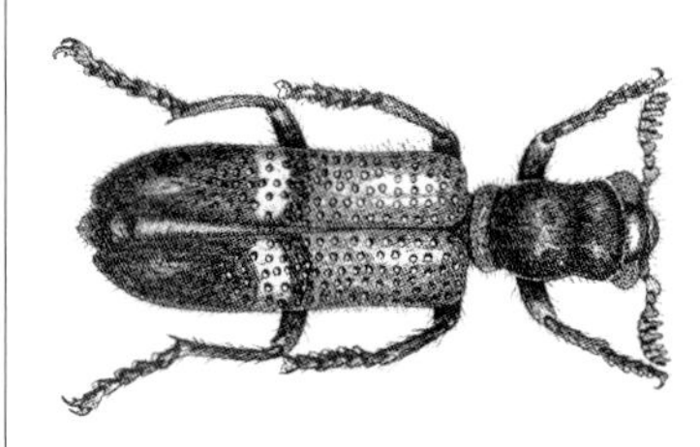

Soft-winged flower beetles

Family: Melyridae

Small to medium-sized (3–10mm). Oval-shaped with a blade-like flattening of the thorax along the sides. Mostly brightly coloured, with prominent erect hairs on body. Larvae are predators; adults feed on pollen. Poisonous. The larvae of the spotted maize beetle (*Astylus atromaculatus*) are sporadic

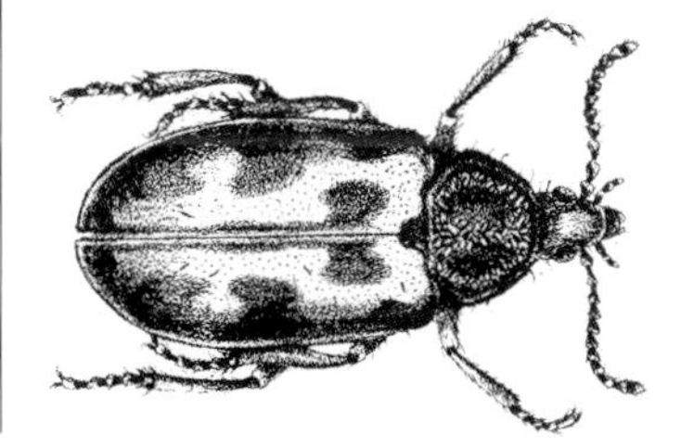

pests on germinating maize and the adults are potentially poisonous to livestock.

- At least 360 species.

Ship timber beetles

Family: Lymexylidae

Medium-sized to large (15–45mm). Long, pliable abdomen, with reduced and protruding forewings and non-foldable hind wings. Larvae are woodborers. Adults attracted to lights at night.

- 3 species.
- Can be confused with rove beetles (Staphylinidae) and flying males of red driver ants (Dorylinae), but ship timber beetles are flatter and have only two non-foldable wings for flying.

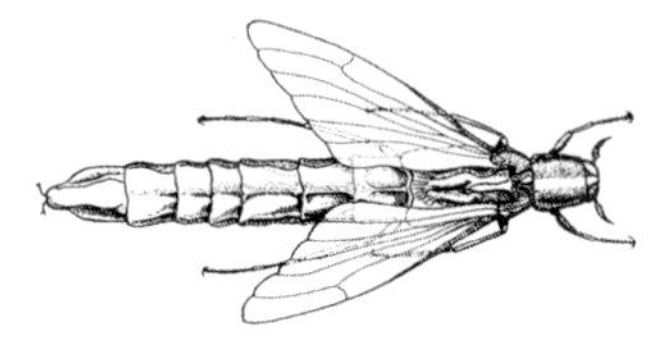

Ladybeetles

Family: Coccinellidae

Very small to medium-sized (0.5–8mm). Hemispherical; black, often with yellow, red or white markings. Larvae and adults are predators, predominantly on aphids. A few plant-feeding species are agricultural pests.

- ±300 species.
- Can be confused with fool's gold beetle (Cassidinae), which also has a shell that covers the legs. Fool's gold beetles are less convex and have a more flattened edge, and the head is completely covered by the pronotum.

Darkling beetles, toktokkies

Family: Tenebrionidae

Small to very large (1.5–60mm). Extremely diverse in shape. Most are wingless and ground-living, including the large and bulky knocking species (*Psammodes* spp.). A small group is winged and attracted to lights at night. Most species are nocturnal, although the small, agile, oval coffee-bean beetles (*Zophosis* spp.) are diurnal. Larvae and adults eat dead organic matter. Larvae are similar to the larvae of click beetles (Elateridae); some are agricultural pests. Very commonly found in the Namib and Kalahari deserts, with extreme adaptations to heat and burrowing in dune sand.

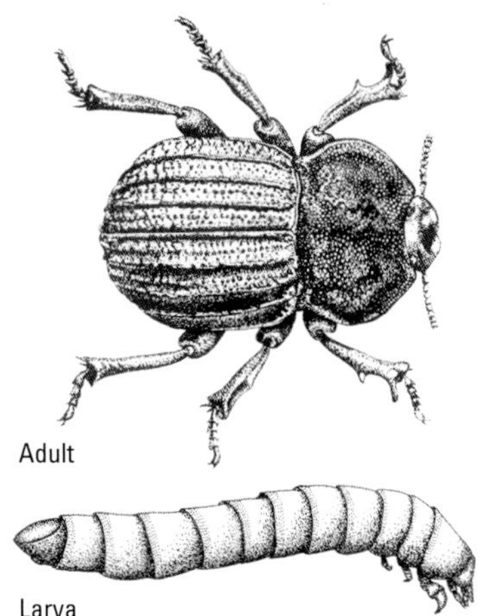

- 3,200 species.
- The best form of identification is by means of elimination. Almost all ground-living and wingless beetles that are not readily recognised as Carabidae, Scarabaeidae or Curculionidae are Tenebrionidae.

Tumbling flower beetles

Family: Mordellidae

Small to medium-sized (2–9mm). Dark beetles with a typical curved shape and pointed abdomen. Adults are generally found on flowers. Larvae of many species tunnel into live or dead stalks of herbaceous plants.

- 3,200 species.

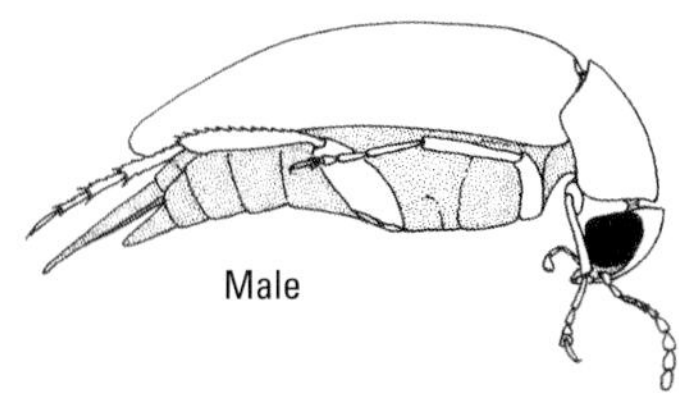

Male

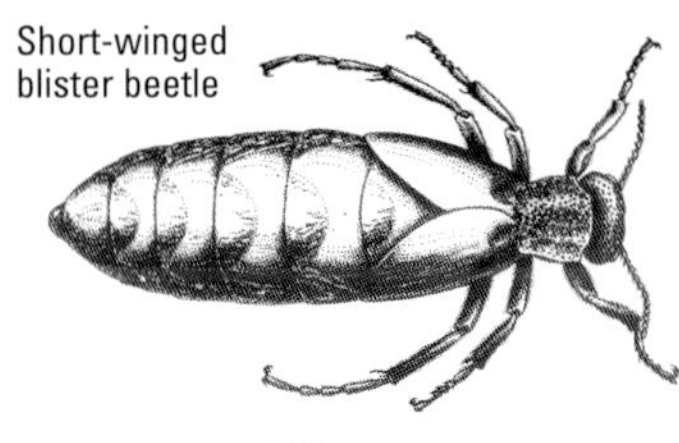

Short-winged blister beetle

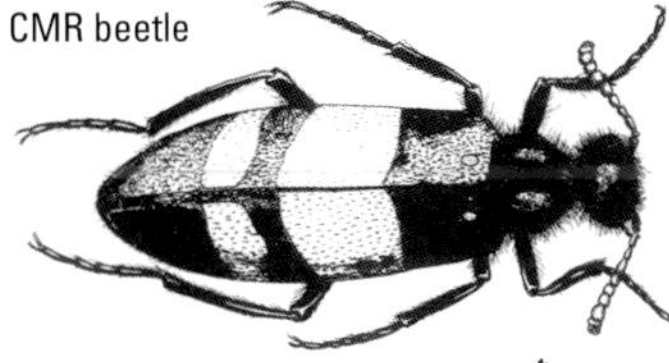

CMR beetle

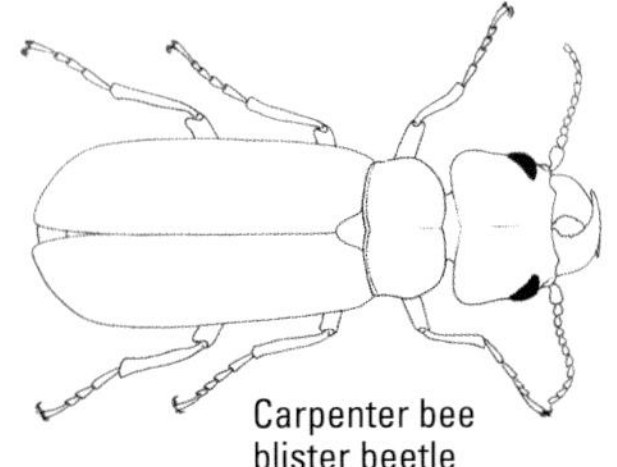

Carpenter bee blister beetle

Blister beetles, oil beetles, CMR beetles

Family: Meloidae

Medium-sized to large (5–40mm). Clumsy, soft-bodied beetles, with a relatively soft shell, small, narrow pronotum and round head. Coloration mostly black and yellow (resembling the colours of the Cape Mounted Rifles, hence the name 'CMR beetle'). Some are blue-black or grey with a red pronotum. A few species are flightless, with reduced forewings that fold across each other. Several insects from other groups mimic these beetles. Larvae of some species have large heads and parasitise nests of carpenter bees (Anthophoridae). The agile larvae lie in wait on flowers, ready for these bees to carry them to their nests. The larvae of other species track down grasshopper egg packets underground and feed on them. All species are poisonous, hence their bright aposematic colour patterns. They contain a heart stimulant, cantharidin, that causes blisters on the skin, irritates the mucous membranes, and results in internal bleeding if swallowed. Can be fatal to humans.

- ±350 species.

Longhorn beetles, timber beetles

Family: Cerambycidae

Small to very large (3–100mm). Elongated bodies, with very long antennae, mostly longer than length of the body (longer in males). Kidney-shaped eyes around antennal base are typical. Virtually all species, including larvae, are woodborers. Larvae, as well as their tunnels, differ from those of jewel beetles (Buprestidae) by their cylindrical shape. Some species are pests in orchards and silviculture.

Giant longhorns

Subfamily: Prioninae

Large to very large (30–100mm). Flattened, brown or black, with forward-pointing head and mandibles and spiky protrusions on the sides of the pronotum. Nocturnal fliers; attracted to lights at night.

- 22 species.
- Can be confused with ground beetles (Carabidae), but these beetles have shorter antennae and lack the giant longhorn's sharp serrated blades on the sides of the pronotum.

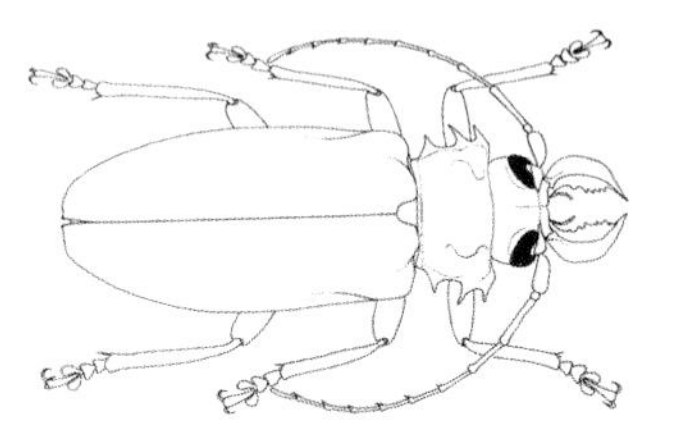

Goat beetles, flower longhorns

Subfamily: Cerambycinae

Medium-sized to large (10–35mm). Slim build, sometimes with reduced forewings, and mouthparts angled downward and forward. Many species are brightly coloured, and several

have a strong defensive smell. Some species visit flowers. Most species are diurnal.

- 150 species.

Leaf-footed species

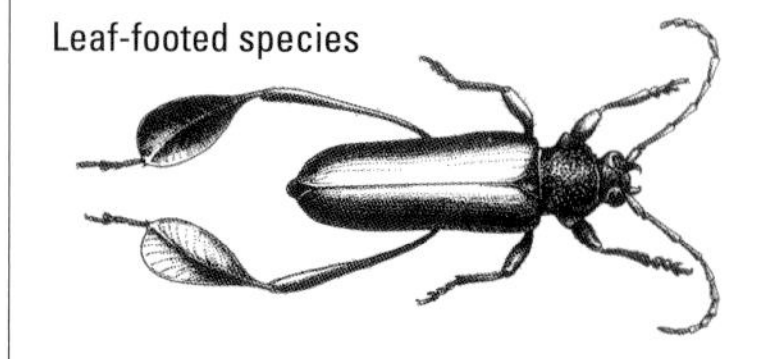

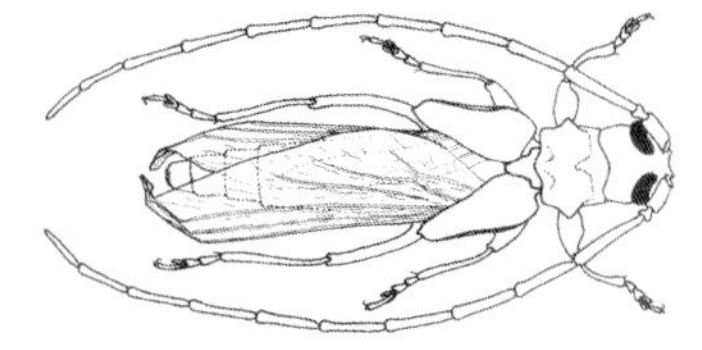

Short-winged species

Common longhorn beetles

Subfamily: Lamiinae

Small to large (3–50mm). Solid, cylindrical body shape; mouthparts directed downward. Diurnal species often brightly coloured; nocturnal species usually a dull grey or brown.

- 475 species.

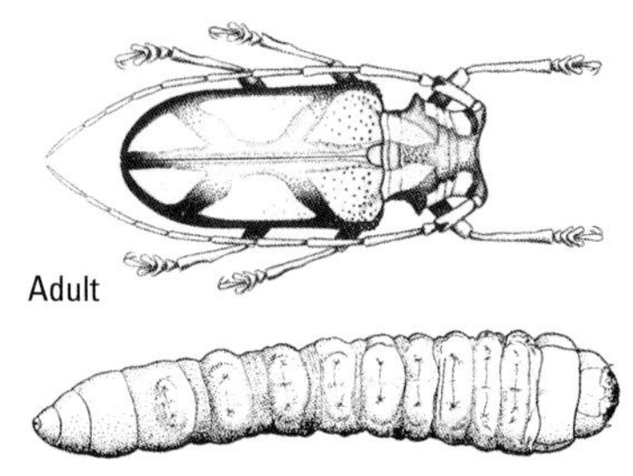

Adult

Larva

Leaf beetles

Family: Chrysomelidae

Large and diverse family. Adults and larvae feed on leaves. Most are very host-plant specific. Larger and more prominent subfamilies are described below.

Swollen-legged leaf beetles

Subfamily: Sagrinae

Medium-sized (12–20mm). Beetles with an elongated body and a markedly thickened rear femur, with spines.

- 4 species.

Cylindrical leaf beetles

Subfamily: Cryptocephalinae (including Clytrinae and Chlamisinae)

Small to medium-sized (3–10mm). Cylindrical beetles; blunted front and rear. Mostly bright yellow or orange with black markings; some brown and textured. Larvae mostly live in cocoons constructed from their faeces and other debris.

- 260 species.

Christmas beetles and their kin

Subfamily: Eumolpinae

Small to medium-sized (3–15mm). More or less cylindrical, but the pronotum is narrower than the abdomen. Subfamily includes the glossy milkweed or Christmas beetle (*Platycorynus dejeani*), which feeds on milkweed.

- 175 species.

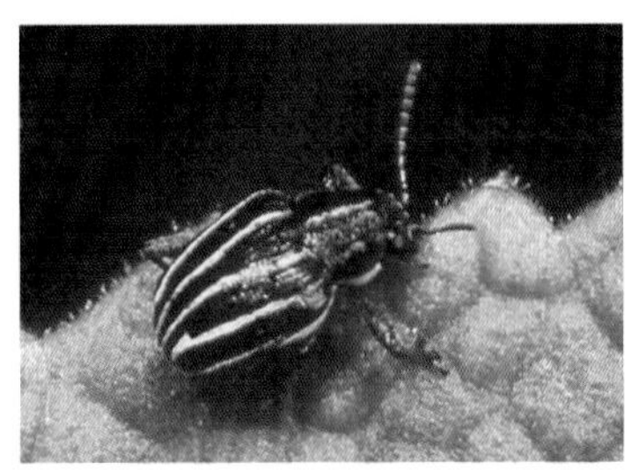

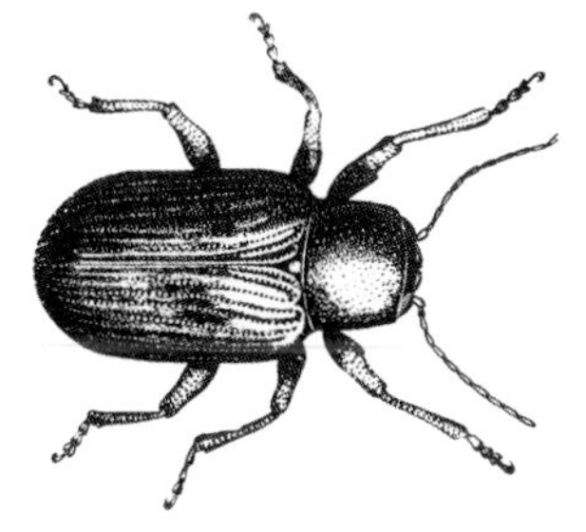

True leaf beetles

Subfamily: Chrysomelinae

Medium-sized (5–12mm). Hemispherical in shape. Some species mimic ladybeetles (Coccinellidae). Many species are poisonous.

- 115 species.
- Can be confused with ladybeetles (Coccinellidae), but in 'true' leaf beetles the mouthparts are pointed more forward and the sharp edge on each side of the thorax is absent.

Soft leaf beetles

Subfamily: Galerucinae

Medium-sized (5–12mm). Most species have a small pronotum and leathery shell. Subfamily includes the Celtis leaf beetle (*Megaleruca* sp.), found in large numbers on white stinkwood trees. (In some classifications, the subfamilies Galerucinae and Alticinae are considered one subfamily.)

- At least 300 species.

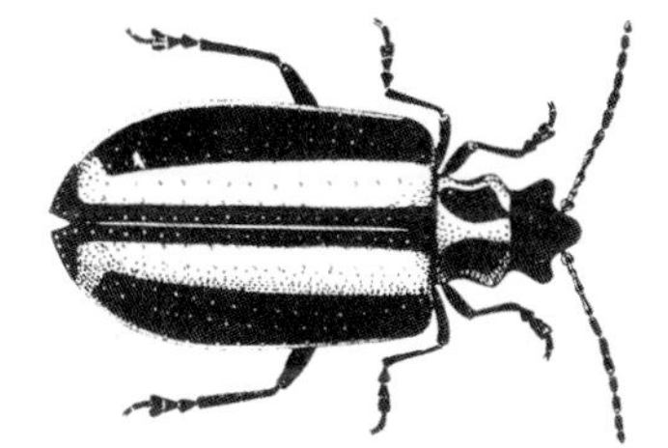

Flea beetles

Subfamily: Alticinae

Small (2–5mm). Oval beetles, with swollen rear femur. Able to take gigantic leaps to escape danger. Subfamily includes Bushman arrow-poison beetles (*Diamphidia* spp.) and *Polyclada* spp. (In some classifications, the subfamilies Alticinae and Galerucinae are considered one subfamily.)

- ±300 species.

Spiny leaf beetles

Subfamily: Hispinae

Small (2–6mm). Characteristically long spines on pronotum and elytra. Larvae are leaf miners. (In modern classifications, the subfamilies Hispinae and Cassidinae are often considered one subfamily.)

- 125 species.

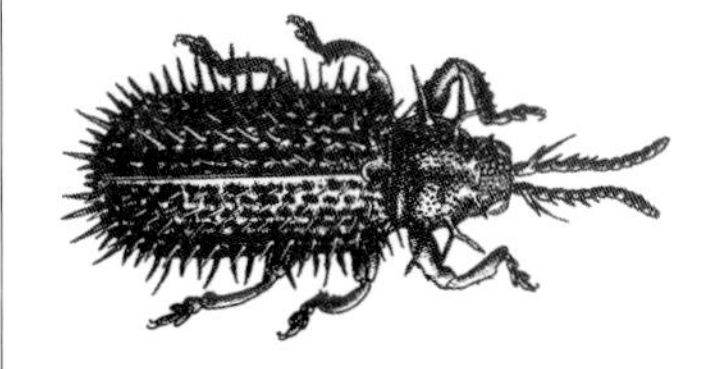

Fool's gold beetles

Subfamily: Cassidinae

Small to medium-sized (4–10mm). Flat and round, with expanded pronotum and elytra covering the head and legs.

Elytra often transparent with gold and green coloration of the layers of the cuticle (epidermis) underneath. The hue can be changed by the beetle. Following death, this coloration disappears. (In modern classifications, the subfamilies Cassidinae and Hispinae are often regarded as one subfamily.)

● 120 species.

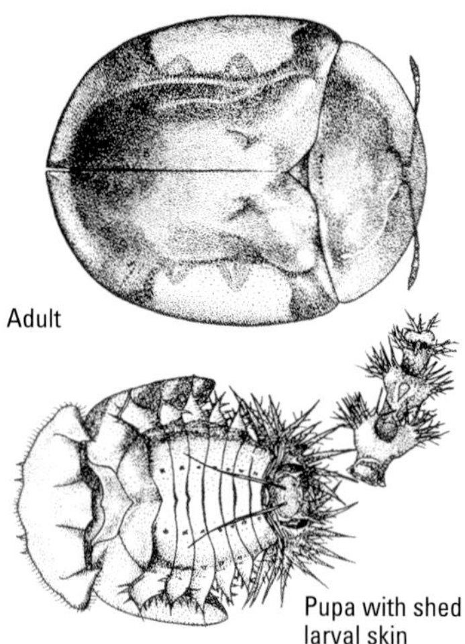

Adult

Pupa with shed larval skin

Pea weevils, bean weevils, seed weevils

Subfamily: Bruchinae

Very small to small (1–4mm). Body covered with hairs, giving a velvet-like appearance. Hunch-shaped, with elytra shortened to expose the end of the abdomen. Larvae and pupae of all species develop in seeds of leguminous plants, for example acacias. Several are pests of stored seeds; others are used to control invasive plants. Some authorities regard this subfamily as a separate family, Bruchidae.

● At least 115 species.

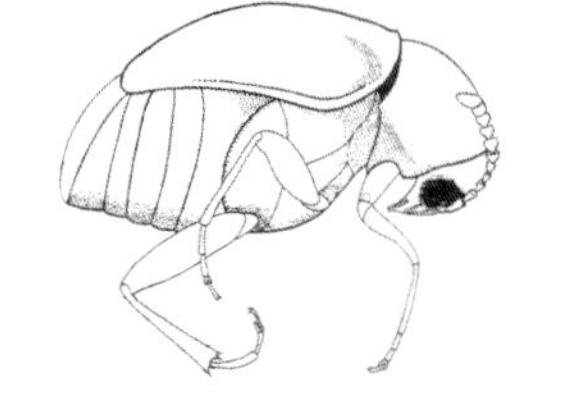

Weevils, snout beetles

Superfamily: Curculionoidea

This group of families is the largest among all insects (five families and 17 subfamilies in southern Africa). Species are almost always characterised by some type of head elongation. They are mostly herbivorous, often with highly specialised niches. Some species feed on fungi. Larvae live in plant tissue and are mostly legless; some are free-living in soil. Four families are described below.

Straight-snouted weevils

Family: Brentidae

Small to medium-sized (4–20mm). Very long, thin beetles with black to brown coloration. Prominent grooves on elytra. Characterised by long snout and elongated head (behind the eyes). In some species males have large pincers at the snout tip. Larvae live on fungi. Family includes unusual forms, such as the cycad weevil (*Antliarrhinus* sp.).

● ±100 species.

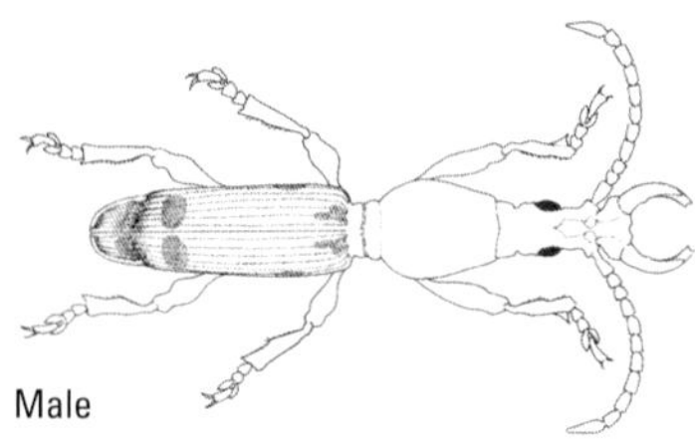

Male

Leaf-rolling weevils

Family: Attelabidae

Small to medium-sized (2–8mm). Short with long 'necks' (eyes placed to the front of the head). Some species have spines on their wings. Make food and cocoon packets for their larvae by rolling up leaves.

● 45 species.

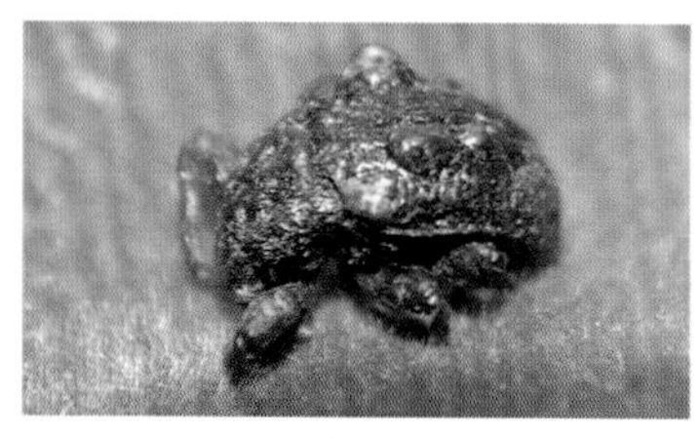

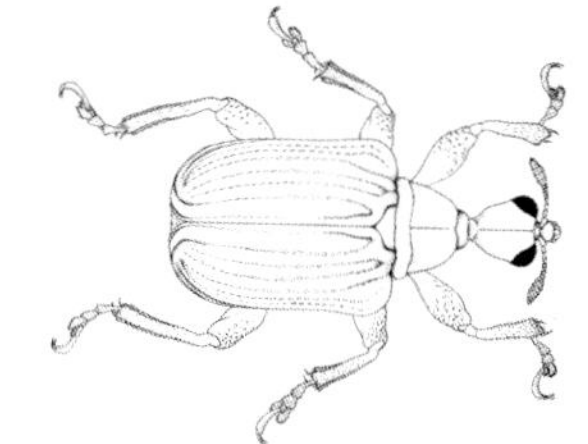

Snout beetles; weevils

Families: Curculionidae; Apionidae

Very small to very large (0.5–55mm). Large and diverse families. Head more or less elongated in the region of the eyes; antennae attached to sides of the snout and pointed forward. Many species are pests. Infest all parts and organs of plants, for example lily weevils (*Brachycerus* spp.) on lily bulbs, beaded weevils (*Protostrophus* spp.) on grass-like plants and maize, and rice weevils (*Sitophilus* spp.) in

seeds. One subfamily, pinhole borers (Platypodinae), contains very small, cylindrical beetles (1.3mm) without snouts – these bore tunnels in wood and grow fungi in them. About 50 subfamilies, but experts disagree on classification.

- 3,000 species (but many more undescribed).
- Pinhole borers (Platypodinae), can be confused with shot-hole borers (Bostrichidae), but they are much smaller and the head is not concealed under the edge of the pronotum.

Adult snout beetle

Larva

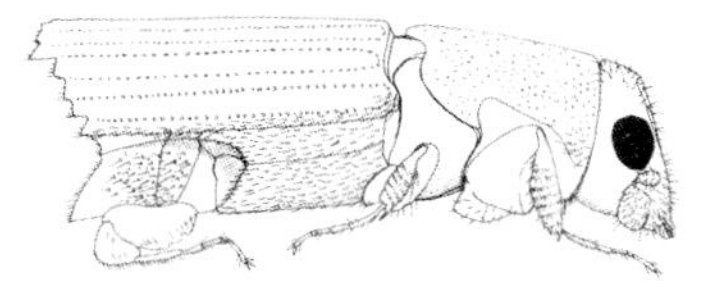

Pinhole borer

STYLOPIDS

ORDER: STREPSIPTERA

Very small to medium-sized (1.5–6mm). These unusual insects were previously classified as highly specialised beetles (Coleoptera), but are now recognised as a separate order. They survive as parasites in other insects; members of seven other insect orders have been recorded as hosts – wasps and bees (Hymenoptera) and plant bugs (Auchenorrhyncha), including leafhoppers (Cicadellidae) rank as the most common. They are seldom seen, but are not rare.

Males and females are sexually dimorphic. Females are wingless and larva-like, and live in their host throughout their life. Males are free-living and look like small flies, with strange bulging 'berry eyes' and branched antennae. Their forewings are reduced to club-like structures; the hind wings are large, membranous and fan-shaped.

- 4 families, at least 11 species (possibly with many more undiscovered species).

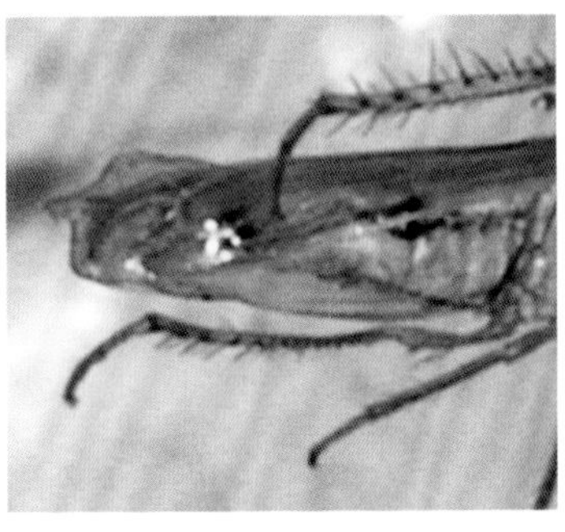

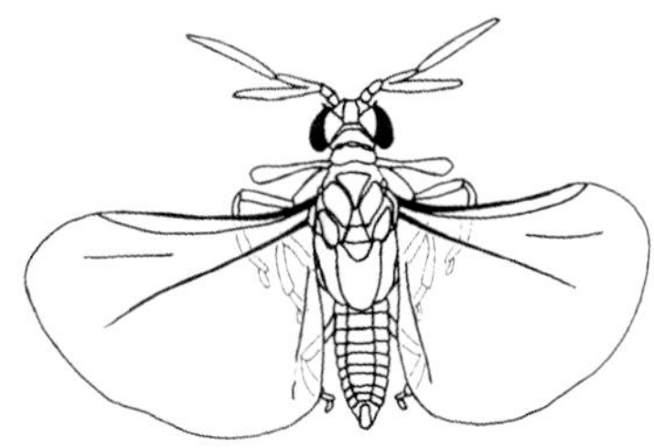

FLIES

ORDER: DIPTERA

All members of this order have only two functional wings, with the hind wings reduced to small clubs (halteres). Mouthparts are piercing or licking, but never biting (with mandibles).

The order is often subdivided into three suborders, of which two are hard to distinguish by sight. The families in these two suborders are discussed under the suborder Brachycera.

- 91 families.

MOSQUITOES AND MIDGES

Suborder: Nematocera

This suborder contains the small two-winged insects known as mosquitoes and midges. Antennae are many-segmented and mostly plumed, do not end in hair-like spikes, and are longer than the head. The most important families are briefly described below.

- 18 families.

Craneflies, leatherjackets

Family: Tipulidae

Medium-sized (10–25mm). Mosquito-like midges, with very long legs. Males form mating swarms. Larvae feed on organic plant waste in water and moist environments. Adults are mainly nocturnal.

- 340 species.
- Can be confused with mosquitoes (Culicidae), but are much larger and lack the piercing-sucking mouthparts of mosquitoes. They also do not lift their hind legs when sitting, like mosquitoes do.

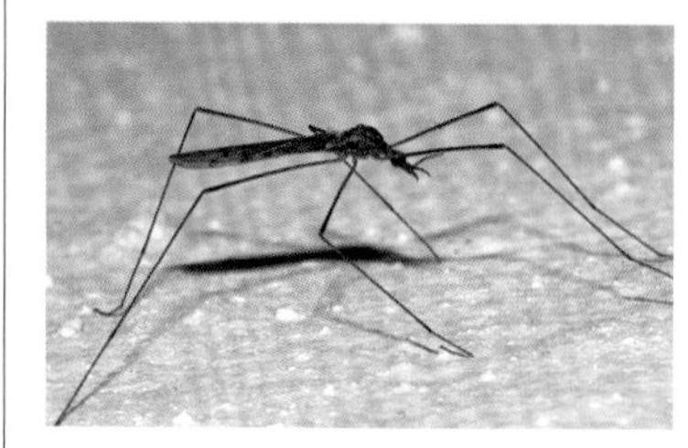

Mosquitoes

Family: Culicidae

Small to medium-sized (3–8mm). Slender insects with long legs and piercing-sucking mouthparts. Distinctive larvae and pupae are aquatic. Adult females are blood-sucking, and are significant pests, as they transmit malaria and yellow fever. Nocturnal, but not attracted to lights.

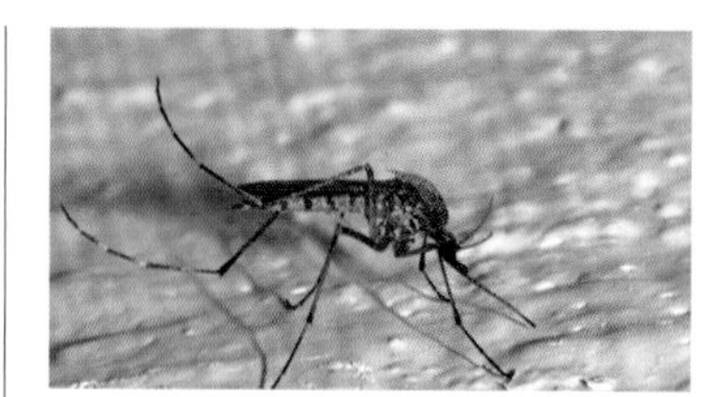

- 150 species.
- Can be confused with craneflies (Tipulidae) and bloodworms (Chironomidae). Bloodworms have long forelegs, while mosquitoes have long hind legs.

Bloodworms

Family: Chironomidae

Small (2–5mm). Unlike in mosquitoes, the front legs are very long. Adults do not feed, and are short-lived. Males have plumed antennae and form swarms. Larvae live in mud

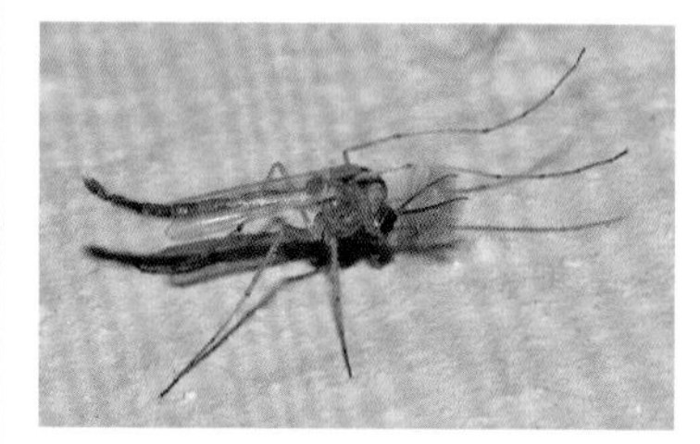

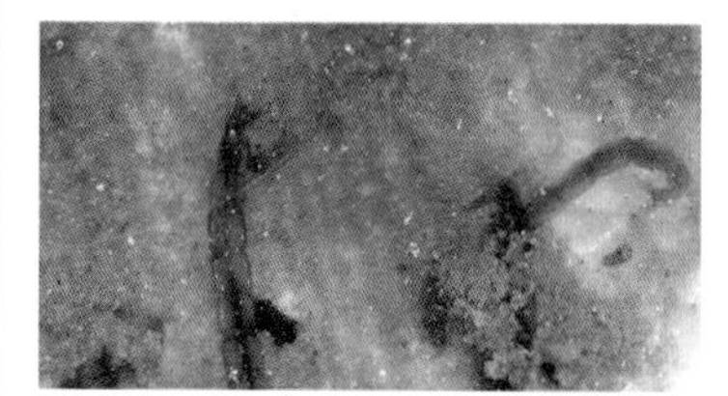

Larvae

sediments under water and are bright red.

- ±400 species.
- Can be confused with mosquitoes (Culicidae).

Blackflies; biting midges

Families: Simuliidae; Ceratopogonidae

Small (2–3mm). Black, hard midges, with a convex thorax. Antennae shorter than the head. Larvae found in running water. Adults are blood-sucking; serious pests of livestock.

- 65 species (Simuliidae); 126 species (Ceratopogonidae).

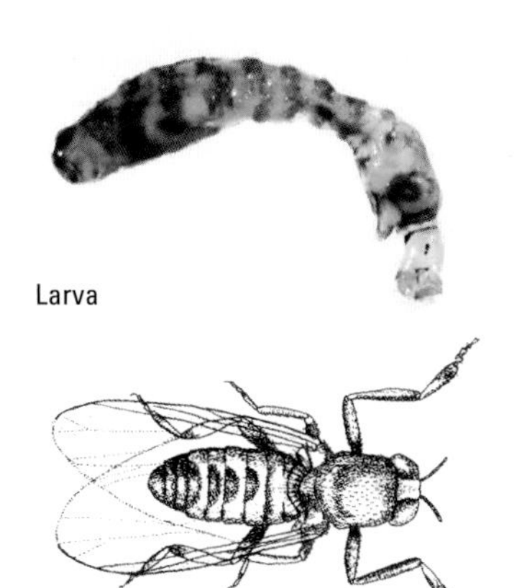

Larva

Moth flies

Family: Psychodidae

Small (2–4mm). Midges with broad, flat, moth-like wings. Adult females suck blood, especially from reptiles. Larvae feed on decomposing matter in water and often colonise drain systems, where they perform a decomposing function.

- 23 species (with many more still to be named).
- Can be confused with whiteflies (Aleyrodidae) or Ricaniidae.

Gall midges

Family: Cecidomyiidae

Small (1–3mm). Mosquito-like midges, but with characteristic thick, pointed abdomen. Most larvae live in plant galls they create. A few species are agricultural pests.

- 26 species (but specialists suggest there are hundreds of species still awaiting discovery).

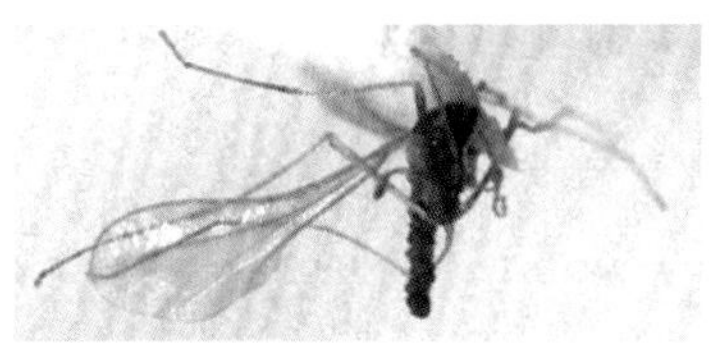

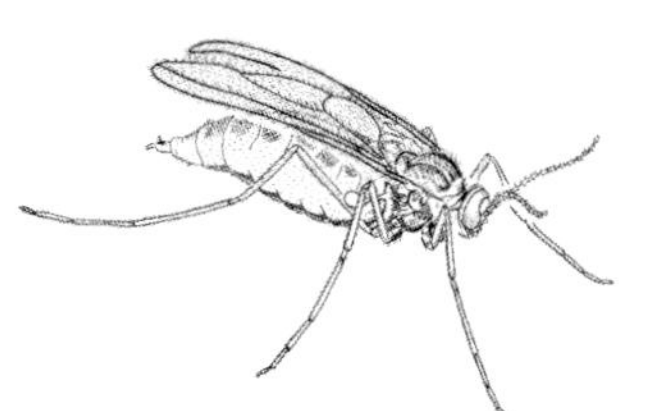

TRUE FLIES

Suborder: Brachycera

Feelers of adults are short and end in a hair spine (arista), which may be plumed. Eyes big and cover the largest part of the head. Larvae are typically legless maggots; thorax, head and body segments indistinct. Suborder includes the majority of dipteran families commonly known as flies and blowflies. The most important families are described below.

- 73 families.

Soldier flies

Family: Stratiomyidae

Medium-sized (10–15mm). Eyes large, practically touching each

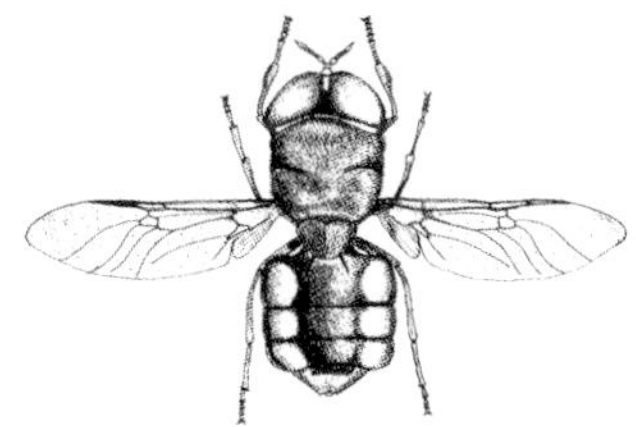

other; antennae relatively long. Wings folded flat over abdomen. May have a transparent patch on each side of the abdominal base to suggest the 'waist' of a wasp: some species mimic paper wasps (Vespidae).

- 90 species.

Horse flies

Family: Tabanidae

Medium-sized (10–25mm). Large, often colourful eyes, triangular head and prominent V-shaped antennae (see illustration below). Piercing-sucking mouthparts are long in some species. Males suck nectar; females suck blood of mammals, but may also suck

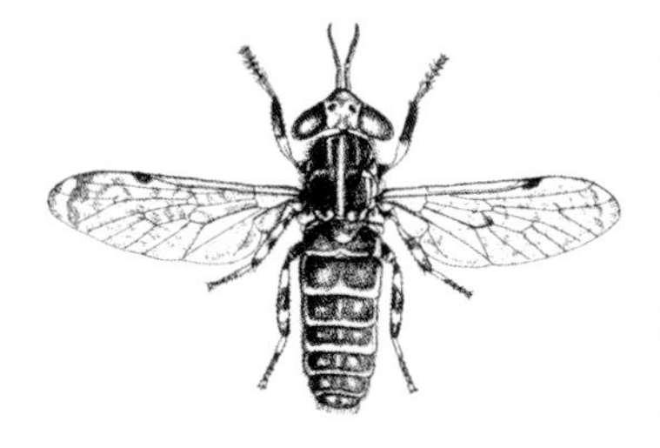

nectar or even drink water when thirsty. Females are carriers of several diseases.

- 250 species.
- Can be confused with bee flies (Bombyliidae) and hover flies (Syrphidae). Species with long sucking mouthparts (rostrum) can be distinguished from bee flies by their lack of long hairs. Species with a shorter rostrum may resemble hover flies, but hover flies have rounder eyes and the abdomen looks like that of a honeybee. See also tsetse flies (Glossinidae).

Robber flies

Family: Asilidae

Small to large (3–40mm). Distinctive, with a long abdomen and narrow wings folded flat over the abdomen. Top of the head hollowed out between the large eyes; piercing-sucking mouthparts point downward. Larvae mostly live in compost, but a few species are predaceous, catching and sucking out the insides of other insects.

- 500 species.
- Although this family is generally distinctive, there are a few confounding mimics. *Hyperechia* spp. convincingly mimic carpenter bees (Anthophoridae), but have a concave head and only two wings. *Leptogaster* spp. mimic hanging flies (Mecoptera), and several large species mimic spider-hunting wasps (Pompilidae); however, the robber flies are easily identified in that they have only one pair of wings. Several genera mimic paper wasps (Vespidae) or may be similar in appearance to thick-headed flies (Conopidae), but the robber fly's smaller concave head differentiates it from other species.

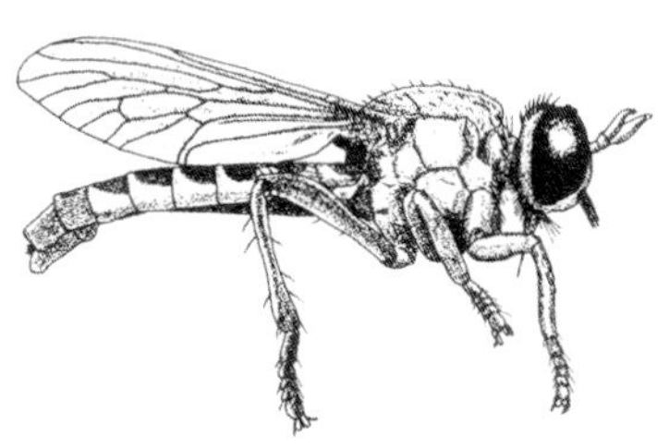

Bee flies

Family: Bombyliidae

Small to medium-sized (3–20mm). Characteristically furry, with a long rostrum. Commonly found on flowers, often hovering while sucking nectar. Very important pollinators of wild flowers. Larvae parasitise eggs, larvae or pupae of other insects, including digger wasps (Sphecidae). The female bee fly will hover over the ground tunnels of a digger wasp, shooting eggs into the nest.

- 940 species.
- Can be confused with horse flies (Tabanidae), as less hairy bee flies can resemble them.

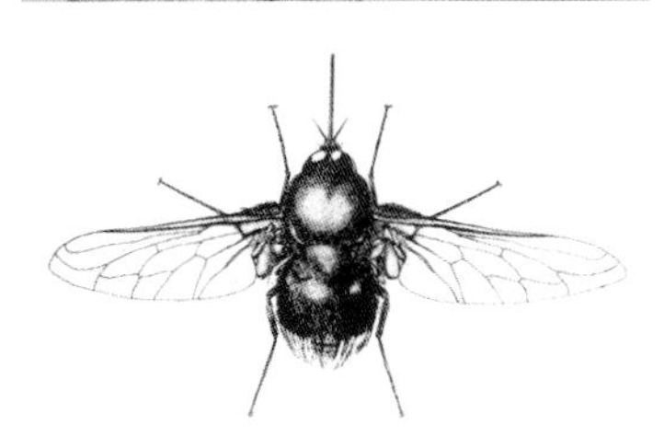

Hover flies

Family: Syrphidae

Medium-sized (6–15mm). Large round eyes. Body and wings very similar to those of honeybees (*Apis* spp.). Maggots have two lifestyles: some are free-living predators of aphids (Aphididae); others, known as rat-tailed maggots, live in mud and have long breathing tubes.

- 165 species.
- Can be confused with honeybees (*Apis* spp.), but are differentiated by their large eyes and only two wings. Sometimes mistaken for horse flies (Tabanidae).

Thick-headed flies

Family: Conopidae

Medium-sized (10–20mm). Characteristically narrow 'waist', relatively long antennae and a very large head. Mimic the coloration of smaller paper wasps (Vespidae). Maggots parasitise, among others, cockroaches (Blattaria) and paper wasps. The female fly attaches her hooked eggs to the paper wasp in flight.

- 65 species.
- Can be confused with paper wasps, but have only two wings and parallel antennae that are pointed forward. Resemble other wasp-mimicking flies, for example robber flies (Asilidae).

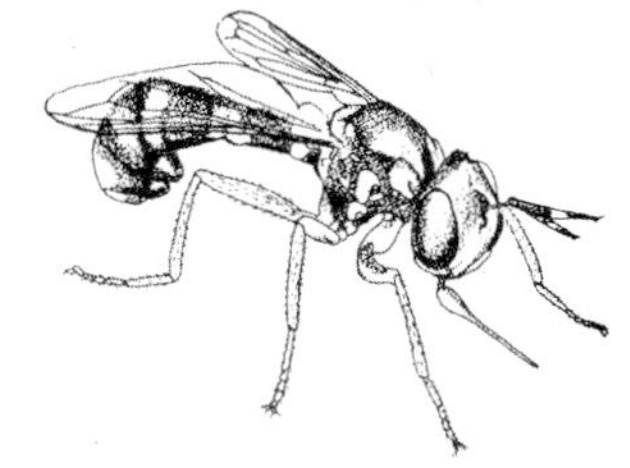

Fruit flies

Family: Tephritidae

Small to medium-sized (3–7mm). Mobile head, eyes often with metallic iridescence. In females, the rounded abdomen ends in

a point. Wings are triangular, usually with brown and black markings. Maggots develop in fruit; many are serious agricultural pests.
- 375 species.

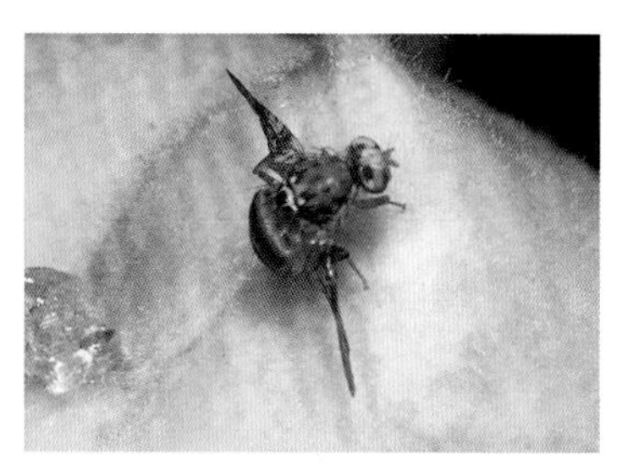

Red-headed flies (also called signal flies)

Family: Platystomatidae

Medium-sized (10–25mm). Sluggish, slow-flying flies with distinctive red or orange heads; body and wings black or metallic blue. Maggots are carrion feeders or feed on decomposing plant matter. Adults sometimes feed on nectar from flowers. Poisonous; avoided by predators.
- 80 species.

Bee lice

Family: Braulidae

Very small (1–1.5mm). Louse-like, wingless, parasitic flies that live on honeybees (*Apis mellifera*).
- 2 species.

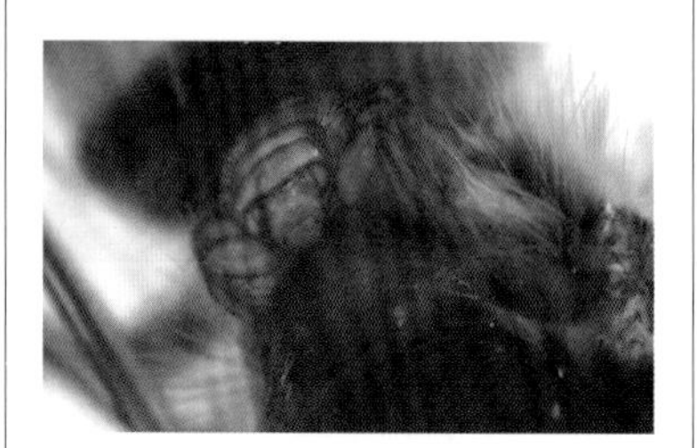

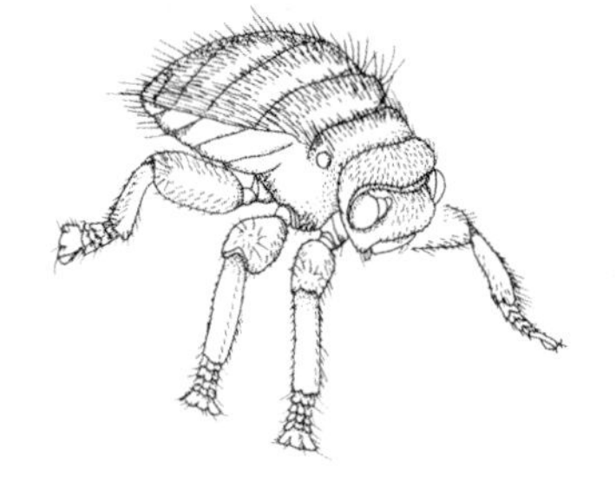

- Can be confused with 'true' lice (Phthiraptera); however, they live only on bees, and bees have no lice.

'Semaphore' flies (also called stilt-legged flies)

Family: Micropezidae

Medium-sized (8–15mm). Long slender legs. Forelegs attached far to the front of the body, often with white tips, and waved about continuously to attract mates. Wings folded over the abdomen. Found in tropical forests.
- 4 species.

Stalk-eyed flies

Family: Diopsidae

Small to medium-sized (3–6mm). Tropical flies with eyes and short

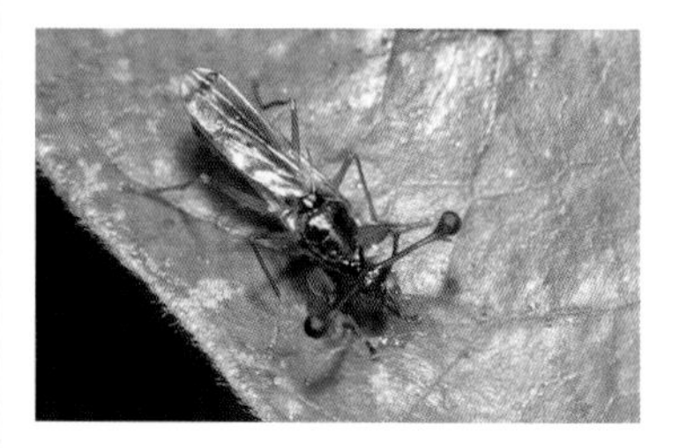

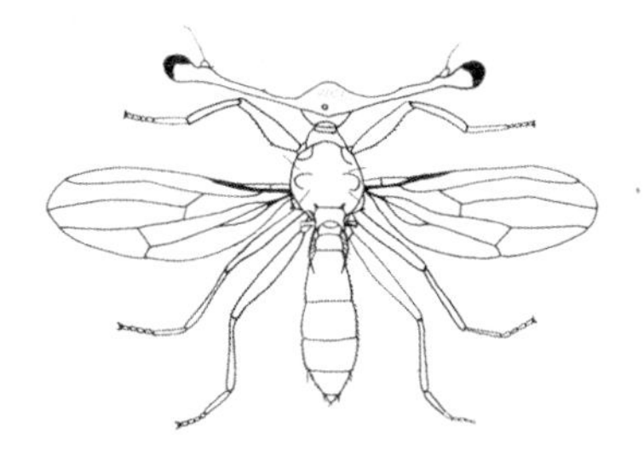

antennae located at the end of long, laterally protruding stalks. Maggots develop in plant tissue.

- 48 species.

Leaf-mining flies

Family: Agromyzidae

Very small (0.5–2mm). Maggots are miners in leaves or stems. Some species are easily identified from the type of mine, or from specific hosts such as agricultural crops (where host-specific leaf miners are present). Many are serious agricultural pests.

- 131 species.
- The leaf-mining habit also occurs in beetles (Coleoptera); moths (Lepidoptera); and wasps (Hymenoptera).

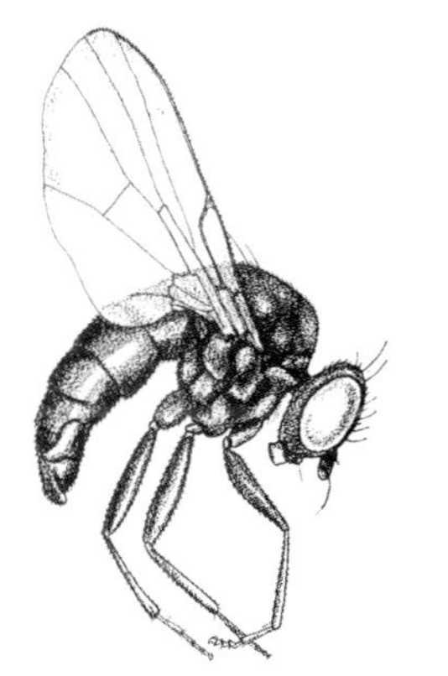

Vinegar flies

Family: Drosophilidae

Very small (0.5–2mm). Adults are yellowish with large red eyes. Attracted to the smell of alcohol or vinegar. Maggots live in rotting fruit where they feed on yeast. The species *Drosophila melanogaster* became famous for being among the first organisms to be used in genetic and molecular biology research.

- 61 species.

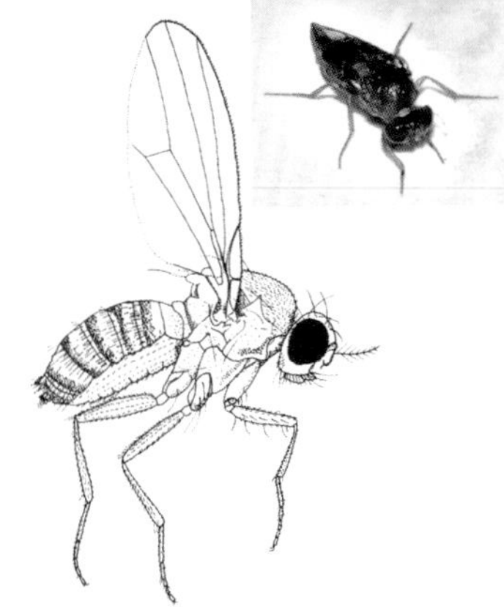

Jackal flies

Family: Milichiidae

Very small (1–2mm). Resemble miniature house flies (*Musca* spp.). Feed on body fluids that leak when, for example, spiders, robber flies (Asilidae) or assassin bugs (Reduviidae) suck juices from their prey. Often ride 'taxi' on on other insects (see photograph below). Maggots live in decomposing plant matter.

- 13 species.

House flies

Family: Muscidae

Medium-sized (5–8mm). Biting types can transmit diseases; licking species, for example the house fly (*Musca domestica*),

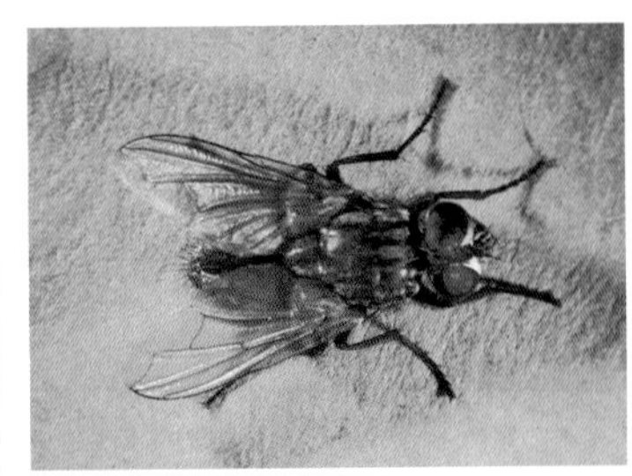

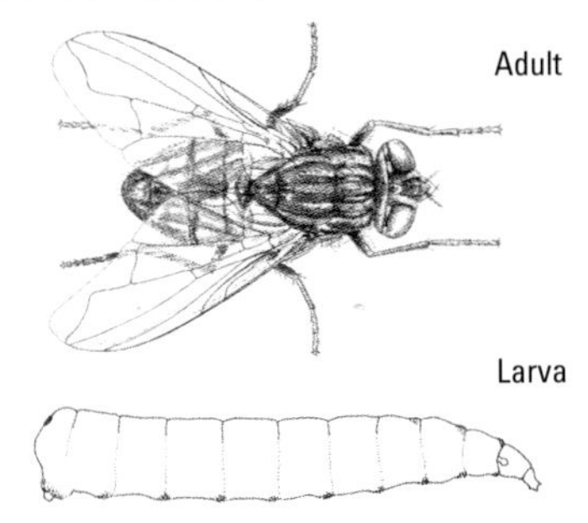

may cause sanitation problems. Maggots develop in any decomposing material. Family also includes the stable fly (*Stomoxys calcitrans*).

- 364 species.
- Can be confused with flesh flies (Sarcophagidae), but these are much larger and have a longer abdomen with white patterns. Other similar flies are much smaller, for example Milichiidae.

Tsetse flies

Family: Glossinidae

Medium-sized (±12mm). Flattened, blood-sucking flies, with dull coloration and forward-pointing mouthparts (proboscis and palpi). Family includes the infamous tsetse fly *Glossina brevipalpis*, which transmits nagana in cattle and sleeping sickness in humans. Eggs hatch inside the female; maggots are born alive and pupate almost immediately after birth.

- 4 species.

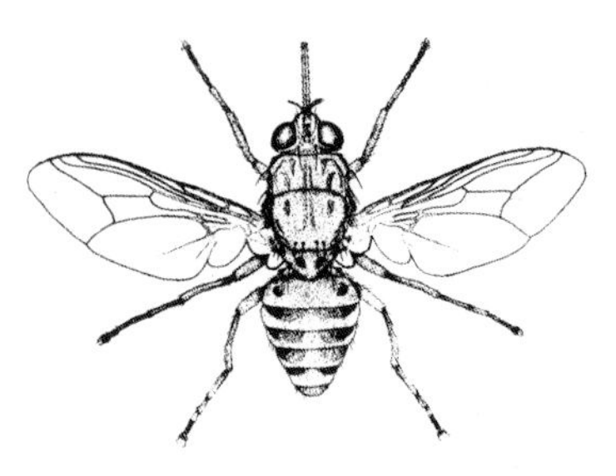

Louse flies

Family: Hippoboscidae

Medium-sized (8–12mm). Very flat, hard flies, with wide grasping legs modified to cling to the hair of mammals or the feathers of birds. Wings sometimes reduced. Blood-sucking. Maggots are born alive and pupate immediately.

- 37 species.
- Can be confused with two related families found mainly on bats. Bat louse flies (Nycteribiidae) have round bodies, are spidery and are always wingless. Bat flies (Streblidae) are also round in shape; some species have wings, but most are wingless.

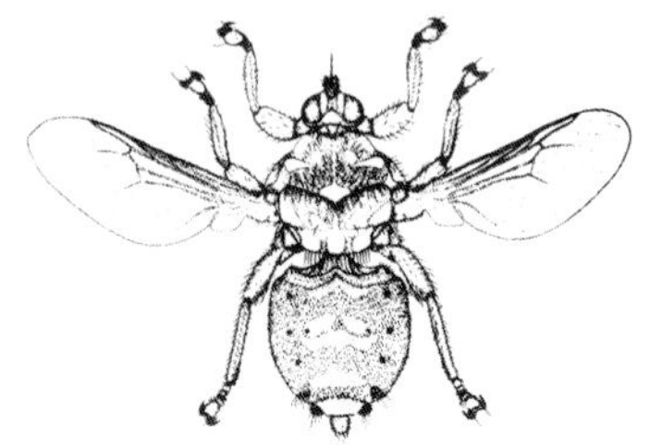

Bluebottles, greenbottles, blowflies

Family: Calliphoridae

Medium-sized (8–12mm). Compact, mostly metallic blue or metallic green, with large red eyes. Maggots live inside rotten flesh or protein-rich faeces, but some attack insect congregations, for example termites or ants, or grasshopper egg packets. Infect shallow wounds (for example sheep blowflies (*Lucilia* spp.) and *Chrysomya* spp.), or actively penetrate the skin of humans and domestic pets, for example the yellow-brown tumbu fly (*Cordylobia anthropophaga*).

- 152 species.
- Yellowish species (such as the tumbu fly) can be confused with tachinid flies (Tachinidae), horse bots (Gasterophilidae) and nasal flies (Oestridae). Tachinids are diverse in appearance, but have more prominent and larger antennae. Horse bots and nasal flies have reduced mouthparts.

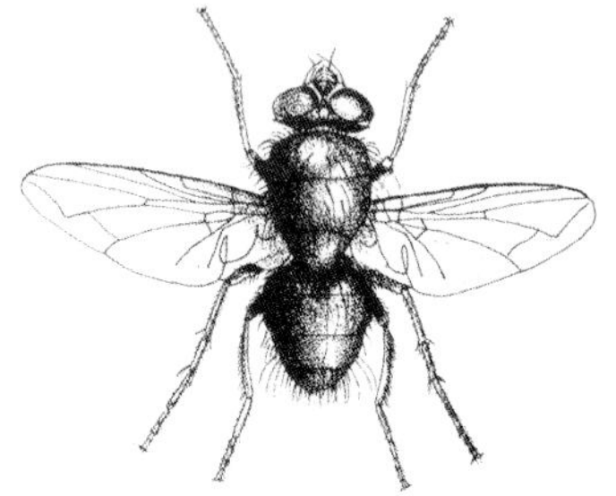

Flesh flies

Family: Sarcophagidae

Medium-sized (9–14mm). Silver-white and black, with elongated abdomen and eyes that do not meet on top of the head. Maggots are born alive, several at a time, and are still underdeveloped at birth. Some are parasites of social or subsocial insects; others feed on meat or protein-rich faeces.

- 157 species.
- Can be confused with house flies (Muscidae) and Oestridae, but species of the latter have reduced mouthparts and smaller eyes.

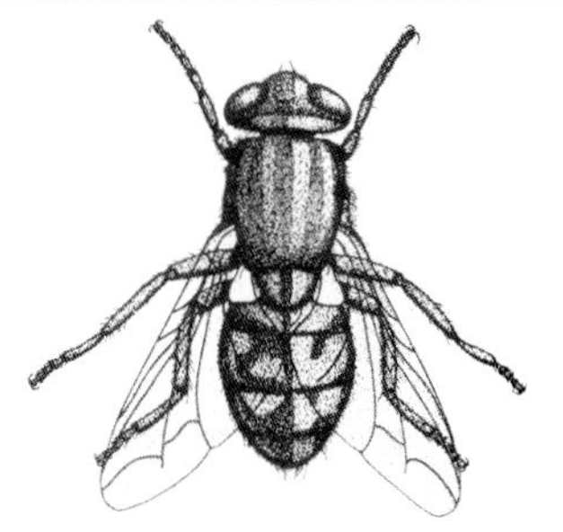

Warble flies, bot flies, nasal flies; horse bot flies

Families: Oestridae; Gasterophilidae

Medium-sized (8–10mm). Maggots of nasal flies develop in the sinuses of sheep, are sneezed out when fully grown, and then pupate in the ground (so-called 'nasal pupae' are not pupae but maggots!). Eggs are laid in the nasal passages of sheep. Maggots of horse bot flies end up in the stomach of the host when eggs are licked off the skin. Fully grown larvae exit their host through its dung and land on the ground where they pupate. All nasal flies and horse bot flies have mammals as hosts and many are livestock pests.

- 17 species (Oestridae); 12 species (Gasterophilidae).
- Can be confused with flesh flies (Sarcophagidae) and hairy tachinid flies (Tachinidae), but Oestridae and Gasterophilidae differ in having reduced mouthparts.

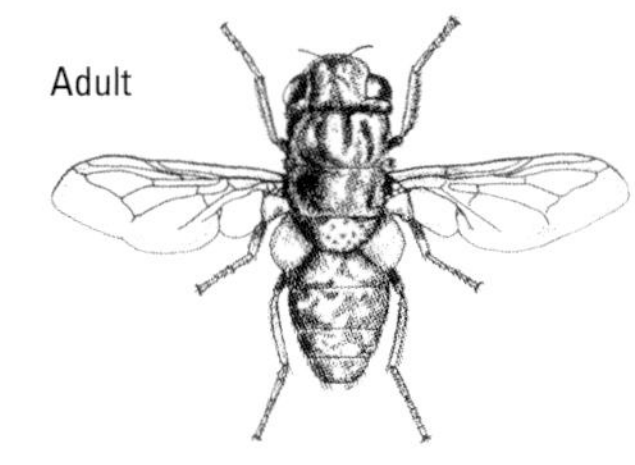

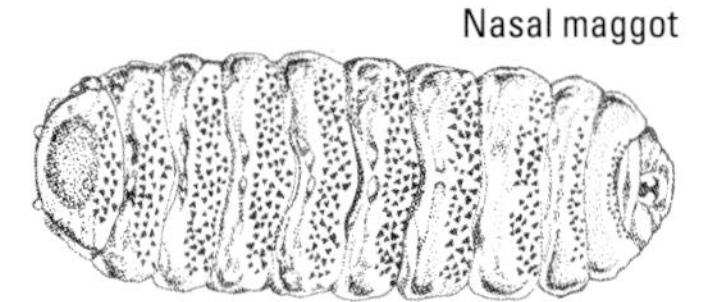

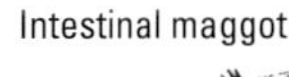

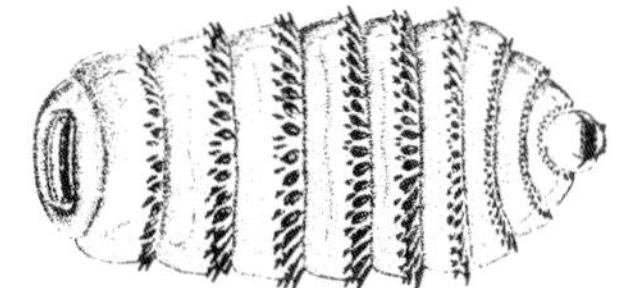

MOTHS AND BUTTERFLIES

ORDER: LEPIDOPTERA

Wings are broad and, like the rest of the body, are covered with scales. Mouthparts are absent or present. Where present, mouthparts form a long siphoning tube (proboscis) that can be rolled up. Larvae are caterpillars with six thoracic legs as well as sucker-like 'legs' on abdominal segments. Almost all caterpillars are herbivorous.

- 89 families.
- Can be confused with caddisflies (Trichoptera) and certain lacewings (Neuroptera).

MOTHS

The species in the 18 families described below are generally called moths, but do not form an official taxonomic group. Along with the butterfly families, they make up the order Lepidoptera. Most species are night flyers. Pupae usually form cocoons.

Swift moths, ghost moths

Family: Hepialidae

Medium-sized to very large (20–60mm). Primitive moths. Brown, some with white markings. Fore- and hind wings are almost the same size. Caterpillars feed on grass or bore in wood, for

example keurboom ghost moth (*Leto venus*).

- 66 species.

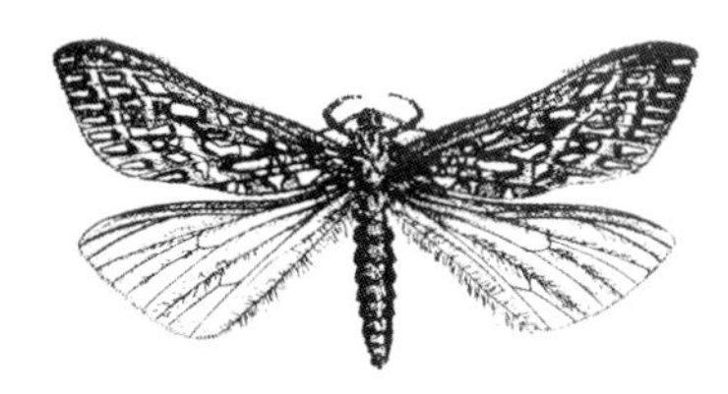

Leaf-mining moths

Family: Nepticulidae

Very small to small (1.5–4mm). Long, hairy fringes on wings, mostly longer than wing diameter. Caterpillars create mines inside leaves.

- 11 species.

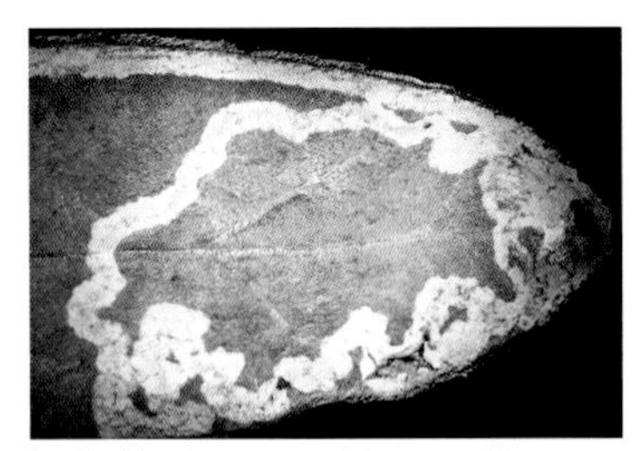

Leaf with mines created by caterpillars

Goat moths, carpenter moths

Family: Cossidae

Medium-sized to large (10–59mm). Sturdy build; normally dull brown or grey with black transverse markings. Antennae are plumed, tips often thin and straight. Larvae tunnel into wood of variable nutritional value. As a result, adult sizes differ widely within the same species. Caterpillars spin together excreted wood pellets, which can be seen on tree trunks (see first photograph below).

- 56 species.
- Can be confused with several families, including monkey moths (Eupterotidae) and owlet moths (Noctuidae), but goat moths and carpenter moths have reduced mouthparts and lack a coiled proboscis.

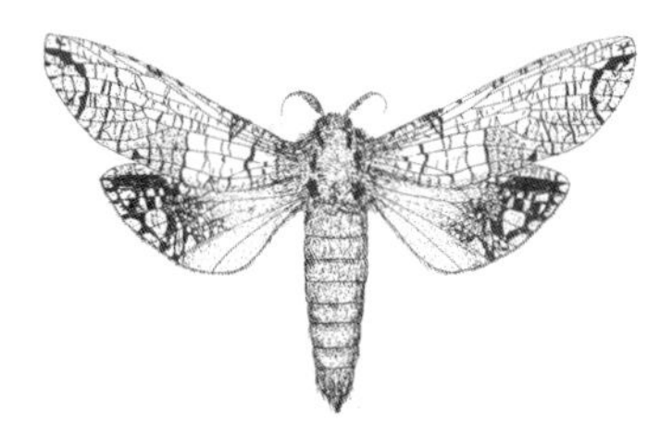

Bagworm moths

Family: Psychidae

Medium-sized (10–20mm). Body black or grey. Antennae plumed.

Males have transparent wings with few scales; females are wingless. Caterpillars spin bags or cases from leaves, grasses, twigs or thorns and carry them around. The bags also serve as cocoons (see photographs). Only the adult male leaves the cocoon – for breeding purposes. Females are fertilised by males in the cocoon, and the eggs are laid in the cocoon. Hatching larvae spin long silk threads; suspended from these threads, they are carried to other plants by the wind. Some species are parthenogenetic, with eggs not fertilised by a male. The exotic wattle bagworm (*Kotochalia junodi*) became a serious pest in wattle plantations.

- 133 species.
- Can be confused with caddisflies (Trichoptera), which spin bag homes – but underwater. Certain clothes moths (Tineidae) and pyralid snout moths (Pyralidae) make portable homes, but they live in dry, dead plant matter or animal tissue, and are much smaller. A few carpenter moths (Cossidae) also make portable cocoons, but they feed only on tree bark.

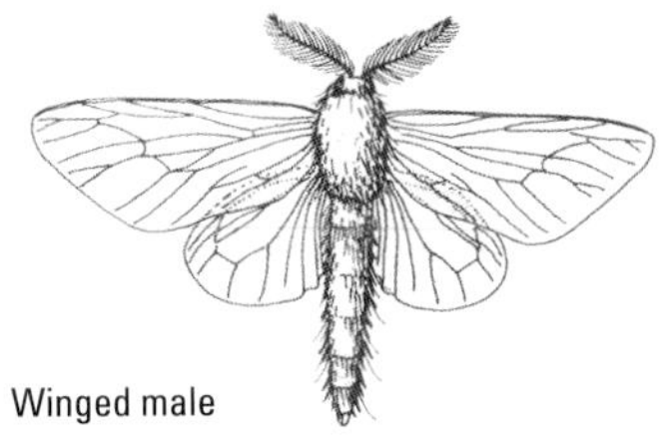

Winged male

Clothes moths

Family: Tineidae

Medium-sized (5–10mm). Long fringes of hair around the narrow wings and a tuft of hairs on the head. Family includes *Tinea* spp.

and *Tineola* spp., other pests of stored goods, and species that bore into horns (see first photograph below), which have pupae that build their cocoons on the surface of the horns (see second photograph below).

- 253 species.

Leaf rollers, codling moths

Family: Tortricidae (including Olethreutidae)

Medium-sized (5–10mm). Forewings are characteristically broad and have blunt tips.

Caterpillars feed inside fruit or seed, or in shelters they construct by rolling up leaves and loosely spinning them together. Several are agricultural pests.

- 258 species.

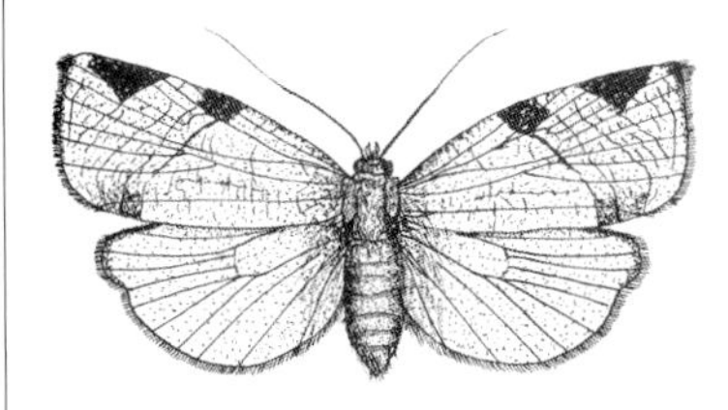

Slug moths

Family: Limacodidae

Medium-sized (10–25mm). Squat, often brightly coloured, with a sturdy thorax. Caterpillars mostly green and look like slugs; move in a slow, wave-like motion. Forelegs are modified into suckers that rest flat on leaves. Body covered with poisonous stinging hairs. Family includes the plum slug (*Latoia vivida*), a pest species.

- 119 species.

Pyralid moths; snout moths and their kin

Families: Pyralidae; Crambidae

Medium-sized (5–18mm). Forewings narrower than hind wings. Palpi on head pointed forward, appearing as a snout or sharp tip. Caterpillars build shelters of silk and debris from the environment; they also pupate in these shelters. Very active when disturbed. Several pest species, including stemborers and pests of flour, chocolate and other stored goods.

- More than 1,000 species.
- Can be confused with owlet moths (Noctuidae) and several other dull-coloured or brown moths. The 'snout head' is the best identifying feature, but it is not always distinct.

Geometrid moths

Family: Geometridae

Medium-sized to large (5–30mm). Mostly dull or light green, but some display striking white or bright green patterns. Several species mimic brightly coloured butterflies. Always sit with their broad wings spread out. Thorax and abdomen relatively slender. Caterpillars have only four sucker 'feet' on the abdomen. Locomotion is accomplished by a series of alternating contracting and stretching movements, as the legs and suckers change hold.

- More than 1,000 species.

Emperor moths

Family: Saturniidae

Large to very large (30–100mm). Wings have transparent 'windows' in the centre, which are usually surrounded by brightly coloured 'eyespots'. Some species have a curved forewing tip or a long 'tail' on their hind wings. Males have wide, plumed antennae. Caterpillars are multi-coloured, with distinctive coloured nodules and spines. Family includes the mopane moth (*Imbrasia belina*).

- 75 species.
- Can be confused with moths with eyespots on wings, such as large owlet moths

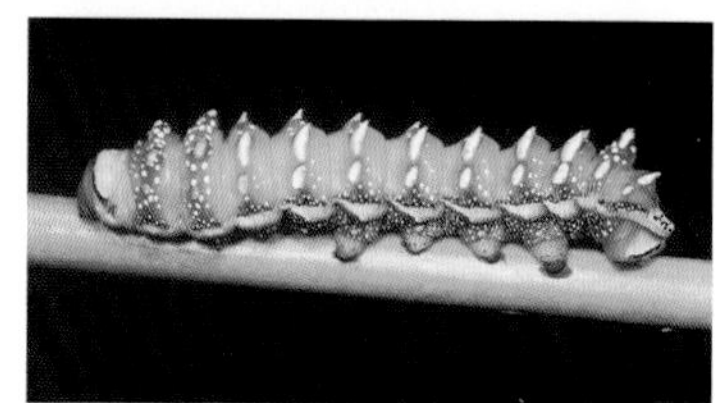

(Noctuidae). However, in other families the transparent 'windows' in the eyespots on the wings are always absent.

Monkey moths, giant lappet moths

Family: Eupterotidae

Medium-sized to very large (17–65mm). Furry and bulky, colour ranging from brown to dull grey. Antennae broad and plumed. Wings rounded with long-haired fringes. Caterpillars covered with long, backward-curved hairs.

- 62 species.

Adult

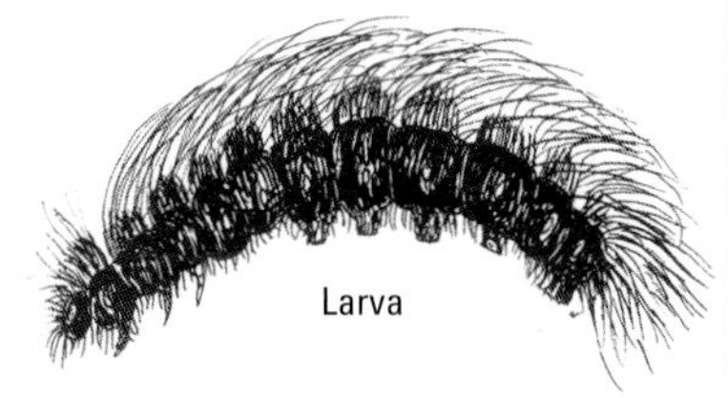

Larva

Egger moths, lappet moths

Family: Lasiocampidae

Medium-sized to large (14–50mm). Mostly dull grey or brown; hind wings lighter in colour. Antennae usually plumed. Front edges of hind wings extend beyond forewings when folded, and are often wavy. Femur and tibia of legs are covered in long hairs. Caterpillars typically hairy, with tufts of stinging hairs and lateral tufts that reach the substrate, hiding their shadow and thus camouflaging the body.

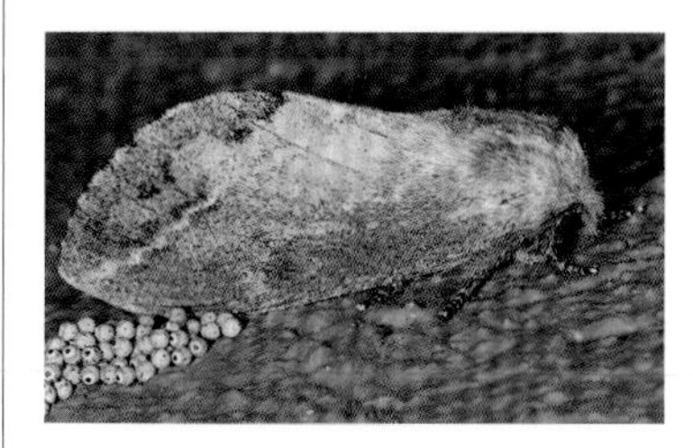

- 127 species.
- Can be confused with owlet moths (Noctuidae), especially when hind wings do not protrude prominently from under forewings. Difficult to distinguish between Lasiocampidae and short-tailed Sphingidae moths, as forewings are significantly longer than hind wings in both families. Antennae of Sphingidae have hooked tips.

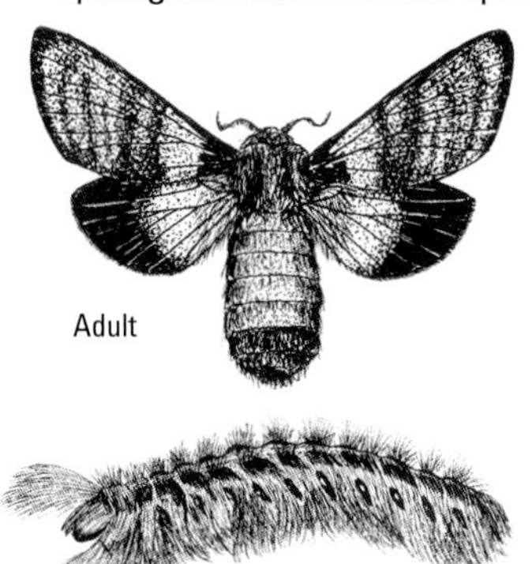

Hawk moths, sphinx moths

Family: Sphingidae

Medium-sized to very large (15–75mm). Small hind wings, about half the length of narrow, pointed forewings. Pointed abdomen, sometimes with tuft of hairs on the end. Antennae have characteristic hooked tips. Proboscis very long. A few species are diurnal fliers, with translucent wings. Caterpillars

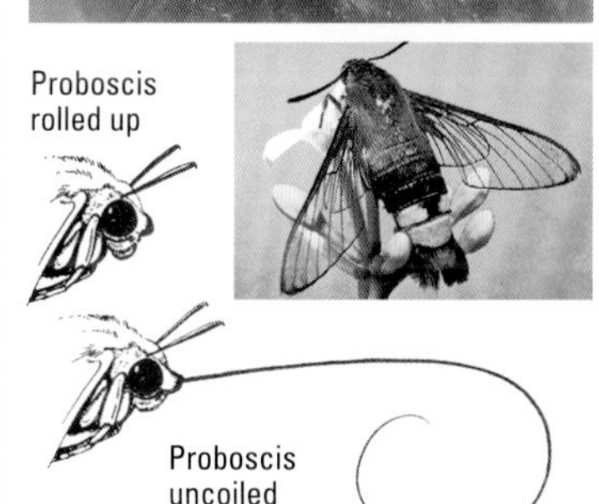

are often brightly coloured, usually have 'eyespots' and always have a 'tail' at the rear end. In pupae, the proboscis protrudes from shell. Family includes the death's-head hawk moth (*Acherontia atropos*).

- 105 species.

Processionary caterpillar moths

Family: Thaumetopoeidae

Medium-sized (15–18mm). Wings mostly white with a network of dark brown lines on forewings. Caterpillars uniformly hairy without tufts. Move from tree to tree in typical trail processions (head to tail). These 'trains' can reach lengths of up to 20m (see Chapter 4). Pupate in a single silk bag that they spin communally.

- 6 species.

Tussock moths, gypsy moths

Family: Lymantriidae

Medium-sized to large (12–30mm). Brownish, yellow or white moths of average build. Caterpillars are hairy, with four distinctive upright bristles on the abdominal segments. Stinging hairs are spun into cocoons and reused by emerging females to serve as protection for their eggs later on. Some are agricultural pests.

- 180 species.
- Can be confused with owlet moths (Noctuidae), except that mouthparts of tussock and gypsy moths are greatly reduced.

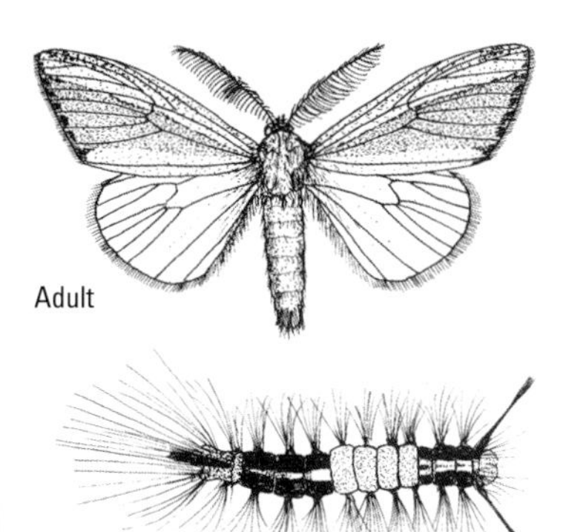

Prominents, puss moths

Family: Notodontidae

Medium-sized to large (15–45mm). Brown, dull grey, white or yellowish coloration. Forewings keel-shaped when folded. Caterpillars very diverse and unusual; some have grotesque shapes or mimic geckos, others have double-horned projections, foul-smelling tails and chemical glands for self-defence. Group aggregations occur in some species ('tent caterpillars'), with the caterpillars covering an entire tree in a silk 'tent' for protection. No agricultural pests.

- 193 species.

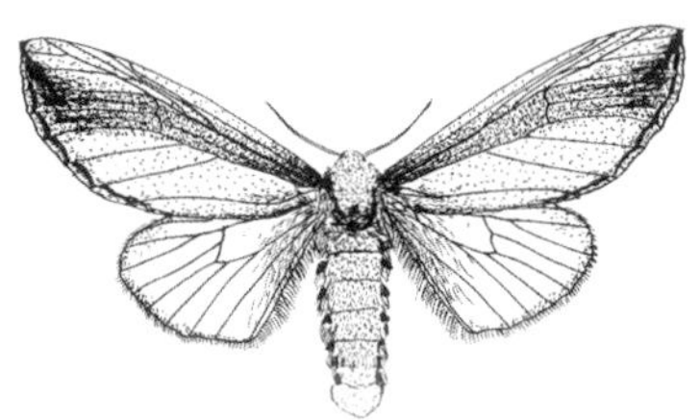

Tiger moths, footmen

Family: Arctiidae

Medium-sized to large (15–40mm). Sturdy moths, mostly bright yellow combined with red, white, black or brown. Many larvae of the subfamily Arctiinae (tiger moths) are very hairy or are brightly banded. Grey and brown species

Adult

Larva

also occur. Many species are diurnal fliers. One subfamily (Ctenuchinae) is exclusively diurnal and has narrow wings and unusually bright blue and purple markings. Caterpillars hairy or brightly banded. Most are poisonous.

- 227 species.
- Only some owlet moths (Noctuidae) and geometrid moths (Geometridae) are as colourful as tiger moths and footmen, but the more dully coloured species are difficult to distinguish.

Owlet moths

Family: Noctuidae

Medium-sized to very large (10–60mm). Dull grey or brown, usually with pale hind wings. A few species have bright colours or eyespots. Caterpillars normally hairless and typically resemble African armyworms (*Spodoptera* spp.). Caterpillars constitute the largest number of agricultural pests by far. Family includes most nocturnal flying moths.

- At least 1,700 species.
- Given the large number of species in this family, the best way of identifying owlet moths is by elimination. If the specimen does not clearly belong to any of the other moth families, it most probably is an owlet moth.

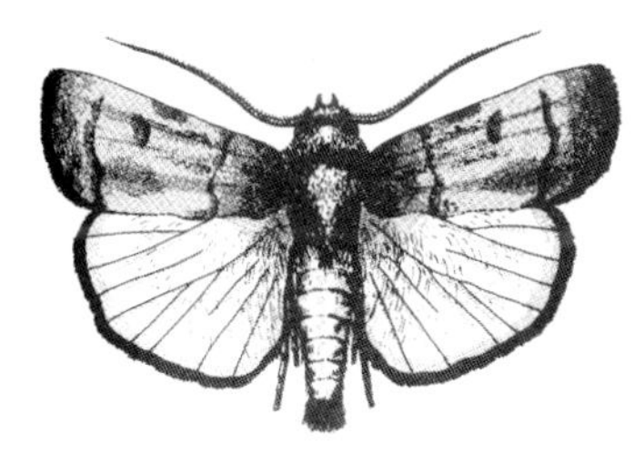

BUTTERFLIES

The following five families are collectively known as butterflies, but do not form one taxonomic group. Along with the moth families, they constitute the order Lepidoptera. All butterflies are diurnal, have club-shaped (capitate) antennae and fold their wings upright when resting. Pupae do not pupate in cocoons.

Skippers

Family: Hesperiidae

Medium-sized (12–25mm). Brown butterflies, often with yellow or white markings. Head and thorax very broad so that

only the tips of the wings touch when folded. Antennae have hooked tips. Fly at dusk; fast and darting flight. Caterpillars spin leaf shelters together in which they eventually pupate.
● 130 species.

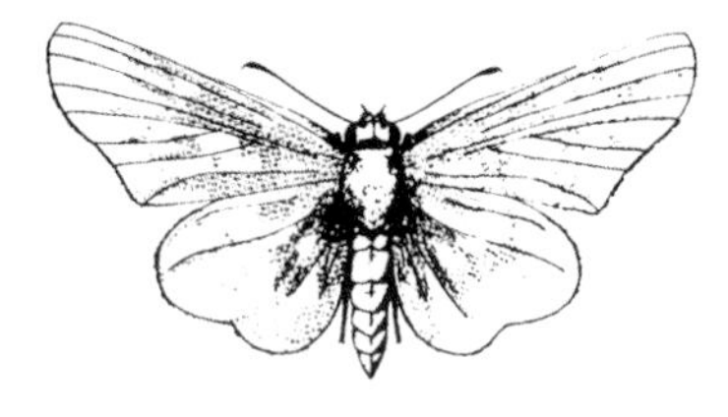

Swallowtails

Family: Papilionidae

Large to very large (40–75mm). Distinctive butterflies with yellow-and-black or blue-and-black coloration and a 'tail' on each hind wing. Females often very

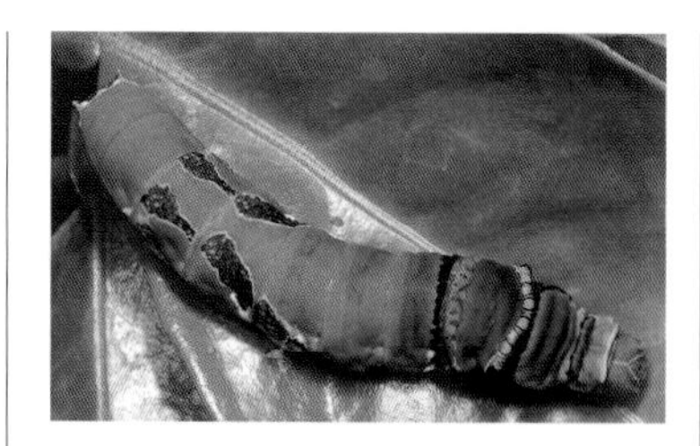

effectively mimic milkweed butterflies (Danainae). Early-instar caterpillars mimic bird droppings and, later , resemble leaves. They have protrusible scent-gland horns. Family includes the well-known citrus swallowtail (*Papilio demodocus*).
● 17 species.

Whites, sulphurs, orange tips

Family: Pieridae

Medium-sized to large (18–35mm). Mostly white or yellow, often with black markings around wing edges and red or orange forewing tips. Wings more or less rounded. Caterpillars mostly green and smooth. Pupae hang

on branches, supported by 'safety belts' spun from silk. Family includes the cabbage white (*Pieris brassicae*) and the brown-veined white (*Belenois aurota*). The latter forms large migratory swarms.
● 60 species.

Coppers, blues

Family: Lycaenidae

Medium-sized (8–20mm). Often brightly coloured, with dorsal side of wings mostly metallic blue or copper with brown markings. Undersides of hind wings often have eyespots and movable false 'antennae' at the rear, forming a false head. Antennal clubs are either flat or hollow on the underside. Some species mimic milkweed butterflies and monarchs (Danainae) or acraeas (Heliconiinae). Caterpillars often have complex life cycles that include nest parasitism of ants.

- More than 400 species.
- Some dull brown species can be confused with skippers (Hesperiidae), but their bodies are more slender.

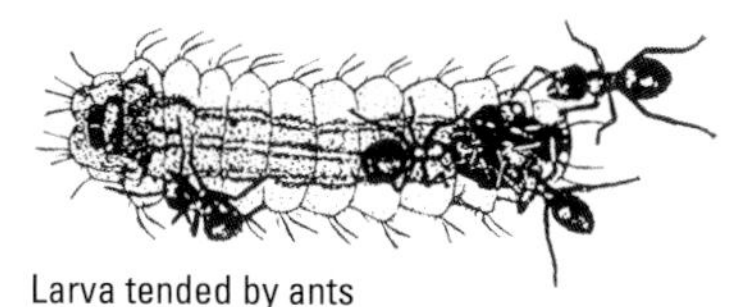

Larva tended by ants

Brush-footed butterflies

Family: Nymphalidae

This family includes most butterflies. It is divided into eight subfamilies, containing 268 species. The most common subfamilies are described below.

Charaxes

Subfamily: Charaxinae

Large (25–45mm). Two thin 'tails' on the hind wings, often with spectacular blue metallic colours and black, white and orange markings on the upper side of the wings (sometimes also orange or light yellow with black). Very fast and strong fliers. Caterpillars often with horn-like protrusions on a head shield and two horns on the abdomen, which tapers towards the end. Found in forests and mountains, where they are attracted to droppings of carnivores and fermenting fruit.

- 38 species.

Brushfoots

Subfamily: Nymphalinae

Large to very large (26–65mm). Diverse shapes and colours. Forelegs form brush-like appendages. Many species mimic acraeas (Heliconiinae), milkweed butterflies and monarchs (Danainae). Some species mimic

dry leaves. Some caterpillars are cylindrical and hairless; others have spiky or hairy protrusions. Family includes most common garden butterflies.

- 70 species.

Milkweed butterflies, monarchs

Subfamily: Danainae

Large (±40mm). Wings orange, black and white, or merely black and white. Forelegs are formed into club-shaped or spiny appendages. Caterpillars

Larva

are banded in yellow and black, and have distinctive protrusions. Adults are mimicked by a large number of butterflies in other families. All species are poisonous; larvae extract poison from host plants like milkweed.

- 7 species.

Browns

Subfamily: Satyrinae

Medium-sized to large (18–40mm). Dull brown, almost always with eyespots on top of and under the wings. Veins markedly swollen at the base of the forewings. They mostly fly around in shaded areas and sit on the ground. A few species mimic milkweed butterflies and monarchs (Danainae).

Caterpillars have short hairs and the abdomen is characteristically forked at the rear end.

- 92 species.

Acraeas, reds

Subfamily: Heliconiinae (formerly Acraeinae)

Medium-sized to large (25–45mm). Characteristically long forewings and short, rounded hind wings, often partially transparent with orange and black markings. Forelegs reduced. Acraeas mimic each other (Müllerian mimicry) as well as milkweed butterflies and monarchs (Danainae). In turn, many other families mimic them. All species are poisonous and are capable of reflex bleeding. Poison is produced by larvae and is not necessarily extracted from host plants. The diederik cuckoo, which preys on acraeas, is resistant to their poison.

- 38 species.

Pupa

SAWFLIES, WASPS, ANTS, BEES

ORDER: HYMENOPTERA

This order contains most of the social insects. The four wings are hairless and translucent, and the mouthparts have mandibles. Hymenopterans have a characteristic 'waist' (petiole) between the thorax and abdomen (except in the suborder Symphyta). In some pupae the limbs are loose from the body.

- 70 families.
- Although the classification of this order is much debated, the traditional subdivision into two suborders, Symphyta and Apocrita, has been applied here. Apocrita is further divided into two 'sections', namely Parasitica and Aculeata.

WOODWASPS, HORNTAILS, SAWFLIES

Suborder: Symphyta

This suborder contains the most primitive hymenopterans. All species are herbivores.

Sawflies

Family: Tenthredinidae

Small to medium-sized (5–8mm). Primitive wasps with a stout abdomen and no visible

'waist'. Females have a saw-like ovipositor. Larvae are slug-like or caterpillar-like, and feed on plant matter. Pear slugs (*Caliroa cerasi*) belong to this group.

- ±100 species.

WASPS, ANTS, BEES

Suborder: Apocrita

The species in this suborder are typical hymenopterans. They have four membranous wings and there is usually a petiole between the thorax and abdomen. An ovipositor is common in females. Larvae are legless.

SECTION: PARASITICA

This group is extremely important in biological control of pest insects, both in the wild and in commercial agriculture.

Small parasitic wasps

Superfamily: Chalcidoidea

Very small to small (0.2–5mm), with a few groups that exceed 10mm in length. Every conceivable body shape occurs. Very specialised, species-specific parasites of other arthropods or plants: different species attack specific stages of host development (egg, larva, adult). Of great importance in biological pest control.

- 19 families (±15 in other closely related superfamilies).
- Not likely to be confused with other hymenopterans, owing to their small size, extremely reduced veins on their wings, and their very large head and eyes.

Small parasitic wasp on eggs

Fig wasps

Family: Agaonidae

Very small (±1mm). Elongated bodies. Males are wingless. All occur within figs, where they develop and pollinate the tiny fig flowers. Each fig species has its own specialised wasp species with special adaptations.

- 24 species.
- Can be confused with at least five other small parasitic wasp families known to be associated with figs.

Large parasitic wasps

Superfamily: Ichneumonoidea

Small to medium-sized (5–22mm). Distinctive long legs and antennae, long ovipositors (in some species) and an

elongated abdomen. Some have a compact body and are brightly coloured. All are parasites of other insects; pupal cocoons are often spun on the host's body.

- 2 families, ±1,000 species.

SECTION: ACULEATA

There are 28 families in this group, with 12 families described below.

Cuckoo wasps

Family: Chrysididae

Medium-sized (5–20mm). Sturdy, textured and armoured body; distinctive metallic green to metallic purple coloration. Roll up into a compact ball when threatened. Larvae parasitise the larvae of solitary bees and wasps, or the eggs of stick insects.

- ±200 species.

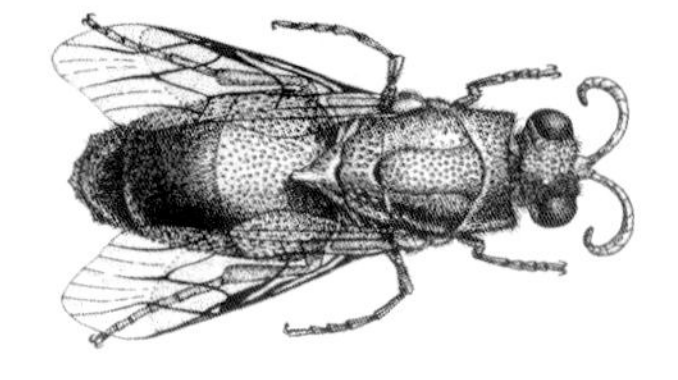

Velvet ants

Family: Mutillidae

Small to large (2–30mm). Females are wingless and heavily armoured, with distinctive red-black and white bodies covered in velvet hairs. Males are winged, often totally black. Females stridulate when threatened. Males sometimes fly around with wingless females. Larvae develop as external parasites on larvae of other wasps or bees; some live on fly pupae or on leaf beetles (Chrysomelidae).

- ±300 species.
- Can be confused with certain beetles (Cleridae) as well as spiders and unrelated wasps that convincingly mimic female velvet ants. Males differ from similar wasps by the absence of eye indentations.

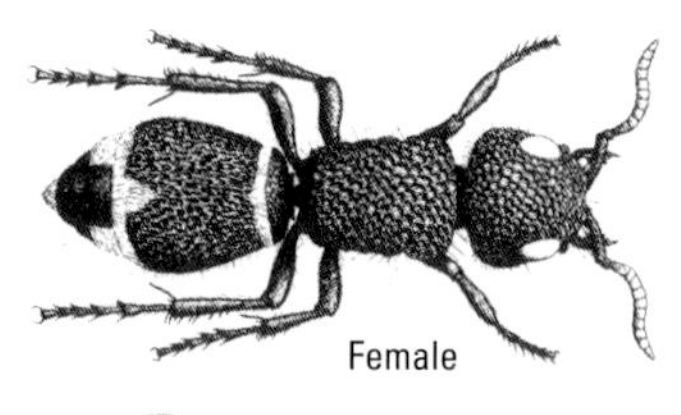

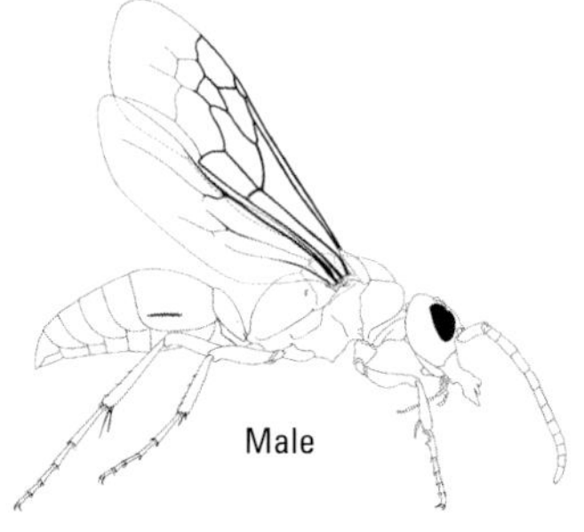

Mammoth wasps

Family: Scoliidae

Medium-sized to large (10–50mm). Black to blue-black hairy wasps with a robust build. Eyes have characteristic indentations that also occur in paper wasps (Vespidae) and potter and mason wasps (Eumenidae). Larvae mostly

live as external parasites on C-shaped larvae of dung and fruit chafer beetles (Scarabaeidae).

- At least 55 species.

Spider-hunting wasps

Family: Pompilidae

Medium-sized to large (5–50mm). Blue-black to black, mostly with long orange legs. Larger species make a rattling sound with their wings when flying. All paralyse spiders, bury them in tunnels and then lay their eggs on them. The eggs develop as internal parasitoids. Some species specialise in hijacking paralysed spiders from their rightful owners. Their larvae first devour the resident larvae and then the spider.

- 200 species.

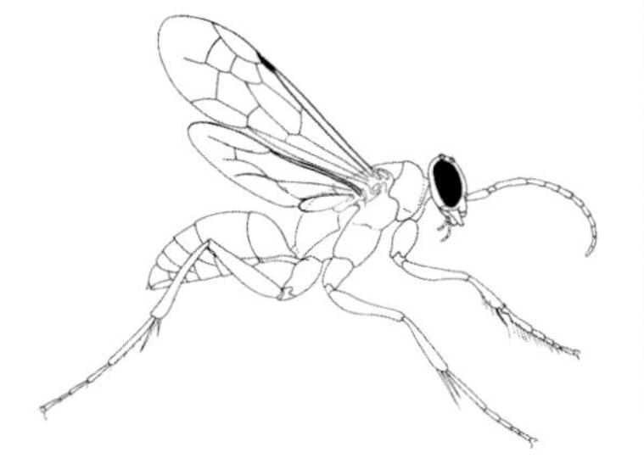

Paper wasps

Family: Vespidae

Medium-sized to large (7–35mm). Mostly red-brown. Forewings are folded double lengthwise when resting (subfamily Vespinae). Live socially and are well known for building paper nests. Workers feed larvae with caterpillars in the nests, where they remain to eventually pupate and develop into adults. Pollen wasps (subfamily Masarinae) are unique to arid parts of southern Africa. So far, 124 species of this subfamily have been described and a further 40 are in the process of description and publication.

- 35 species (Vespinae);
  124 species (Masarinae).

Potter wasps, mason wasps

Family: Eumenidae

Medium-sized to large (6–30mm). Some have a compact body shape; others have long, thin petioles. Often brightly coloured. Eye indentations and wing fold pattern similar to paper wasps

(Vespidae). All are solitary and store food supplies (mostly paralysed caterpillars) for their larvae in subterranean tunnels, clay nests or clay pots.

● 120 species.

Mud daubers, sand wasps

Family: Sphecidae

Small to large (2–40mm). Prominent 'collar' on the front of the thorax; eye indentations absent. Display same nesting behaviour as potter and mason wasps (Eumenidae). Nests are made in existing tunnels or are dug in soil or built from clay. Nests with larvae are often progressively supplied with food. Prey varied but species-specific; includes caterpillars, cockroaches, beetles, crickets, bees and spiders. Some species parasitise other solitary wasps.

● 736 species.

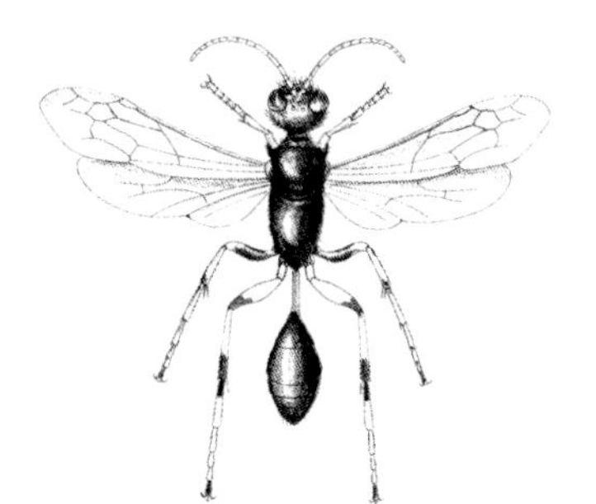

Ants

Family: Formicidae

Small to medium-sized (workers: 2–20mm). Antennae characteristically angled and a 'waist' is always present between the abdomen and thorax. Males and reproductive females have wings for the purpose of mating flights. The females (future queens) will eventually shed their wings. A variety of worker and soldier castes are normally found within the same nest. Most ants are omnivorous, but some specialise in collecting nectar or honeydew from leafhoppers and

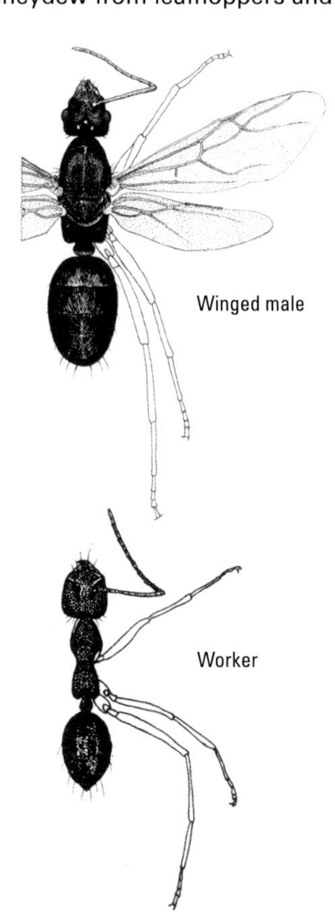

aphids (Auchenorrhyncha and Sternorrhyncha). Parasitic species preying on the food stores, nests or workers of other ant species also occur.

● 11 subfamilies, 620 species.

Bees

Superfamily: Apoidea

A 'tongue' between the mandibles is used to suck nectar. Hairs are branched. Most have 'pollen baskets' – special bristles around a collecting area which are used to transport pollen. The 'pollen basket' is located on the outside of the enlarged first segment of the hind tarsus. Nectar and pollen are fed to larvae. All lifestyles, from solitary to social, occur.

● 9 families.

Sweat bees, flower bees

Family: Halictidae

Small to medium-sized (2–15mm). Species are either solitary or social. They make nests in subterranean tunnels. Some parasitise nests of the same family or of other families. Some species, such as the so-called 'mopane flies' found in the Kalahari and Namibia, are attracted to sweat (for moisture).

- 70 species.

Leafcutting bees, mason bees, carder bees

Family: Megachilidae

Small to medium-sized (3–23mm). All are solitary bees. Parasitic species occur. Head exceptionally large. Pollen baskets located under abdomen and not on rear tarsi. Nests are made in existing or new subterranean tunnels and are often lined with pieces of green leaves cut from live plants. Some species build 'cotton-wool' nests out in the open. These are constructed from fine plant fibres that are so densely packed that nectar can be stored in them.

- 200 species.

Carpenter bees

Family: Anthophoridae

Subfamily: Xylocopinae

Medium-sized to large (20–40mm). Robust bees, characteristically hunched, with a thick covering of hairs ventrally. Males totally yellow; females black and white. Nests are communally bored, and protected, in dead wood or cane, but bees do not eat the wood. Bees carry pollen and honey to the nest, and each female supplies her own brood with food. Females house mites in a hollow between the thorax and abdomen, the function of which is unknown.

- 100 species.

Honeybees

Family: Apidae

Small to medium-sized (2–12mm). The well-known honeybee (*Apis mellifera*) is representative of this family and has 'pollen baskets' on the outside of the dilated first segment of the rear tarsi. Other species are small and without a sting, for example mopane bees (*Meliponula* spp.), and build nests in the ground or in hollow tree trunks.

- 10 species.

Index

Page numbers in **bold** indicate pages on which the topic is illustrated.

C

D

E

F

G

H

I

J

K

L

M

N

O